Coming Forth by Day

Note to Readers

This workbook is for entertainment purposes only. It is not a substitute for medical, legal, or financial counsel. The author and publisher assume no legal or moral liability for damages, losses, or other consequences of reader decisions subsequent to, or based upon, the contents and activities presented herein.

Coming Forth by Day
A System of Khemetic Magic
Book One

Storm Constantine

Megalithica Books
Stafford, England

Coming Forth by Day: A System of Khemetic Magic Book One.
By Storm Constantine
First edition © 2019

MB0203
ISBN 978-1-912241-11-8

Editor: Louise Coquio
Cover Art: Danielle Lainton
Interior Illustrations: Ruby, pages 60, 61,62, 72, 92, 110, 124, 142, 154, 164, 180, 200, 220, 221, 240, 264, 282, 300, 318, 334;
Storm Constantine, pages 12, 16, 20, 26, 54, 80, 135, 136, 141, 153, 179, 192, 199, 219, 263, 281, 317, 333 (some of which are adapted from Khemetic wall paintings and bas reliefs).
Ennead Family Tree by Danielle Lainton, page 88

Author's Web Site: www.stormconstantine.co.uk

A Megalithica Books edition
An imprint of Immanion Press
www.immanion-press.com
info@immanion-press.com

Coming Forth by Day
A System of Khemetic Magic
Book One

Storm Constantine

Megalithica Books
Stafford, England

Coming Forth by Day: A System of Khemetic Magic Book One.
By Storm Constantine
First edition © 2019

MB0203
ISBN 978-1-912241-11-8

Editor: Louise Coquio
Cover Art: Danielle Lainton
Interior Illustrations: Ruby, pages 60, 61,62, 72, 92, 110, 124, 142, 154, 164, 180, 200, 220, 221, 240, 264, 282, 300, 318, 334;
Storm Constantine, pages 12, 16, 20, 26, 54, 80, 135, 136, 141, 153, 179, 192, 199, 219, 263, 281, 317, 333 (some of which are adapted from Khemetic wall paintings and bas reliefs).
Ennead Family Tree by Danielle Lainton, page 88

All other illustrations and plate pictures are from the author's personal collection or from the public domain. Every attempt has been made by the author to clarify the ownership of illustrations used in this book. Any oversights or omissions will be corrected in future editions.

Author's Web Site: www.stormconstantine.co.uk

A Megalithica Books edition
An imprint of Immanion Press
www.immanion-press.com
info@immanion-press.com

This book is dedicated to my dear friend Louise Coquio, with whom I have embarked upon many strange and wondrous journeys into the magical and mysterious for several decades. Here's to many more extraordinary excursions!

Acknowledgements

Thanks to the following fellow travellers who also helped me to create this book:

Danielle Lainton and Katie Kesterton – weird sisters, who along with Louise tested all the workings in this book with me and made very helpful suggestions

Andrew Collins and Graham Phillips – erudite brothers, both for answering my questions and verifying information, and Andy particularly for providing photographs for me to adapt into illustrations

Ruby for illustrating the divine so divinely

My husband Jim Hibbert who, when I told him exultantly I had finished writing this book after talking about it constantly for over a year while I worked on it, said, 'What book?'

Contents

Introduction 9

Part 1: The Magic of Khemet

The Fascination with Ancient Times 13
The Book of the Dead 17
Temple of the Soul 21
Beliefs and Customs in Khemet 27
Modern Khemetic Magic 35
Magical Practice and Principles 47
The Importance of Colour in Khemetic Magic 55
The Sacred Enclosure 59
Heka: Neter and Magical Power 63
Ur Heka: Words of Power 81

Part 2: The *Neteru*

The Roles of Male and Female Neteru 89
Evolving Ancient Deities 91
The Creation Myth of Heliopolis 93
    Visualisation: Witness to the Creation of Life 104

The Children of Atum
    Tefnut: Neter of Moisture and Coolness 111
        Visualisation: Meeting the Primal Being 113
        Ritual: Tefnut's Mysteries 116
    Shu: Neter of Warm Air and Dryness 125
        Visualisation: The Birds of Imagination 127
        Ritual: The Quest for Self-Knowledge 129

The Children of Shu and Tefnut
    Nut and Geb – Lady of Stars and Lord of the Earth 137
        Visualisation: The Marriage of Earth and Sky 138
    Geb – Lord of the Earth 143
        Ritual: Sinking into the Earth 148
    Nut – Lady of the Sky 155
        Ritual: Rising to the Stars 159

The Children of Nut and Geb
    Isis – Great of Magic 165
        Visualisation: The Dawn Rite of Isis 172
        Ritual: The Teachings of Isis 174
    Osiris – Neter of Growth, the Afterlife and Rebirth 181
        Visualisation: Purification in the Fields of Aaru 186
        Ritual: The Flourishing Grain 193

Nephthys – Lady of Night   201
    Visualisation: Eyes in the Dark   209
    Ritual: Revealing That Which is Hidden   213
Set – Lord of Chaos   221
    Visualisation: Signs in the Storm   230
    Ritual: What Lies Beneath the Mask   234
The Sons of Osiris and Their Families
Horus: Boy King of Khemet   241
    Visualisation: The Trials of Horus   252
    Ritual: Birth of the Sun   258
Serket – Scorpion Queen   265
    Visualisation: The Venom That Purifies   271
    Ritual: Drawing Out Poison   275
The Sons of Horus and Serket   283
    Visualisation: The Chamber of Healing   290
    Ritual: Guardians of Healing & Great Protection 294
Anubis: Intermediary for the Dead   301
    Visualisation: A Visit to the Ancestors   308
    Ritual: Festival of the Dead   312
Anput: She-Jackal Assassin   319
    Visualisation: Slaying the Monster of Ill-Intent 324
    Ritual: Festival of Sopdet   328
Kebechet: Neter of Freshness & the Celestial Realm   335
    Visualisation: Swimming with the Serpent   339
    Ritual: The Great Sky River   343

Further Journeys   348
Appendix: Breathing Exercises   349
Resources   353
About the Author   354
Books by Storm Constantine   355

Introduction

I have taught courses in alternative spirituality, magic and healing for over thirty years, with a lifelong interest in the unseen and strange. My industrious imagination as a child led to me eventually becoming a professional writer of both fiction and non-fiction – but my work is always touched by the uncanny, influenced as it is by my personal interests and experiences.

In 1998, I wrote a book with my friend and colleague, Louise Coquio, called *Bast and Sekhmet: Eyes of Ra*, which was published by Robert Hale in 1999. This was our intensive study of the leonine and feline deities of Ancient Egypt, with whom we worked regularly in a magical sense. The book was the first of its kind, concentrating as it did on these particular goddesses and providing copious visualisations, rituals and spells to commune with them. We were guests at a Fellowship of Isis conference in early 2000s and there performed one of the visualisations from the book before a participating audience of hundreds, including Olivia Robertson, the founder of the Fellowship of Isis.

In the wake of our book's success we ran courses in paganism and witchcraft, as well as workshops in Egyptian Magic and other pagan belief systems. We had our own regular magical group, which ran for many years, until life commitments – not least the arrival of Louise's son – meant these regular meetings, and the preparation required for them, had to take a back seat for a while. However, our interest in magic and Ancient Egypt never waned. For me, it led on to developing a healing system called Sekhem Heka, a book on which was published through Megalithica Books in 2008 (*Sekhem Heka: a Natural*

Healing and Self-Development System). I also created a correspondence course in Egyptian Magic, which was well received. When I eventually 'retired' that course as – with the expansion of Immanion Press, as well as my own writing commitments – I no longer had the time to work with students on the coursework, I decided to rework it as a book. This volume in your hands is the result. It differs in some ways to the original course, but draws upon its content, as well as work Louise and I undertook with our magical group. But most of the rituals and pathworkings are new, written especially for this book.

I've steered clear of the leonine and feline goddesses in *Coming Forth by Day* because Louise and I will be working on a revised and expanded edition of *Bast and Sekhmet: Eyes of Ra* in the near future, and I want to keep its content separate from this book. (The only exception is Tefnut who is part of Heliopolitan dynasty.) *Coming Forth by Day* focuses upon the Ennead, the gods and goddesses who comprised the prominent figures in the creation myth of Heliopolis – Atum, Tefnut, Shu, Geb, Nut, Osiris, Isis, Set, Nephthys, and Horus the Younger, the son of Isis and Osiris. I've also explored some close relatives – Horus's wife Serket and their sons Qebehsenuef, Hapy, Duamutef and Imsety, as well as Anubis, the son of Osiris and Nephthys, Anubis's consort Anput, and their daughter Kebechet. This was more than enough material to fill one book.

I had to cut a large amount of the work that originally appeared in the correspondence course, since it didn't fit the theme of this book, but plan to release all of it eventually, in revised and expanded form, along with a great deal of new pathworkings and rituals, over two or three volumes.

Storm Constantine, April 2019

Part One
The Magic of Khemet

From a Temple Bas Relief

The Fascination with Ancient Times

During the decades in which I've practiced and taught alternative belief systems and philosophies, I've observed that the majority of interested people resonate with the beliefs of ancient times and feel empathy with the deities who presided over them. Often, this is what draws them to the practice of magic in the first place. One early belief system that particularly intrigues people is that of Ancient Egypt. Perhaps they are drawn by the apparent noble elegance of the Egyptian people of those times. We seem to know so much about them, yet ultimately so little. Their mysterious deities – beautiful yet sometimes monstrous, or both – have power because they affect us profoundly, whether with inspiration, fear or curiosity.

The original name for Egypt was Khemet, so throughout this work I'll refer to Ancient Egypt as Khemet and Ancient Egyptian as Khemetic. I'll use the term Khemetu to refer to its people. This is to differentiate the past from modern Egypt and means I don't have to qualify each use of the word Egypt and its derivatives with the adjective 'ancient'. Khem literally means 'black' and refers to the dark, rich, fertile soil around the River Nile, which enables the country to thrive. Egypt was originally known as the Black Land and the Red Land – the latter being the searing desert, inhospitable to life. Khemetu therefore translates as 'people of the black land'.

I have chosen to use the later Greek/Roman renditions of the *neteru*'s names, rather than their original Khemetic forms. For example, Isis rather than Aset. This is a personal preference, but I do provide the original forms for practitioners who would prefer to use them instead.

The system of magic presented in this book, (or indeed any modern system), can only ever be *inspired* by the beliefs of the Khemetu. No one can reproduce in entirety the rites and mind-set of this vanished race. The only remaining evidence is the often very formalised texts on the walls of tombs and temples. Much of Khemetic life shown in these paintings can only be stylised and representative rather than providing a precise record of the past. You cannot see into the minds of living Khemetu and learn for yourself the way they thought, lived and believed, even though through meditation and visualisation you can attempt to glean inspired information about the way things might have been. Much of the evidence for mundane, daily life in Khemet has been lost, mainly because its people used imperishable stone only in their ceremonial buildings. Houses, and even palaces, were generally constructed from mud bricks, which have been destroyed over the millennia.

In creating the material for this book, I incorporated several techniques and skills that I'd learned and used before, such as visionary questing, meditation, visualisation and colour correspondences. Although, as far as we know, these weren't techniques used by the Khemetu, (although colour did play a great part in their rituals), they fitted very comfortably into the work.

It would be inappropriate, if not impossible, for modern practitioners of magic to try and reproduce to the letter the way in which the people of Khemet interacted with their deities and practiced magic. Not only are we very different from them psychologically and culturally, but some concerns that drove the Khemetu do not have the same relevance for us. A large part of the Khemetic belief system revolved around the Underworld and what happened to people once earthly life was over, as well as the yearly inundation of the Nile upon which their livelihood depended. It might appear they had a deep preoccupation with death and the afterlife, but as most surviving evidence consists of carvings and inscriptions on tomb walls, this can't offer us the full picture – tomb paintings will inevitably depict death and what might follow. There are no personal diaries of common people to examine and interpret. In the ancient past, dying young was far more likely than it is now, but despite that the Khemetu must have been equally concerned with love, money, work and childbirth, which we're of course still concerned about today. These timeless aspects of life provide a link between the past and the present, but it must be accepted that modern life is very different to how people lived in Khemet.

As I'll explain in more detail later in the book, few of the Khemetic deities had full length biographies. With certain exceptions, such as the Ennead, stories about the lives of the gods and goddesses were scant. Sometimes, the most we can learn about a deity is the meaning of their name, which gives some indication as to what aspect of life they personified or prevailed over. As I believe that all gods and goddesses of the world sprang from human imagination, (and more of that later too), I've used my own to flesh out those Khemetic deities who lack depth and significant purpose. In order for a system of magic to be pertinent to our modern lives, its god forms need to more than just a name and to have a purpose. But I also believe it's important for such embellishments to feel authentic, to fit with the original belief system and not drastically change it to become something else. If we do that, we might as well invent a new system entirely with completely new gods and goddesses. There's plenty to work with in the Khemetic system, while remaining true to the core of its original tenets. I've aimed to uphold that standard throughout.

From an Original 'Book of the Dead' Papyrus

The Book of the Dead

The Book of the Dead was a collection of 'spells', written as a 'handbook' for the recently-deceased. Its name in Khemetic has been widely translated as *The Book of Coming Forth by Day*. It could also be translated as something like *The Book of Emerging into the Light*. The Khemetu did not see death as the end of existence, but the start of a passage towards rebirth. It's a long and complicated procedure, with lots of asides and sub-plots along the way, but here are the basics of the journey through death:

Before the newly-dead could enter the Underworld (the Duat), they would be judged as to whether they were worthy of continuing. This involved their hearts being weighed against the feather of Maat (truth). If the heart was heavier, it meant their negative acts in life outweighed the positive and they'd be denied permission to go forward. There were other nuances and details to this procedure, but that is the basic sequence of events. The successful candidates entered the Duat, and here their bodies regained the ability to move and speak, as the first step of rebirth. During their stay, they would meet a host of deities and demons. The spells in the funerary texts were designed to protect the dead by informing them on how to deal with whatever challenges they encountered and how to address the entities they came across in the correct manner.

While in the Duat, the dead were reborn, so they could rise with the morning sun, after which they travelled across the sky in the Boat of the Sun. In the evening, they returned to the Duat and were granted an audience with the King of the Dead, Osiris. If they met with his satisfaction, ultimately, they rose again as gods – more properly as *neteru* – a divine force with limitless faces. They would abide with Osiris in the Fields of Aaru, (which meant The Field of Reeds) an idealised version of Khemet itself. The Khemetu did not see Paradise as something different to their earthly lives – it was a luxury version of the land and life they loved. They had no concept of hell – in that some people were denied a comfortable afterlife and cast into torment. While the dead were indeed judged, those found wanting simply weren't allowed to proceed to an afterlife. They were denied rebirth.

While a number of the spells have been – and were – collected into something resembling an actual book, such as scrolls of papyri, the term 'book' here more properly refers to a body of knowledge. Many of the spells were carved into tombs walls and painted upon shrouds, rather than written down, and the collation and numbering of these spells into one volume is something that was only attempted quite late in Khemetic history. It's doubtful all the funerary text spells have ever been put together in a single, ultimate guide to the Duat. We can look upon the *Book of the Dead* translations available to us as anthologies of these ancient spells rather than one cohesive text.

I named this book *Coming Forth by Day* to describe the process of what all serious practitioners of magic strive towards – enlightenment. Emerging into the light. While the drives and ambitions of the Khemetu were obviously different to those of modern humans, there is still within us the belief that, through diligently applying ourselves to the task, we can evolve into something greater than what we are. If we are willing to try, we may overcome weaknesses and failings. We may expand our awareness. We may enlarge our ability to feel compassion and tolerance. If we learn all these lessons, perhaps we'll gain at least some understanding of the whole unruly mess that the modern world seems to be and how to live in it. Even more – we might learn how we each, in our own small way, can make it a better place.

However, it's vital to remember that self-evolution does not equal evangelism. The true adept of magic understands that every individual has their own way to the light and accepts also that others might choose never to seek self-awareness at all. It is not anyone's place to judge. If we should choose to lecture and criticise, to impose our own 'enlightened' way upon those we might consider as the ignorant masses, while at the same time being dogmatic and narrow-minded, then we are no better than the worst of those we seek to condemn. In effect, we become that which we most despise.

In a similar vein, the 'evil magicians' of fiction and film who possess extreme and ultimate power for the sole purpose of harming others cannot exist. The simple reason for this is that should a practitioner of magic attain such levels of self-awareness and control over their reality to affect the lives of others to such a degree, power over others will have become meaningless to them. The desire to control others derives from a core of terror and ignorance, the fear of 'the other'. It has no place in the heart and mind of a true adept.

Of course, people without self-awareness, who might believe they're better than everyone else but aren't, can still have power over others in a physical sense and through the force of negative emotions and reactions. They might be charismatic and through that draw followers to their sides. They might have a host of privileges others do not enjoy. But that is not magic.

Soul Temple

Temple of the Soul

When you embark upon any magical or spiritual work, you should have a clear view of what you're hoping to achieve and why, and in this case have an appreciation of how the Khemetu worked their magic and interacted with their deities – as much as we can discern from surviving evidence. Some people might turn to ancient belief systems because they feel disappointed and unfulfilled by modern conventional religions. They find comfort and inspiration in deities that mean more to them than the stern and oppressive gods of patriarchal belief. Others are drawn to systems inspired by the past from a purely magical perspective. They are not looking for comfort so much as understanding; of themselves and the universe around them.

The Nature of Deities

Gods and goddesses have been created throughout human history to help people try and understand the mysteries of the universe. Deities can be imagined as the masks we place upon the unfathomable forces within creation. While some people might regard this idea as a scientific reality we have yet to penetrate, others might veer more towards the belief that an ineffable intelligence moves the heavens and creates life. My personal thoughts on this are that *if* something, someone, or a number of someones is/are in charge, it's so far beyond our comprehension that it's better to visualise it/them as gods and goddesses. Deities give the unimaginable a face we can relate to, but I believe the appearance and character of deities derive from *us*, our own thoughts and expectations: a user interface between humankind and the forces of the universe.

If a god or goddess loses their followers, perhaps they cease to exist. Maybe only human imagination and the intention this pours into them causes them to endure. The gods and goddesses of Khemet have been pulled from the sands of time by modern practitioners who feel strongly attracted to them, but it's important to accept that inevitably some reinvention and embellishment has taken place and continues to do so. I don't think this modification matters, as long as it's respectful to the original. It's equally important that the deities with whom we resonate are pertinent to our modern lives. They should reflect our ideals, hopes and aspirations. The process of encountering them – and creating them – is unending: there is no limit to what you might discover, remember and imagine.

Magic vs Religion

Are religion and magic compatible, or do they mutually exclude each other? First, the difference should be defined. By using magic, practitioners seek to change or affect mundane circumstances or events. To do this, they might invoke certain god-forms or spirits to act on their behalf or aid them in their tasks. Someone who adheres to the neo-pagan belief system of Wicca might address Celtic deities such as Cerridwen and Cernunnos. Magicians who favour high Enochian magic might invoke angelic forms. A shaman might commune with nature spirits or ancestors. Practitioners of magic believe that by performing ritual actions in a particular order, with the appropriate sequences of words, empowered by specific emotions and will, they can affect reality and achieve the results they require.

But magic is not just about causing effects and achieving results. It can, and *should*, involve the search for self-knowledge and self-awareness, whereby you gain wisdom, not just about yourself, but others and the world in general. If you aren't aware of what makes you the person you are, and why you behave as you do, how can you hope to understand others, or indeed effect positive changes in the world?

Self-knowledge arises naturally from making a study of yourself – performing visualisations helps achieve this. All that you are, all that you aspire to and believe in, exists within your mind. Meditating in a relaxed state can release buried thoughts and feelings, which may have been subtly affecting your daily life. Such information usually comes in symbolic form. In this calm, objective state, free of condemnation and judgement, you're able to examine those thoughts and feelings *honestly*, and perhaps work out how they originated. This aspect of magic is self-evolution.

In its pure sense, magic does not involve worship – the praise of an individual god or goddess, with the hope of swaying their favour on the practitioner's behalf. By contrast, religion usually revolves entirely around worship and the attempt to live up to proscribed ideals. In the most rigid religions, believers do not imagine themselves to possess autonomy or self-responsibility, and the idea of practising any form of ritual to 'play god' with reality is seen as abhorrent or blasphemous. Deeply religious people might feel they are subject only to divine will rather than their own. They often adhere to rigid rules and behaviours, forever in fear of the 'forces of darkness', from which their piety will protect them.

Although unlikely to be thought of in this way by the religious, prayer is a form of magic – it puts intention and will out into the universe. Through prayer – and usually the medium of a priesthood – people can appeal to their deity to have their requests granted. But as part of organised religion this is more a case of '*please* do this for me' rather than the 'I *will* this to be so' practiced in magic.

A religious priesthood generally regards part of its role as providing moral education for its congregation. In some religions, there is also an emphasis on the concept of sin or ungodly behaviour, which the practitioner seeks constantly to overcome or, more accurately, suppress within themselves. So-called sins might arise from quite natural impulses in the mind and body, often connected with sexuality. In magic, the concept of being sinful or somehow 'not good enough' as a person is irrelevant. The correct ritual actions will work regardless of the political or moral codes of the practitioner. The practitioner takes responsibility for their own actions, believing in free will.

The force behind magic is impartial, even if human beings rarely are. Magical systems can, and many do, also involve some form of worship, although this should be regarded as separate from the working of magic. Spirituality, however, (which I regard as separate from religion, although can be part of it), is inherent in magic – it would be difficult to perform magic without some form of spiritual belief. Spirituality is a feeling of connectedness with all things, the wonders and mysteries of the universe. True spirituality comes from a centre of freedom, not from fear or guilt or any other form of negativity, intolerance or oppression that is often inherent in organised religion.

The rites and pathworkings within this book provide a framework through which you can interact with the universal energy, of which gods and goddesses are but frequencies. You can interact with these frequencies to develop as an individual, understand more about your species and your culture, as well as effect changes in reality.

Because so much energy and belief have been invested into these entities over the ages, it's equally important to approach them with respect. The depthless pool of human will and intention has given them a form of mundane (in the sense of the earthly world) existence. For ancient deities and beliefs to have relevance and context in a modern society, they deserve to be kept alive by reinterpretation. Everyone has the right to their own spiritual beliefs and is responsible for them. By working magic, free of dogma and with self-responsibility, an unending sense of wonder and the curiosity of a child, you create the Temple of the Soul. And what lies beyond its threshold is immeasurable.

Khemetic Family Hunting in the Marshes

Beliefs and Customs in Khemet

The mythology of Khemet is fragmented. Unlike the myths of the Greeks and the Romans, which often describe the acts and relationships of their deities in great detail and have survived intact until now, (even if they have been embellished over the centuries), it is more difficult to piece together all the stories about the Khemetic gods. Quite often, the most information available about a deity is the names by which they were invoked, or the circumstances under which they were appealed to. There are several different versions of the creation myth, from different areas of Khemet, and a host of sometimes contradictory stories about the goddess Isis, her consort Osiris and their immediate families. But myths about some deities are non-existent, such as in the case of the cat-headed Bast, and there is only one detailed story about lioness-headed Sekhmet. Some goddesses appear to be interchangeable, yet their characters are very different, such as Hathor and Sekhmet. Hathor is a benevolent goddess connected with love, music and dancing, and the animal with which she is most closely associated is the cow, yet the lioness-headed Sekhmet is often portrayed as a ferocious creature to be approached with extreme caution.

The Khemetic gods can have many different faces, all of which might have different parents, different children and different functions. There are thousands of them, from the prominent deities revered in temples, down to the innumerable beings who presided over the minutiae of life in the Duat – the Khemetic Underworld. Similar deities were revered all over Khemet but were known locally by different names, different aspects of the same god or goddess, who had been subjected to local preferences. The deities might have been imagined differently at various times of year, or else reinterpreted and reshaped to help with a particular predicament, such as war, famine or plague. It's impossible to impose a rigid, chronological framework upon Khemetic mythology, with so many stories and characters over-lapping and interchanging. Also, later Greek and Roman writers embellished the myths, in particular those of the Heliopolitan Ennead, of which Isis and Osiris are a part. The best that can be achieved now is to examine the known material and attempt to perceive a coherent storyline within it.

Neteru: The Names of the Divine

Part of why there might be such confusion in the stories and names of Khemetic gods, (or what seems to be a casual interest by the Khemetu in observing a linear narrative for them), is that the divine principle was imagined as one force with many different names. It could be everything, everywhere, and all at the same time. The Khemetic word for a divine being was *neter* or *netjer*, (plural: *neteru*), and this term included all the different aspects of divinity, both male and female. Because *neter* is one limitless idea, it can have inestimable guises and immeasurable functions. It can be in countless places at the same time. It has no boundaries.

It's possible the Khemetu might not have imagined the *neteru's* life stories for the simple reason they didn't believe their deities *had* personalities that would contribute towards biographical narratives. Other cultures created personae for their deities that strongly reflected the human condition – such as those found in the dramatic 'lives' of the Greek gods. Perhaps we could even go so far as to consider that the Khemetu believed in the *force* of the divine and did not feel it appropriate to restrict this force into small vehicles that resembled their own bodies, racked by destructive or petty emotions. While some myths, especially those associated with the family of Isis and Osiris, do involve vengeance, murder and infidelity, these stories were expanded at a time in history when other races and cultures had begun to influence the Khemetic way of life and spirituality. These writers saw parallels between the Heliopolitan Ennead and their own god forms and sought to fit the *neteru* into their own system.

Magic and Religion of the Khemetu

In Khemet, religion and magic went hand in hand. The priests were regarded as specialists in magic as well as intermediaries with the gods. They were paid for their services and performed magical rituals as part of their daily duties. Many were also physicians.

As in modern magical practice, the Khemetic priests believed in the inherent power of words and images, which, when utilised correctly, possessed their own creative force. The priests were also concerned with understanding and interpreting the true nature of objects and living things. They sought to discern correspondences, similarities and connections between them. These shared properties would include colours and the sounds of names. For example, a red flower or herb might be regarded as related or relevant to a fiery *neter* associated with the colour red. Correspondences therefore arose between them, and that plant was then believed to share the qualities of that deity. This is similar to practices in modern magic. For example, a bark such as red sandalwood would be one of the incense ingredients used to help invoke the presence of a fiery or solar deity, such as Ra. The influence that the moon has on the tides gave rise to the correspondence between the moon and water, so a plant that grows in or near water, such as the iris (orris), would be an ingredient of a lunar or watery incense, used in rituals to invoke a moon deity, such as Khonsu.

A great part of magical study and practice revolves around tables of correspondences that students of the art have compiled over the millennia. The Khemetu also believed it was possible to cause an effect upon one thing by performing ritual actions on an object that possessed the same qualities. This is known as sympathetic magic, and one example is creating a small doll-like representation of a person, to perform magic upon them, whether for good or bad.

As well as the priests, who would be affiliated to various temples, other practitioners worked among the populace, providing everyday spells to deal with ailments or troubles.

Heka: Energy of the *Neteru*

The Khemetu believed the force that the creator deity – the source of *neter* – used to make the world was called *heka*. When people worked magic, they reconnected themselves to the primal creative process.

It's commonly thought that the Khemetu worshipped their gods as statues, but this is not exactly the case. The statues, often with bizarre animal heads, were regarded as potential vehicles for *heka*, providing a means for the *neteru* to speak directly to the priesthood. The priests made offerings of food, drink and incense to these votive statues, and recited invocations to animate them with *heka* of the *neter* they wished to commune with. Through the offerings, and a certain amount of flattery, they coerced a *neter* to enter the stone. In this way, a statue became a tool of magic. The priests did not have to visualise the gods as pictures in their heads, but could focus upon them as living beings, resident in the stone before them. *Heka* was not just a force but also a *neter* in his own right, who will be explored in more depth later on.

Khemetic Books and Spells

Workers of magic, both male and female, who provided services for the general population and who were part of the community, would have had a largely oral tradition of magic, of which scant information has survived to modern times. It's doubtful the secular magic-worker would have had access to the prestigious esoteric books compiled by the priests, mainly because ordinary people would have lacked the education to be able to read them. Similarly, because they could not write, they wouldn't have recorded their own techniques. Most information about Khemetic magic known today derives from the written script of temple priests that was preserved in stone and on papyri. The magical 'books' of the priests were scrolls, lengths of papyrus or calf vellum that could be rolled up. These books were sacred and secret, not for the eyes of the common people. Some were said to have been found in forgotten tombs and hidden caskets, and to record the actual words of the *neter* Thoth, or legendary sages and priests.

Early Khemetic spells and rituals were written mainly to be spoken aloud, with few instructions as to what actions should be performed, but as writing developed, and the format of rituals perhaps became fixed, the instructions grew ever more detailed and specific. They listed the actions a practitioner should perform and a script for the speaking part. Repetition of meaningful phrases was very important, and it's believed rituals and spells were chanted or sung to differentiate them from common speech.

Some magical workings required the practitioner to paint appropriate hieroglyphs onto papyrus, which would then be dissolved in beer or water. The resultant mixture was then consumed by the magician. In this way, they absorbed the *heka* of the spell into themselves. Physician-priests used a variation of this technique. They would pour water over a written spell and collect it in a vessel. The *heka*-charged water would then be given as a medicine to their patients. Images of *neteru* might be inscribed onto the skin of a priest or their client. A spell or invocation would then be recited to attract a *neter* into the image, whether to heal, give strength or perhaps even make someone more attractive to a person they desired.

Archaeological finds have revealed that the average person in Khemet spent a lot of their income on spells and amulets, which were used extensively, especially by women and children. They were worn as pieces of jewellery representing various *neteru*, everyday objects, or parts of the human body. They could be used as protection, but also to promote success in various ventures, be it in love, work or the conceiving of a child.

Women and Magic in Khemet

The official religion in Khemet was run by the state, and women appeared, in the earliest times, to have had few established roles within it. Few goddesses had priestesses to serve her, but one who did was Hathor. Her priestesses were generally women of noble birth, the wives of high-ranking officials. As Hathor was believed to decree the fate of all new-born children, it's possible her priestesses had a similar seeress function in pronouncing the future.

While women might not have had led rituals in the state temples, they had other roles within them as musicians and dancers. To a modern practitioner this might appear a demeaning, inconsequential role, but to the Khemetu it was an important aspect of temple proceedings. The priesthood sought to please the *neteru*, most of whom were believed to enjoy the same activities enjoyed by humans. Therefore, dancing and music would have helped persuade a *neter* to enter and animate their sacred statue in the temple. The term *henutet* (masculine: *henuty*) referred to a woman who worked in a temple and is thought to mean 'servant'. It is not known what the *henutets'* duties were, although from inscriptions it's clear that none of them were high-ranking in everyday life. A female musician was known as a *shemayet* and this word was generally followed by the name of the *neter* for whose temple the woman worked. Therefore, a musician of Isis would have the title *Shemayet Aset*. The woman who was in charge of a musical temple troupe was known as *weret khener*, which means 'great one of the musical performers'. This role was held by a high-ranking woman, again probably the wife or relative of a temple official.

The most likely reason women didn't become lector priests is because of the Khemetic view of 'cleanliness' in a spiritual sense. All bodily secretions were regarded as impure. Because women menstruated and gave birth to children, and the blood of these processes was believed to be unclean, they would have been considered vulnerable to the influence of malign spirits, which would not have been appropriate for a temple official conducting rites.

Even though Khemetic women didn't have a major role in the temples, it appears they had a magical tradition of their own outside them, more concerned with day to day life rather than politics and war. The term *sau* referred to a magic worker of either gender in the community. Women who acted as midwives, or who cared for the sick, were said to 'make protection' for those in their care.

Certain women were described as *rekhet* or 'knowing ones'. They were believed to be able to speak with the dead; an ability that could have had various functions in a magical sense, whether to ask for advice or information or to coerce an ancestor to work magically on behalf of the living. *Rekhet* were said to be able to sense which *neter* or spirit was responsible for a person's misfortune or illness.

Although few records have survived about women's role in magic and religion, it's likely that every community had their own *rekhet* and *sau*. The Khemetu were not misogynistic. Women had legal rights and could own property and were neither cloistered nor restricted. Some of the most powerful *neteru* were female, revered, respected and sometimes feared.

Modern Khemetic Magic

The Purpose of Magic and Ritual

There are many different systems of paganism, drawn from different areas of the world. Khemetic magic is just one of them, and there are other systems of Egyptian-themed magic that differ from this one. The point of following the practices of a particular system is to develop yourself, through imagery and techniques that appeal to you emotionally, aesthetically and spiritually. A belief system that's right for you feels natural – you are drawn to it. This system is for people drawn to ancient Khemet. Performing rituals and other magical workings enables you to learn more about yourself. They encourage you to look inward and to discern how your experiences have shaped you. If there are areas of yourself that you want to mend or grow, your belief system provides a familiar and comfortable framework to work within.

Another aspect of a magical system is to perform rituals to help with life's difficulties, whether for yourself or for others. Or you can perform rituals simply to celebrate, whether at seasonal festivals or for more personal occasions.

The Record of Learning and Experience

Nearly every system of magic advocates keeping a journal of your activities, thoughts and experiences. Even if this is simply a folder of documents on a computer, it's useful to keep an account of your magical work and its results. If you don't record your visualisations soon after you've completed them, the details will slip away and be forgotten. Also, you might experience dreams related to your work; these too should be saved as their meaning might become clearer over time. Keeping a detailed magical journal up to date allows you to refer back to earlier work, add to your findings, and expand upon various workings and meditations.

Sacred Space and Place

Before performing a ritual or visualisation, practitioners of most traditions prepare the space in which they'll work in advance. This might involve no more than breathing exercises to induce a calm, tranquil atmosphere, or it could involve more complicated procedures using ritual props and actions. (Breathing exercises are provided in the appendix to this book, should you need instructions.)

Sacred space refers to an environment in which you have projected your will and intention to remove that area temporarily from the mundane, to infuse it with meaning and power. This can be a room in your home, an ancient site in the landscape, or any other location that feels appropriate. It is your intention that makes a space sacred, although if you do utilise a traditional site used by many others, such as a stone circle or ancient ruin, it will have been invested with the will and intention of practitioners over a long period of time, thus making it a kind of permanent sacred space.

Many of the techniques in this book are adapted from the Western Mystery Tradition of magic and the influences from other cultures that have been adopted, adapted and become part of it.[1] I'm not suggesting these methods were ever used by the Khemetu. For example, in the Western Tradition, the casting of a magical circle generally involves invoking elemental beings associated with the four quarters or compass points. While the Khemetu did assign various sets of *neteru* to the cardinal points, this wasn't to utilise their *heka* to 'guard' or empower a ritual space. No evidence remains of how – or even *if* – magical practitioners in the community created sacred space, or whether the quarter points had significance in ritual. But I found that including directional deities during the creation of sacred space added to the atmosphere of rites, no doubt because it's a ritual action I've used and liked for a long time and it feels natural for me to include it.

Part of what gives the practice of magic an emotional impact is its theatre. The speaking of invocations, the powerful words, the feelings they invoke, the smell of incense and the evocative light of candles, all contribute to changing your state of consciousness, so that you feel set apart from the mundane world while you work magic. In this system, the ritual space you create for this is called the 'sacred enclosure', which is a term used to describe part of an ancient temple regarded as particularly relevant to the divine.

The Altar

Any of the rites in this book can be performed without an altar, should circumstances prevent having one, but generally its preferable to include one. An altar provides a focal point for the ritual, contributing towards the ambience of your sacred space – as well as providing a surface on which to place any items you might be using during your work, particularly the image or statue of a *neter*. An altar can be made from an item as humble as a cloth-covered box, a small table, a shelf, or any flat surface upon which you can arrange ritual items.

You can place upon your altar objects that hold particular relevance to you, or that are pertinent to the working you're engaged in at the time. This can include votive candles in various colours, feathers, stones, gems, or any other items you feel are appropriate. Your altar is personal to you, so be as creative in its design as you like.

Vessel for the *Neter*

As attracting the *heka* of a *neter* into a statue was a significant component of Khemetic magic, you should include a symbolic image of the *neter* in any rituals you perform. It is very easy to acquire statuettes of just about any Khemetic deity online, and at reasonable prices, but even so, the number of *neteru* explored in this book most likely makes it prohibitively expensive to obtain a statue for each of them. If it better fits your budget, you could either acquire a few to represent the *neteru* with whom you most resonate and will work with in the future, or else simply find two figures to represent male and female *neteru* (but lacking particular animal heads or head-dresses) that will be suitable all magical workings. Alternatively, you may substitute a picture instead, or utilise decorative ornaments or pieces of jewellery to represent various *neteru*. For example, you could use a mirror for Isis or Hathor, ornaments or models of various animals for *neteru* who have animal associations – hawk/falcon for Horus, snake for Kebechet, jackal/black dog for Anubis and Anput, and so on. As with all magical endeavours, focused will and intention are the real tools behind the symbol.

The Light of the Enclosure

To augment the atmosphere in the sacred enclosure, place candles or lanterns at the four compass directions, as well as on the altar, on either side of your deity image/statue. If your budget permits, you can acquire Khemetic-themed candlesticks from New Age and magical suppliers, but any candle holders will suffice.

Aromas Fit for *Neteru*

For thousands of years, incense and other types of perfume have played an important role in ritual, both as a tool to aid communication with the gods and for purification. Frankincense was valued as highly as gold by some societies, including that of Khemet where the *neteru* were said to 'live on perfume'. The Khemetu believed that the smell of incense attracted the *neteru*. Incense smoke was also used before each rite in the temples to fumigate the space and purify the celebrants. These fragranced fumes were believed to carry the wishes of the priests, and of those whom they represented, to the realm of the *neteru*. The priests were also anointed with perfumed oils during purification rites.

You should burn air-filling perfume for any ritual or visualisation to help create the appropriate atmosphere. Ideally, you should use loose incense, which you burn on charcoal blocks, but you can use incense sticks or scented oils or candles instead. You'll find suggestions for appropriate scents for each *neter* in the section devoted to them, but you may purchase incenses created specifically for various neteru online or in magical shops. You may also use a more easily acquired zodiacal incense for each neter that you feel smells appropriate.

Natron

The Khemetic priests would wash themselves with natron to purify their bodies. They would also rinse out their mouths with it before addressing the neteru and uttering their divine names. Natron was also cast upon the floors of Khemetic temples, as it was believed this would purify and cleanse the area, in the same way that salt and water is used in the Western Tradition. Natron is nothing more exotic than bicarbonate of soda (baking powder) and water. It was also a key ingredient in mummification for purification and preservation.

In this system, you'll use natron to purify sacred space and yourself. You'll draw the ankh symbol on your forehead with it and dab it on your tongue to symbolise cleansing of the mouth. If you prefer, for the latter, you can rinse your mouth with a solution of natron instead, but that is entirely optional.

You should prepare your natron by consecrating it. Fill a suitable receptacle with spring water and using a spoon reserved for magical work, add the bicarbonate of soda to the water. The ratio is one teaspoon of bicarb for around a third of a pint of water. Hold your hands over it and say: *'I consecrate this natron in the names of the neteru.'* To further consecrate it, you may leave it out in the light of the moon for a night.

Offerings to the *Neteru*

Offerings played a great part in the religion of Khemet and is therefore an important component of this modern interpretation. Rituals include a feast, when the participant(s) consume appropriate foods and drink that are considered appealing to the *neter* who's the focus of the ritual. A portion of each type of food is set aside as belonging to the *neter* and will be disposed of appropriately once the ritual is concluded.

Nowadays, people might have restrictions or life-style preferences concerning what they eat and drink, so if this applies to you, you'll have to be creative about what you include in your ritual feast. Colours are important, so if you can't eat fish, for example, you can substitute pale, delicately flavoured food. Wine and beer are the drinks of choice for Khemetic ritual, but this can be substituted for fruit juice, flavoured water, non-alcoholic beer or wine, or milk, where applicable. The important thing is that your feasts are comprised of items you enjoy yourself, because as you consume them, so the *neter* with whom you're communing will share that pleasure. That is the nature of making an offering of this type.

Divination

The ritual to Nephthys you'll find later in this book includes the use of Tarot cards, and the ritual to Kebechet is enhanced by placing a particular Tarot card upon your altar. After a working, my magical group often spends some time in divination while we relax and continue to feast and celebrate. Divination using the symbols of Tarot feels appropriate to Khemetic magic. While some practitioners are convinced the Tarot originated in Khemet, I'm not sure this can be definitely proved. But, however or wherever they originated, the symbols within the cards have been influenced by the imagery of Khemet so they don't feel out of place in this system. You can use any deck for Khemetic magic, but there are quite a few available that have an Egyptian theme. You could purchase one of these and keep it solely for your Khemetic work. The deck can be charged with *heka* as you would for an altar statue, making it a permanent *heka*-infused part of your magical equipment.

Raising Power

The Sistrum

As part of creating the sacred enclosure, you'll use a rattle called a sistrum, which was a musical instrument in Khemet. It often featured a representation of either Hathor or Bast on the handle and was used in rituals, most particularly for Hathor. The *shemayet* of the temples would certainly have used them, as its sound was believed to ward off the powers of chaos. The sistrum was called *shesheset* and was a favoured

instrument in many religious ceremonies. Its shape resembles the *ankh*, the symbol of life. The sound of the sistrum was supposed to placate and please the *neteru*, and it's thought that originally sistra would simply have comprised bunches of dried papyrus heads.

You can acquire sistra and ethnic rattles from many craft and New Age shops, but you can also make your own. Rice grains or pasta pieces in a small container or a glass jar work just as well – you can decorate the containers with relevant pictures and symbols.

The Magical Voice

When you address the *neteru* in your sacred enclosure, you should use your voice in an authoritative and commanding manner. It is far better to learn the speaking parts of a ritual by heart, rather than recite from a script, because then you can concentrate on putting feeling and power into the words, rather than simply reading them. To see this for yourself, note the difference in feeling and intensity when you read the words from a page in comparison to when you speak them from memory. Mumbling the words in a flat monotone won't conjure a feeling of magic and energy. Throughout history, sound has been used in ritual. Try to 'be' in the moment, standing in your own temple, speaking to the *neteru*. Your voice is a powerful tool: use it.

A chant in Khemetic to raise power is often included as part of the rituals in this book. Begin speaking it in a whisper, gradually increasing speed and volume, until you are virtually shouting.

While you do this, shake the sistrum, and visualise energy being stirred around you, swirling in a clockwise direction. Feel this energy building up. When you sense it has reached a peak, release it by throwing up your arms with a final cry of the chant, and visualise it speeding off to do its work.

Ground any remaining energy by placing your hands upon the floor. Visualise that it is soaked up by the earth.

Symbols in Khemetic Magic

The Khemetu considered pictures to be – in a way – alive. For this reason, certain hieroglyphs were defaced on tomb walls, to prevent them leaving their place and causing harm. In ritual, symbols can act as a powerful focus.

The ankh and the Eye of Horus are always pertinent for any working, although you may include the hieroglyphs of each *neter*'s name and use them too. To bring the energy of a symbol into your enclosure, draw it in the air with the first two fingers of your dominant hand, using sweeping movements of your arm. As you draw, concentrate upon the meaning of the symbol. Imagine it hanging in the air before you, formed of blue-white light.

The Ankh

The ankh was a symbol of life and immortality. It's one of the most recognisable motifs of Egyptian art. It can be imagined as a kind of 'power' symbol. It can also be viewed as signifying the union of male and female: the female being the loop, the male the vertical stroke. It is sometimes known as the Key of the Nile. It's used in this system to symbolise *heka* and magic itself, to vitalise your sacred space. It's also employed as a symbol of protection.

The Eye of Horus

According to Khemetic myth, Set, the *neter* of chaos, cut out one or both of the eyes of his nephew (in one version, brother) Horus during a fight. They were restored to Horus by the goddess Hathor, who used gazelle's milk to do this. Each of the restored eyes then became a symbol for perfection and soundness. The right eye is known as the *utchat* eye, and is said to represent the sun, while the left eye is known as the *wedjat* eye and represents the moon. The eye is depicted as being lined by cosmetics, with the cheek markings of a falcon descending from it. The Eye of Horus is also a symbol of protection.

Visualisation, Meditation & Pathworking

These practices are generally part of any system of magic or self-development, and if they're new to you it's important to be aware of their differences. Visualisation means using the imagination to see pictures in the mind, rather like telling a story. Essentially, when you visualise, you create a mental image, projected upon what can be called 'the blank screen of the mind'. So it can be likened to watching a film. In a visualisation, you might put yourself into the story and become part of it, or you might observe events as a witness.

Meditation means reaching a relaxed state of being, during which you empty and rest the mind to attain an altered state of consciousness that is different to its normal waking state. Meditation may be part of a visualisation, but visualisation is not strictly a part of meditation. Simply put, visualisation is thinking in pictures, meditation is emptying the mind and waiting to see what thoughts or impressions might come to you.

Pathworking was originally the practice of exploring the connecting paths between the different spheres (or sephiroth) of the Kabbalistic Tree of Life, imagining these explorations as visualised journeys, upon which the practitioner might gain knowledge and meet and speak with entities. Nowadays, any visualisation involving the following of a narrative may be referred to as a pathworking. The word implies a kind of progression – travelling and exploring – rather than remaining in one spot. The terms visualisation and pathworking are often used interchangeably nowadays to mean the same thing.

The instructions for the visualisations in this system are merely guidelines. You might feel you want to expand or slightly change certain parts of them. You can pause to concentrate on the imagery when it feels appropriate. You might be inspired to explore different aspects of the inner landscape or converse with any beings you meet. Just follow the paths your imagination wants to take.

If you are reading for a group, you should do so slowly, pausing often so that the group has time to fully imagine what you're describing to them. You are not simply reading a story to them; you are leading them on a journey, and they need time to look around and experience the imagery fully.

Especially when leading a group, you'll probably feel it's natural to 'ad lib' here and there. Again, there is no strict, set way to perform the rituals and pathworkings in this system, other than to read slowly and clearly, with regular pauses. You don't have to read aloud or recite from memory exactly what's written in this book, word for word. Go where you want to travel. Remember also to leave adequate time (several minutes) for people to freely visualise their personal interactions with the *neteru*. Call everyone back to the main visualisation when you feel it's right to do so or they have signalled to you that they are ready to resume.

Part of preparing to meditate or visualise is to spend a few minutes performing breathing exercises to relax you and to help you focus on the imagery you'll be exploring. Examples of such exercises are included in the appendix of this book for those who have not done them before.

Note:
1. The Western Mystery Tradition consists of magical beliefs and practices of an Oriental nature, principally those of Judaism, Hinduism, Buddhism, Classical mythology and the religion of ancient Egypt, as seen through the eyes of ceremonial ritualists and occultists of the second half of the nineteenth and early part of the twentieth century. The key to this inspiration were the rituals and teachings of the Hermetic Order of the Golden Dawn, the Theosophical Society of Madame Blavatsky, and later influential groups such as the Society of Inner Light, founded by Dion Fortune. Indeed, Fortune's writings, more than any other, carried forward the Western Mystery Tradition into the modern era. Also inspirational to its success in later years were the writings and practices of Aleister Crowley, who although much derided by purists had an unquestionable impact on the spread of the Western Mystery Tradition in the second half of the twentieth century. Much later proponents of this tradition were individuals such as Gareth Knight, who continued Dion Fortune's legacy, combining Celtic mythology and the medieval Grail tradition, and also Kenneth Grant, who wrote a series of books expounding the deeper philosophies and magick of Aleister Crowley.

Andrew Collins

Magical Practice and Principles

Working Solo or With Others

All the rituals and pathworkings in this book can be performed alone or with other people. While circumstances might not always allow it, I do recommend working magically with at least one other like-minded person, if you can. Members of a group can be designated to acknowledge each of the directions and share other aspects of creating the sacred enclosure. They may also share speaking parts in the rituals when appropriate. Group members can take turns to read the pathworkings aloud, which is perhaps the most helpful part of working with others, for reasons explained below. A group, however small, brings more of a sense of occasion to any magical working, and also provides useful feedback among members. Groups can also pool resources to acquire altar statues and other equipment.

If you prefer to work alone or cannot be part of a magical group for any other reason, you might find it easier to record the workings to replay while you're performing them. This is because they would otherwise require a lot of memorising beforehand. The workings in this system include the instructions – the details of what you will be visualising and any actions you take in the visualisation – and the speaking parts, which include invocations, requests and thanks. If you're unable to make recordings, you may come out of a visualisation temporarily to read a speaking part, or to remind yourself of the imagery, before closing your eyes once more and resuming where you left off. If you perform the workings regularly, you will soon know them well enough not to need detailed instructions.

If someone is reading the pathworking to a group, everyone can repeat the words of speaking parts, line by line after the speaker, without opening their eyes.

Come out of a visualisation when necessary, but always imagine that a part of you remains in the imagined, inner world with the neter you are communing with. The statue or image of the neter on your altar acts as conduit between inner and outer reality, so that the neter can be imagined as being with you in reality as well as in your imagination.

When to Perform Magic and How Often

The workings for each *neter* can be performed as and when you want to. The pathworkings particularly lend themselves to multiple visits. It's unrealistic to expect one pathworking to expel a lifetime of accumulated conditioning, negative emotions, lack of self-esteem and so on. You can build up a relationship with a *neter* through the visualisation associated with them, perhaps gradually changing and expanding it over time, as imagery comes to you.

As for the rituals, these are themed towards a specific outcome, although in most cases I've aimed to include within them a more general use. Some address certain problems you may encounter in life, which might not apply to you at the current time. Yet as part of experiencing this system, you should undertake a ritual with each *neter* within it, adapting the words and imagery as seems right to you. If there are other people who you think would benefit from the ritual, you can direct the energy you raise to them, with their consent (see below).

Seasonal Rites

The Horus ritual is designed to be performed at the winter solstice, since this was a festival time for him in Khemet. I've also included a ritual to Anput (Anubis's consort) that's appropriate to perform at Lammas (Lughnasadh), since she's associated with the heliacal rising of Sirius and the Dog Days of July/August. I've not included rituals for other major Western Tradition pagan festivals, because the only members of the Ennead to whom such an association most aptly applies are Horus and Anput.

As far as other festivals are concerned, if you already follow the pagan wheel of the year and its rites, you might like to adapt some of them to have a Khemetic theme. The summer solstice was a festival of Wadjet, the autumn equinox involved Hathor and the spring equinox was a harvest festival in which a number of *neteru* were venerated – you could perhaps dedicate this rite to Osiris. Obviously, the seasons were different in Khemet to those observed in the Western Tradition. There were only three of them, and the implications for farming, upon which the pagan festivals are based, were also very different. The Khemetu did not observe the fire festivals, or cross quarter days, as this is a northern European practice. However, you could perform a rite to Anubis at Halloween/ Samhain, (Oct 31st) because of his association with the dead and, in this system, with ancestors. Anubis and his consort Anput are also strongly connected with the 'Dog Days' when the star Sirius rises with the sun, so a ritual to Anput would be suitable for Lammas/Lughnasadh (Aug 1st).

Ethical Magical Practice

I do not like the idea of finger-wagging or telling people what to do, treating them as if they haven't the sense to work things out for themselves or if I somehow have superior knowledge to them. I believe in self-restraint and free will and am suspicious of those who are compelled to lecture others on how to behave. But because I think the responsibility of a magical practitioner is a big one, and not everyone who reads this book will be a long-time practitioner who's very experienced, I feel obliged to cover the ethics of practice for the benefit of those who are new to magic. These are the ethics I practice myself – learned over the years through my teachers, and also through trial and error and in some cases disagreeable experience!

When working magic, you should always do so for the greater good, but people's idea of what the greater good actually *is* can vary considerably. The tenet of most magical systems is that whatever you do returns to you threefold – whether in respect of positive or negative actions. This is a good principle to follow. The Khemetu abided by the rule of Maat – balance, justice and truth. You should never act magically on impulse. If something happens that makes you (or others) angry or miserable, or physical harm was involved, your instinct might be to make a wrongdoer pay for their actions. But you should always allow a cooling off period. Acting in the moment is rarely advisable, simply because intense emotions and reactions influence the situation, and this can lead to action you later bitterly regret. (You will see this reflected in several of the stories of the *neteru* that come later in this book.) When you leave the dust to settle for a day or two, you usually feel differently – calmer and more objective. You might still decide magical action is needed, but that distance of a few days will encourage you to proceed with impartial consideration rather than lashing out. This also applies to others who might seek your help. As a rule, inform people you will only use magic to help them once a period of at least three days has passed and then you will discuss the matter with them again. The single exception to this is when urgent action is required, perhaps when someone has been injured and healing energy needs to be sent at once or the safety of a person is of high priority.

Workers of magic should practice under the rule of 'do as you will, as long as it harms no one'. You should never, under any circumstances, attempt to control the will of another person, no matter how much you might feel they are in the wrong and it's your job to stop them. If you try to impose your will over others you are – whether you stand by the threefold law or the rule of Maat – making yourself vulnerable to being influenced by others yourself. You should always seek to ameliorate bad situations in indirect ways – by providing protection to the vulnerable or making them 'invisible' to those who might wish them ill, so that the perpetrators simply lose interest and walk away or are distracted by something else. The most you should attempt in terms of retaliation is constructing a magical mirror – a visualised reflective shield – so that negative energy is reflected back to whoever sent it. It is also appropriate to ask the *neteru* to act as guardians to prevent harm. Simply the presence of aggressive protective energy like that of the *neter* Anput, for example, can be enough to deter wrongdoers, even if they don't know *why* they feel compelled to change their plans.

Love spells – just don't. For all the reasons given above.

Sometimes, you might have to use your own judgement in a situation, but you should be very careful when doing so. You might think that, because in the distant past the *neteru* were asked to smite enemies, curse people or make them fall in love, it's acceptable to work with them similarly today. But the *neteru* were part of the moral climate of Khemet when it was considered the norm to act in that way; to work with Khemetic deities now they should be part of the *modern* moral climate – what is seen as 'good' and acceptable to the majority.

Ultimately, to become a wise worker of magic, you have to maintain an objective stance, never act impulsively, never seek revenge, or act through negative emotions and situations such as envy, resentment, fury, jealousy, disappointment in others, or unrequited love. People will be people: they will often annoy, hurt, confuse and obstruct you. You might, even unintentionally, do the same to others. It's human nature. Part of life is dealing with its ups and downs, including the people we have to live and work with. You don't need magic to succeed at that – merely common sense, fairness and objectivity. Magic should be used with consideration. It can help smooth the path of life, connect you with the natural world, assist with making bad or broken things better and to help you evolve, but it must never be used as a weapon or a method of mind control.

Seeking Consent

Another rule that's important to follow is that you should never act magically for another person without their consent. It's possible that one day you might find yourself in the situation where a friend or loved one is in trouble, and you've offered to help, but they've told you to keep out of it. It can feel unbearable to stand on the sidelines and watch people get hurt, unable to step in, but if they've said no, they've said no, and you must respect that. To do otherwise is a violation of their free will. This doesn't mean you can't speak with the person and ask (gently) why they don't want help. It might be something they haven't considered themselves and it would be beneficial for them to explore the question, but as a general guideline don't assume you know what's best for people and certainly don't try to browbeat them into submission. This rule also applies when people are ill, and you wish to send healing energy to them: always ask first.

The only exception to this is when someone is in a coma or in some other way unable to give their consent. In that case, you should visualise a meeting with Isis or Osiris (or both for that matter), whose attributes include empathetic benevolence and the desire to make things better. Explain that you wish to send healing but cannot seek permission from the person you want to help. Ask the *neteru* to do that for you on a higher level, beyond the physical world. Do this with a completely open mind, not with a set, desired outcome. Then meditate to receive an answer – or you could go for a long walk in the countryside and be alert for signs. The *neteru* might tell you not to proceed. If that should occur, then you must go with their advice. The *neteru* are part of us all. Our 'higher self' or unconscious mind – whatever you believe it to be – speaks to us through them.

Magical ethics can be a tangled business, and there are of course many grey areas. The best you can do is to use your judgement with caution and act with the best intentions.

From a Khemetic Wall Painting

The Importance of Colour
in Khemetic Magic

In any magical system, colour correspondences play an important part, and influences the choice of hue for altar cloths, candles, gem stones and any other items included as altar decoration. In this system, you'll follow the correspondences used in Khemet. These differ slightly from the typical Western Tradition understanding of the primary colours, but there are also similarities. Although the Khemetu might have broadened their ritual palette by mixing certain colours together, the basic shades and their symbolic meanings are as follows:

Black (*khem*)

The colour black had dual meaning. While it was used to represent death, the Duat and the night, it also symbolised resurrection, fertility and life. The colour of the rich soil around the Nile is black, so intrinsic to the welfare of the Egyptian people. Egypt was split into the Red Land (the desert) and the Black Land (the fertile areas around the Nile and the Delta). In some respects, the colours black and green are interchangeable, both being associated with the idea of fecundity. The *neter* Osiris is sometimes depicted with green skin, and sometimes with black skin to represent his various aspects. Black stone was used to create 'healing' statues that were carved with powerful spells.

Blue (*irtiu* and *khesbedj*)

Blue signified rebirth and life. It was also the colour of the heavens and the primal flood that brought about the first life on earth, so it symbolised both water and sky. In addition, blue represented the waters of the Nile and the crops that grew in the fertile black soil around it. Blue pigment was used to colour figurines and amulets that characterised these attributes. Certain sacred animals were often depicted as being deep blue in colour, even if they were naturally of a different hue. This includes the baboon, the heron and the ibis. Blue was also strongly associated with the *neter* Atum, (the androgynous creator deity in the Hermopolitan creation myth), who was often shown with blue skin, as were other *neteru* connected with them.

Green (*wadj*)

Green symbolised growth – life bursting abundantly from the land. It was also the colour of resurrection, (hence Osiris sometimes being depicted with green skin), and of all things wholesome and benevolent, including good health and vitality. Khemetu would refer to acts of goodness as doing 'green things', while more unpleasant acts would be referred to as doing 'red things' (red being primarily a negative colour). The Khemetu used green malachite in their art to represent positive attributes and objects, such as in the Eye of Horus, and certain *neteru* were strongly associated with the colour, such as Wadjet, whose name literally means 'green one'.

Red (*desher*)

While the colour red represented blood, the fiery sun, life and regeneration, it was also indicative of hostile forces beyond the control of ordinary people. The chaotic *neter* Set was said to have red hair and eyes, and the colour of the Egyptian desert, inimical to life, was also red. It was known as the 'Red Land'. Red meant anger, destruction and chaos, and was also associated with the fiery 'Eyes of Ra', *neteru* such as Sekhmet and Pakhet, who could wreak havoc if unleashed. Words in Khemetic such as *desher ieb*, which meant 'furious', can be translated literally as 'red in heart'. The word for wrath, *desheru*, also clearly derives from the same source. When the priests inscribed hieroglyphs that they regarded as 'evil', such as the names of demons, they would use red ink instead of the usual black.

White (*hedj* and *shesep*)

This hue, while apparently colourless but consisting of all colours of the spectrum, represented purity and cleanliness, especially in respect of the priesthood. In the majority of wall paintings, Khemetu were shown as wearing garments of this colour, most likely to indicate their purified nature. White was the colour of the sacred: vessels and items used in temples, such as bowls and even mortuary tables, were generally fashioned from white alabaster. Sacred animals were also depicted as being white, in particular the Apis bull, baboons, cows and hippopotami. As gold and yellow were used to represent the sun, so white and silver represented the moon. Only sacred objects, apparel and creatures were depicted as white, not *neteru* or people.

Yellow (*khenet* and *kenit*)

This is the colour of gold, and since the *neteru* were believed to have flesh and bones made of this substance, yellow was regarded as a divine colour. Statues of the *neteru* were fashioned from gold, not just because of its value, but because of its symbolic colour. Gold was seen as everlasting, so yellow also represented the eternal, that which did not decay.

Wall paintings of the *neteru* generally show them with yellow skin, which differentiated them from ordinary people, whose skins were depicted in various shades of brown, their natural colour. It's possible that some of the priests, particularly those who had dedicated themselves to Anubis, painted their skins yellow when they were involved in funeral rites. The depictions on tomb walls of a black-headed Anubis with yellow skin might well represent priests who had assumed this costume for embalming the dead.

Yellow, along with red, was also associated with the sun, and solar deities. It was interchangeable with white as it shared many of that colour's attributes. 'White Gold', the composite of gold and silver known as electrum, was regarded as having equal purity to gold.

The Sacred Enclosure

The creation of the sacred enclosure comprises a set of actions designed to transform your working area from the mundane to the magical. I have taken inspiration from ancient practices when devising the ritual actions for this system, but as no one knows exactly how things were done in ancient times, I don't claim these methods are historically authentic – merely inspired by Khemetic traditions.

The first action in creating sacred space is to purify the area, since cleansing ceremonies were an important part of Khemetic ritual. The purification rites held at the temple of Horus at Edfu incorporated the sprinkling of natron, the burning of incense, the shaking of rattles and the opening up of the shrine to the light of the sun. The priests believed that once these preparations had been done the area would be set apart as a place that was pure enough for the *neter* Horus to reside in, and where chronological time had no meaning.

Here is an advance overview to constructing the sacred enclosure, which I'll describe in more detail later. You'll begin by shaking a sistrum to enliven the energy in the atmosphere. After this, you'll carry incense around your working space to purify it and to attract the favour of the *neteru*. Then you'll walk around the area sprinkling natron to purify it further. Next, you'll recite an invocation to open a portal to the realm of the *neteru*. Then, you'll address the directional goddesses.

In the Western Tradition, the four elements of air, fire, water and earth play an important part in ritual. Generally, the spirits of these elements are invoked into the four quarters at the beginning of any working. The Khemetu did not have a system of elemental correspondences, but they did acknowledge *neteru* of the four compass directions. In this system, these *neteru* are invoked as keepers or sentinels of the directions. I have included, however, as part of their invocation the time of day most relevant to each quarter. When the sentinels of the directions have been acknowledged, you'll state that the construction of the enclosure is complete and light the altar candles. The ritual may then begin.

The Goddesses of the Directions

Bast: East

Bast (also known in Khemet as Ubaste, Bastet or Baset) is represented as a cat-headed woman – the famous depictions of seated cats are representations of her sacred animal, and not meant to personify Bast herself. Her main cult centre was in Bubastis in the Delta region, although she was venerated throughout the Two Lands, reflected in one of her epithets: 'Life of the Two Lands'. The hieroglyph of her name includes the motif of a perfume jar, which has given rise to the belief that she was strongly associated with perfume. One of her sons, Nefertum, was also related to perfume. The Greek historian Herodotus wrote about Bast's festivals, describing them as occasions of riotous excess. Although Bast was originally a fierce Eye of Ra, warrior of the sun god and the pharaoh, she later became more 'domesticated', and was associated with music, love, dancing and merriment.

Nekhbet: South

The vulture goddess Nekhbet was originally the patron deity of a town called Nekhb, but over time her role grew until she was the patroness of the whole of Upper Khemet, which was the south of the country. Nekhbet was a guardian of mothers and children. Like many other *neteru*, she could be depicted in several forms. Her sacred creature was the vulture. When represented as a woman, she was shown wearing the crown of Upper Khemet or a vulture head-dress. She could also be shown as a woman with the head of a vulture. Another of her forms was the serpent. From the eighteenth dynasty, she appeared in the uraeus on the headdresses of Khemetic queens, symbolising their protection. Nekhbet and Wadjet often appeared together in carvings and paintings.

Neith: West

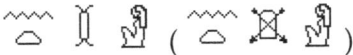

Neith (also known as Nit, Net or Niet) was a goddess of both war and weaving, which might seem a little at odds. She was the patroness of the city of Sais, and also associated with the Red Crown of Lower Khemet (the north). Perhaps one of her most interesting aspects is that of an androgynous creator

deity, who had both male and female aspects. She was seen as the mother of the gods, the primeval waters from which the sun god rose each morning. In one story, she is credited with creating the world by weaving it with her shuttle.

Neith was usually shown as a woman, carrying her sacred emblems, which could either be a shield and two crossed arrows, a bow and arrows, a sceptre and an ankh, or else the shuttle of a weaving loom. She generally wore the red crown of Lower Khemet. Very occasionally, she appeared in the form of a cow.

Wadjet: North

Wadjet (known also as Uatchet) is Nekhbet's northern counterpart, in that she was the goddess of Lower Khemet. She had several titles, one of which was 'Eye of Ra', but she was also known as 'She of Papyrus and Freshness'. Like Nekhbet in the south, Wadjet eventually became a personification of the land in the north. Her name means 'The Green One'.

Wadjet also had multiple forms. She can be depicted as a woman wearing the red crown of Lower Khemet, a cobra with a woman's head, a winged cobra or a lioness-headed woman. As a cobra, she was shown rearing up to strike the enemies of the pharaoh. Wadjet was a *neter* of fire and heat. As a cobra, she could poison the enemies of the pharaoh, and as an 'Eye of Ra', she could shoot out flames as deadly as her poison. She was closely connected to the papyrus plant, which was said to have derived from her.

Acknowledgement Rather Than Invocation

In the Western Tradition, directional entities are invoked as protective influences, and then dismissed at the end of a ritual. I do not find this practice quite so relevant for a Khemetic-themed system. The directional *neteru* are always in their positions, so do not have to be called in but rather acknowledged and asked to turn their faces – or attention – towards you. Similarly, they don't need to be dismissed at the conclusion of the ritual, since they can hardly be removed from their habitual positions. Therefore, at the beginning and end of a rite, you will simply acknowledge the presence of each *neter* in her direction. At the beginning, you will ask her to empower your work; at the end, you will bid her farewell, until you work in the enclosure again.

Hetepu Neter: Caring for the *Neteru*

Within the temples of Khemet, there were different officials and staff who took care of the daily tasks essential to the *neteru*'s wellbeing. There were lector priests and the *shemayet* who danced for the gods. There were *maatiut*, which means 'speakers of truth' who sang the hymns that the *neteru* found pleasing. The *hepetuit* were those who were responsible for the offerings made to the *neteru* every day.

All *neteru* were treated as if they physically resided in their temples, so that their statues (i.e. the earthly bodies they occasionally chose to inhabit) were bathed, perfumed and dressed, and they were symbolically put to bed and woken up each day. The offerings, or *hetepu neter* ('divine offerings of the temple'), were considered essential to the *neteru*, as they provided them with sustenance. Depending on the circumstances, and whether they were enacting a small or a full-scale ritual that involved the pharaoh, the *hepetuit* would make sure the desired offerings were present.

As a part of funerary rites, physical offerings in tombs were eventually substituted with paintings on the walls. It was believed that the right magical words, or *ur heka*, could activate these paintings so that they became, in reality, the object they represented. So great was the Khemetic belief in the power of magically inspired pictures and hieroglyphs that they were occasionally defaced in order to stop them 'walking'.

Each *neter* has preferences in terms of offerings. The most basic *hetepu neter* would be incense, bread and beer, substances acceptable to any *neter*. They also appreciate flowers, (particularly perfumed blooms), whether as decoration within the temple and on their altar, or worn by their priests and priestesses, as well as scented oils. These staples can be offered in any rite. Suggestions for ritual foods and offerings for particular *neteru* will be given in the appropriate sections.

When you make offerings, consume a part of them yourself, so that the *neter* can enjoy the experience through you, but leave a portion of everything you eat, which should later be cast outside on the soil, where wild creatures may consume them.

The Ritual of the Sacred Enclosure

The sacred enclosure may be constructed at any time you wish to perform magical workings or meditation in a space prepared specifically for such purposes.

You should learn the invocations by heart and practice creating and dismantling the sacred enclosure, so that you can do so fluently. When you address the directional *neteru*, visualise them standing before you clearly. Put as much feeling and intention into the procedure as you can. Feel the enclosure building around you, the atmosphere changing.

Before creating your enclosure, you should prepare the space physically – making sure the room (if working indoors) has been freshly cleaned and thoroughly aired. You can scent the air beforehand with oils, incense or candles. You can also mix your natron beforehand, making a small ritual of its creation.

Equipment:

- Sistrum or rattle
- Natron in a bowl or chalice
- Incense (lit)
- 2 Altar candles
- 4 candles placed at the compass directions at the edge of your working space

To begin, stand in the centre of your sacred space and perform a breathing exercise for a couple of minutes to help change your state of consciousness.

When you feel ready, raise your arms and shake the sistrum to enliven the natural energy in the atmosphere. (If you are in a group, all members should face outwards towards the boundary of the enclosure, enlivening the space from the centre to the perimeter.) Then draw an ankh, and the Eye of Horus in the air before you – there is no set way to draw them, just go with what feels natural to you. Visualise these protective symbols glowing with blue-white light.

Now, go to your altar and draw an ankh over the natron, visualising that the energy of the symbol goes into the fluid. Then sprinkle a few drops over your altar and say: *'I purify this altar with consecrated natron.'*

Dip a finger into the natron and draw an ankh on your forehead, saying, *'I purify my body with this consecrated natron.'*

Dip a finger into the natron again and dab your tongue with it, saying, *'I purify my mouth with this consecrated natron.'*

(For a group, a small cup or chalice of natron, poured from the altar receptacle, can be provided for each member to perform these personal purifications.)

Take up the incense and walk around the enclosure in a circle, saying: *'With this perfume, I purify and sanctify this sacred enclosure.'*

Now, walk around the edge of the enclosure, drawing an imaginary line with your hand and say:

'I draw the boundary of the sacred enclosure.
Open the gates of the heavens!

Raise the gate of the sky!
Let the neteru come forth
And shower their blessings upon me!
Open, oh heaven!
Let the doors be flung wide,
That the neteru may come forth from their horizon,
On the boat of the morning and the boat of the evening.
Open the gates of the heavens and raise the gates of the sky!'

Visualise this circle of enlivened energy around you. Then proceed to acknowledging the *neteru* of the directions.

Go the east, shake the sistrum, raise your arms and say:

'Hail to the Great Cat who stands in the East,
Bast, Lady of the Rosy Dawn,
Mistress of Ankhtawy (ank-taw-ee)
Life of the Two Lands,
Turn your face towards me from the East.
Look upon me with gentleness and empower my work.'

Light the candle.

In the south:

'Hail to the Venerable Vulture who stands in the South
Nekhbet, Lady of the Bright Noonday, (nek-bet),
Mistress of the Excellent Shrine,
Queen of the White Crown,
Turn your face towards me from the South.
Look upon me with gentleness and empower my work.'

Light the candle.

In the west:

'Hail to the Creator Neter of Sais (say-iss),
who stands in the West.

Neith, Lady of the Shadowy Dusklight, (Neeth)
Mistress of the Arrows
Lady of the Primal Waters,
Turn your face towards me from the West.
Look upon me with gentleness and empower my work.'

Light the candle.

In the north:

'Hail to the Royal Serpent, who stands in the north
Wadjet, Lady of the Dark Midnight, (Wad-jet),
The Green One
Mistress of the Living Uraeus, (you-ray-us),
Turn your face towards me from the North.
Look upon me in gentleness and empower my work.'

Light the candle.

Now, take up the natron and, starting in the east, sprinkle it around the boundary of the enclosure, saying: *'I purify this sacred enclosure with natron. Let no ill enter in.'*

Light the altar candles and say:

'By the light of these illustrious flames, my ritual has begun!'

The enclosure is now ready for you to work in.

Dismantling the Enclosure

When you have finished your magical work, dismantle the enclosure by bidding farewell to the directional *neteru*.

In the east, shake sistrum and say:

'Hail to the Great Cat who stands in the East.
Bast, Lady of the Rosy Dawn,

Mistress of Ankhtawy,
Life of the Two Lands,
I acknowledge your power.
You are ever welcome in my enclosure,
Until we meet again, I bid you farewell.'

Repeat in the other quarters:

'Hail to the Venerable Vulture who stands in the South,
Nekhbet, Lady of the Bright Noonday,
Mistress of the Excellent Shrine
Queen of the White Crown,
I acknowledge your power.
You are ever welcome in my enclosure.
Until we meet again, I bid you farewell.'

'Hail to the Lady of the Primal Waters who stands in the West
Neith, Lady of the Shadowy Dusklight,
Mistress of the Arrows,
I acknowledge your power.
You are ever welcome in my enclosure.
Until we meet again, I bid you farewell.'

'Hail to the Royal Serpent, who stands in the North
Wadjet, Lady of the Dark Midnight,
The Green One,
Mistress of the Living Uraeus,
I acknowledge your power.
You are ever welcome in my enclosure.
Until we meet again, I bid you farewell.'

Put out the altar and quarter candles, and say:

'The sacred enclosure is dismantled; my work is done. May the
light of the mighty neteru go in my heart, until I come once more
to walk the path to ancient Khemet. Ta-keper sem.'

(Ta-keper sem is a Khemetic phrase that approximates the
Western Tradition ritual blessing of 'blessed be'.)

Stirring the Energy in Your Enclosure

Although the use of a sistrum or rattle is part of the construction of a sacred enclosure, you may also use it to enliven the natural energy in the environment beforehand. This is especially beneficial if you're using a room that's used commonly as a living-room or other communal space where people spend time together in everyday activities. This brief meditation helps change the atmosphere of a room into a place of magic.

Before performing a ritual or visualisation sit down in the centre of the room and spend some time shaking the sistrum. Relax and empty your mind, letting yourself drift into a meditative state. Extend your senses to feel the energy around you, experience it 'waking up' and coming alive, its everyday purpose and the perhaps busy nature of it fading away. When you feel the task is done, leave the room for a while in peace before returning to begin the construction of the enclosure.

Sacred Space for Less Formal Workings

There are times when you might not want to perform a full ritual, but merely meditate or follow a pathworking. At such times, it's not necessary to go through the whole process of creating a sacred enclosure – although of course this is down to the individual and circumstances. What follows is merely a suggested alternative. I've termed it 'lesser' sacred space, which is not meant to imply it's any less effective or significant than a fully created sacred enclosure. It's simply a term to denote the simpler, less formal procedure.

Some of the visualisations in this system are imagined

journeys to investigate and experience various *neteru* or locations. For these, you can erect a temporary temple. This is especially useful if you want to work outdoors

Prepare the site (whether a room in your home or outside) by visualising white light filling it – the power of *heka*. You can call upon this energy in your mind. The light of *heka* touches everything, filling every object around you. It serenifies the atmosphere, encouraging relaxation and the ability to meditate.

Breathe deeply while you are doing this, taking the light into yourself, imagining it cleansing your body within. If it's convenient for your location, you can burn incense. If working at night you can have a lantern or candles to provide ambient light. Once you feel the space is sufficiently purified, let your mind relax for a minute or so. Let everyday thoughts drift away from you. When it feels the right moment, imagine your environment fading away into a mist. Then visualise this mist clearing, and a new landscape forming before your inner eye – the particular location you wish to explore.

When you have finished your visualisation, simply withdraw from the scene, by focusing your awareness back upon your physical body. With eyes still closed, imagine the mist reappearing so that the visualised world disappears into it. Then the mist clears, and with eyes still closed visualise the world as it really is around you. Move your fingers and toes a little to re-establish contact with reality, and in your own time open your eyes.

Heka:
Neter and Magical Power

...to me belonged the universe before you gods had come into being. You have come afterwards because I am Heka.
Coffin texts, spell 261

Heka was one of three creative powers that the sun god, Ra, used to bring about Creation. It is divine energy, literally the life source. The others are *Hu*, which are Ra's divine utterances, and *Sia*, his divine knowledge. *Heka* was also personified as a male *neter*, who was depicted standing in the boat of the sun to protect Ra, or else holding various ritual implements.

Although the word *heka* can be translated literally as 'magic', it's probably best to think of it in terms of: Life Force in Action. The priests used *heka* to connect with the *neteru*, and for maintaining cosmic order and balance. As a term, it can denote all manner of supernatural powers and magical events as well as the energy behind them. It is the essence of the gods, life force itself. *Heka* is energy. The Khemetu had great respect for words and their inherent power. One of the titles of Isis is *Weret Hekau*, which means 'great of magic'; a title applied also to Sekhmet and other female *neteru*. The Khemetu believed that knowing a thing's, or a person's, name meant that you had power over it.

Heka was not regarded as possessed only by the *neteru*, since all living beings possess life force. People who were different in some way, such as dwarves, were believed to possess an abundance of *heka*. Humans can use *heka* to connect with the divine and to effect changes in their lives.

The *Neter* Heka

The *neter* Heka was the son of the lioness deity Menhit, who was associated with war, and the ram *neter*, Khnum, who was a creator deity. With his parents, Heka formed the divine triad of Latopolis (Esna) in Upper Khemet. Another of Heka's functions was to protect Ra as he journeyed across the sky, making sure all hostile entities were kept far from the *Neter* of the Sun.

Heka was the patron of magicians and physicians, and the latter were often called 'Priests of Heka' and were believed to act under his influence. His regalia included two serpents, and even today this motif can be seen in the caduceus, the symbol of medicine.

Vses of *Heka*

In Khemet, medicine was as close to religion as magic was. Doctor-priests would act as any modern physician in establishing the immediate cause of an illness or injury and prescribe the most effective treatment, but it was also their job to interpret the *ultimate* cause, which might well be the malevolence of a deity or spirit, or even a human enemy.

Magic was then performed to deal with this ultimate cause.

All *neteru* possessed *heka*, but the god who was considered to have the most *heka* of all was the ibis-headed Thoth, who was credited with inventing both magic and writing and was the patron deity of scribes. Thoth's temple at Hermopolis possessed an acclaimed library of magical texts and ancient records.

Workers of magic used *akhu*, which means 'magical power'. This is also a word that refers to a spirit of the dead, once they have passed through various transformation stages in the underworld. *Akhu* spirits were the most powerful and possessed great *heka*. But, in its magical sense, *akhu* can be regarded as spells, enchantments and the ritual acts required to access the *heka* of the gods. Both *heka* and *akhu* were seen as impartial powers that could be directed towards creative or destructive purposes. If you can accept the *neteru* as simply masks through which you can interact with the universal energy, you can see that the Egyptian priests used this energy directly to produce specific effects.

Many belief systems incorporate the idea of a universal, life-giving energy. The ancient Chinese called it *chi*, and it was the principle behind the practice of *Feng Shui*, still used today. In *Feng Shui*, objects are placed strategically in order to improve the flow of *chi* around the environment, in the belief that it is beneficial for all who live within it. Blocked *chi* causes pools of stagnant energy that can have detrimental effects upon the individual. Islamic *sufis* believe in a force they call *barraka*, which is an energy possessed, to greater or lesser degrees, by living things, places and objects, especially such items regarded as strange or exotic. In the western world, we find a belief in earth energy, a network of linear channels of power that form a matrix throughout the land and gives rise to the concept of ley lines or spirit lines, and the power immanent in sacred sites. Practitioners of Wicca cast a magical circle to raise the natural energy in the environment, which they will then direct towards their intention or desire. Different cultures have their own interpretation of this energy, with various attributes and terminology, but as the Egyptian priests sought to perceive connections between things, you can appreciate their belief in *heka* is similar to the concept of universal energy espoused by many modern pagans and magicians.

> *Magic was considered by the Egyptians to be a substance stored in their bellies and produced by their intellects (Heart Ab). It had a flavour and a luminosity. It was the motive power for the universe and was created in abundance in primeval times. The longer Heka had been up and running, the more powerful it was… Heka can also be made to enter the bodies of others, either to cause influence (Baw) or as a poison (Metwta). At a certain stage of development, persons could become Heka itself, and not need to resort to magical practice to bring about results. Magicians are called Hekau. A pun the Egyptians were fond of is that Heka is Akh. Magic is effective (Akh). A common word for spells is merely Akhu 'effective things'. The dead, who have become Akhu 'effective spirits', are assumed to have magical power.*
>
> From: 'An Egyptian Lexicon'

Inviting Heka into a Ritual Statue

If you have one male and one female statue to represent the various *neteru*, you can perform this small rite to reconsecrate the statue to the relevant neter at the start of each ritual you perform. Its purpose is to 'persuade' the *heka* of the relevant *neter* to enter the stone so that you can speak with them 'face to face'. Do this in between creating the sacred enclosure and the start of the visualisation. This procedure mirrors the way Khemetic priests persuaded the *heka* of *neteru* to inhabit their cult statues in the temples. It's not appropriate to apply this to a picture or some other representation – only a statue used for ritual purposes.

Light incense. Kneel before the altar and the statue of the *neter* and raise your hands to around shoulder height, palms facing outwards.

Concentrate upon the statue and recite several times the chant appropriate to that neter, e.g. (for Isis): *Ast, weret hekau.* (Chants will be found for each *neter* in the sections dedicated to them.)

Pick up the statue and pass it back and forth through the incense smoke. Say:

'Oh, (neter's name and epithets),
Hear me and awaken to my presence.
May the heka of your divine spirit enter into this stone.
I open your mouth that you might speak.
I open your eyes that you might see.
I open your ears that you might hear.
Abide here in gentleness.
Abide here in power.
I ask this in your name, Oh (name of neter).'

Holding the statue, imagine that it begins to glow with the *heka* of the *neter*. See this as a soft glow coming down from the centre of creation. Visualise the *neter* coming to inhabit their vessel in your enclosure. When you feel the presence of the *neter* is with you, place the statue back on the altar. Then bow to the *neter* and welcome them in your own words.

Permanently Enlivening a Statue with *Heka*

Khemetic priests believed the cult statue in a temple served as an earthly body that a *neter* could choose to inhabit at any time. Therefore, the priesthood tended to the statues as if they were tending to the deities themselves. Statues were 'woken' at dawn with sunlight and the music of sistra. They were offered food and drink and were anointed with perfumed oils and unguents. Priests censed them with purifying incenses and 'dressed' them with clothes of specific colours. At night, the statues were 'put to bed' and their shrines were locked until the morning when everything began again at dawn. The statues also underwent special ceremonies, sometimes known as the 'opening of the mouth'. During this ceremony, priests would coax the *heka* of the deity into the statue, thereby transforming it from an inanimate piece of stone into a vessel for the essence of the *neter*.

If you have a permanent representation of a *neter*, rather than statues that represent different *neteru* at different times, they can be cared for in a similar way. When you first acquire the statue, enact the consecration rite for inviting *heka* into the stone. When you have finished, anoint the statue with oil and wrap it in cloth of appropriate colour, leaving it on your altar overnight.

Thereafter, when not 'in use' the statue can be kept in a 'shrine', perhaps a cupboard or on a shelf designated as its home within your household. You can put fresh flowers beside it, as well as crystals or other magical artefacts. You can adorn the neck of the statue with a necklace of an appropriate colour. If you wish, you could also make daily offerings of food that you may later feed to pets or place outside for wild creatures to consume. You could anoint your statue with perfumed oil or burn incense near it. Small libations of fresh water or cups of wine are also appropriate. At night, you could cover the statue with a cloth reserved for that purpose.

As you undertake these actions, visualise strongly that the

representation of the *neter* subtly alters to become a suitable and permanent receptacle for divine energy that the *neter* can inhabit when you wish to communicate with them.

Communing with the *Neter* Heka

For most of the *neteru* with whom you'll commune through this system, you'll visualise visiting them in their temples. Heka did not have temples dedicated to him, so in this case the visualisation is different.

In order to commune with Heka, create your enclosure as usual and sit in the centre of it. Breathe deeply and evenly for a minute or so to alter your state of consciousness for visualisation.

Take yourself to a visualised location of your choice, somewhere in ancient Khemet – an oasis, a courtyard, a quiet part of a village, or in the desert. Visualise that you shake a sistrum to call Heka to you. Feel the energy in your environment being stirred by this action.

The *neter* appears before you, carrying the twin serpents. These entwined creatures are symbolic of DNA. Thus, the *neter* who represents the power of the universe also holds the secret knowledge of creation. Spend some time communing with Heka. Ask him to share his knowledge with you.

Return to normal consciousness in your own time, and then dismantle the enclosure.

Vr Heka: Words of Power

Spellcasting was common in Khemet, and a large number of descriptions have survived on stelae and scrolls to tell us much about the magic of those who made them. It was believed that words were powerful; they possessed a life of their own. Hieroglyphs were pictograms loaded with meaning and energy and were known as *ur heka* – literally words of power. Words played a great part in the construction of spells, as they still do today in the Western Tradition.

When a physician-priest acted to heal someone, he might paint the inside of a bowl with relevant hieroglyphs, fill it with water and then make his patient drink the water, so that they'd take the *heka* of the words into themselves and thus be healed. Or a patient might be required to wear a linen strip, inscribed with hieroglyphs, to achieve a specific effect.

The Khemetu used love spells, and remains of these have been found that appear somewhat sinister. For example, in order to sway the affections of a woman for a male client, a priest fashioned a 'doll' of the woman and then pierced it with iron nails. This suggests the worst kind of malign magic, perhaps a spell to kill, but this was not the case. Through piercing the doll with nails, the priest sought to secure the affections of the woman for his client. The ethics of this seem dubious if not repellent nowadays, as it's considered wrong to influence another person's will by magic, but the Khemetu had a different world view, so their actions shouldn't be judged by modern standards.

A spell is a symbolic act with intention, designed to achieve a particular objective. It's a small working you might do within your designated sacred space as part of a ritual, although spells can be cast at any time, in any place. The only tools required are your concentration, focus and desire.

When casting spells, either within or outside the sacred enclosure, you can use Khemetic hieroglyphs as part of the process. Dictionaries of Egyptian/English translations give both the pronunciation and the hieroglyph for Khemetic words. Alternatively, you can use other 'ingredients' for your spell and ask a particular *neter*, (especially Isis, as magic is her province), to empower it for you.

As to why you'd cast a spell, the reasons are limitless. You might want to help a friend in need or help yourself. You might want to heal a person or an animal. You might want to influence conditions around a certain situation. In some circumstances, you might need to protect yourself or others from hostile acts and intentions.

A Word on Hexing

Casting a spell to limit the actions of another, typically an enemy who wishes you or someone else harm, is regarded as 'hexing'. There is much debate in the pagan community about the ethics of this, but my personal opinion is that everyone has the right to protect themselves. As long as you perform the binding spell with the right intention, i.e. to protect and not to harm another, your intention is good. You should never wish harm upon someone else, no matter what they've done. The best approach is to ask for the enemy to lose interest in you or a situation; in essence, to hide you from them. A common practice in protection spells is to use a mirror to reflect any evil intention back to its perpetrator, so they get a taste of their own medicine. Ultimately, you should ask the *neteru* that any enemy learns from whatever you send their way, so that they're not harmed but given awareness. Your aim should be that they'll see the folly of wanting to harm others.

The Basic Formula for Minor Rituals

Spells can be termed minor rituals, as opposed to a full-length rite when you interact with specific *neteru*. When casting spells, you should draw upon your own instincts and imagination to determine what actions and components will be most effective under the circumstances. But here is a general overview of the process:

First, decide upon the objective of your spell.

Choose the materials you'll use as the focus of your spell. This could include significant herbs, items that belong to someone, pictorial/word representations of your goal, gem stones or any combination of these. You can write words or hieroglyphs on a piece of paper and symbolically burn it, or else wrap the ingredients in a pouch and bury it, or hang the pouch in an appropriate place. You could include any other item that feels pertinent, but spells generally involve small items rather than large ones.

Decide which *neter* you will call upon as part of the spell.

Devise a rhyme or a set of phrases to chant as you combine the ingredients. You could write particular words or hieroglyphs on a scrap of paper or cloth. This could be something as simple as 'Isis, Great of Magic, empower this spell and aid my desire.' Or, if you prefer and it seems appropriate, you could devise something longer and more complicated.

Gather your materials and imbue them with *heka* to empower them. You can do this by visualisation, or by passing them through incense smoke and sprinkling them with natron to purify them.

You can include any ritual actions that seem pertinent such as creating a 'poppet' to represent a person who is the object of a spell. A poppet can be bound with ribbon to represent the restriction of their actions or clothed in a colour to promote health and healing. You should use your imagination and creativity to the full when composing and performing spells.

When all the items are ready, place them upon your altar. Focus upon your intention, and chant to raise energy. Direct this energy into the components or focus of the spell.

Place the spell components somewhere you've previously decided upon or burn them.

Forget about the spell. Let it do its work.

To dispose of a poppet, wait until you feel it's done its work and is no longer needed. In your sacred enclosure, declare that the work is done and that the poppet is no longer a tool of magic. Cleanse it with natron and incense smoke. Thank the *heka* that resided in it for its assistance and state that you release it. State that the poppet is now an empty vessel of no import. Then either bury the poppet or burn it.

Formulating Intention for Greater Rituals

Before any ritual, you should be clear in your mind about what to want to achieve. You will send visualised images to the *neter*, and these must be as precise as you can make them. For example, if you want help with a forthcoming job interview, you must show the *neter* images of the outcome you want to achieve. The person interviewing you could have a label on their clothes saying 'employer'. You could visualise a document being signed which is called 'contract of employment for (your name).' You should also show yourself as being pleased and contented, having got what you desire. Similarly, if you should do a ritual to help alleviate financial difficulty, show the *neter* a bank statement with your account on it, with the healthiest balance you can imagine.

In ritual, the intention should not be about hope so much as about an outcome already received. For moments within the enclosure, removed from everyday reality, you must *believe* utterly that what you want is already yours. Then, when you dismantle the enclosure and return to mundane reality, simply forget about the task you undertook. Let the energy you raised go off and do its job.

Magic will take the path of least resistance, so you must be as specific and detailed in your visualisation of the goal as possible. You must not allow for any unwanted side effects to occur, such as asking for help with finances and then it coming to you in a way you'd not want, such as a legacy after a death or compensation for an injury. Remember: *It must harm none...* This phrase should be the foundation stone of the words of your requests.

Part Two
The *Neteru*

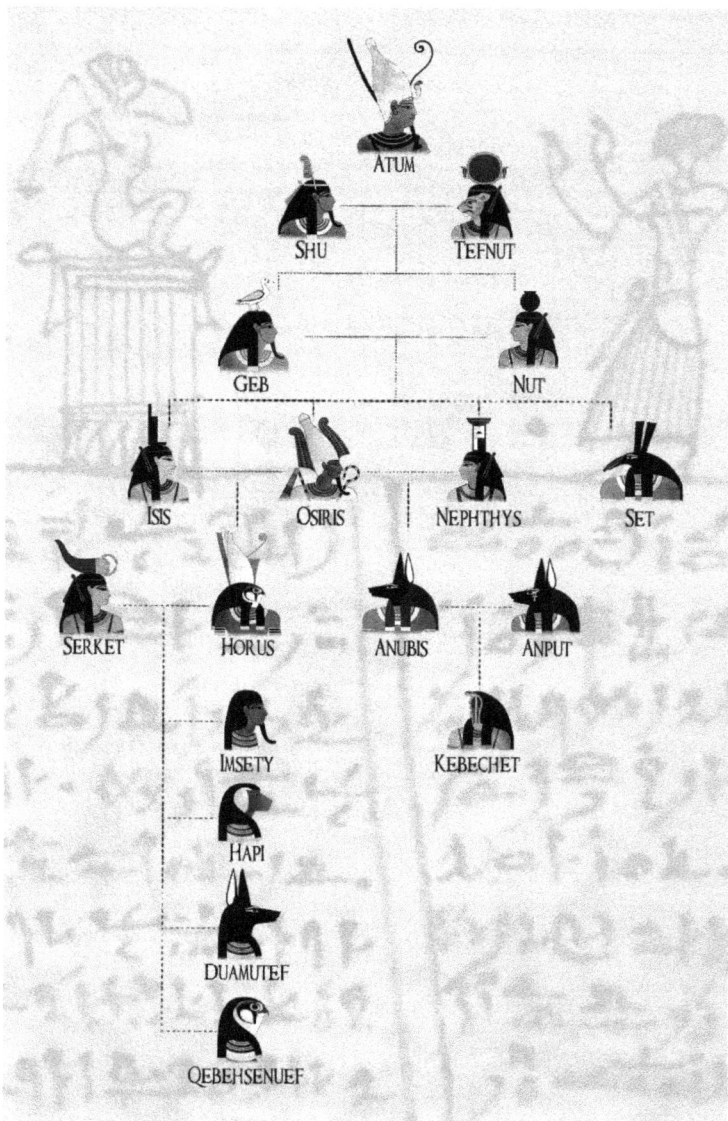

The Family Tree of the Heliopolitan Neteru

The Roles of Male & Female Neteru

Within the Western Tradition deities often have set roles
assigned to their gender. For instance, deities of the earth are
frequently regarded as female, since women give birth to
children and perpetuate human life. The moon is also most
commonly seen as female. The cool white light that guides
the tides is mirrored in the cycles within women's bodies. The
sun is generally imagined as male, a bright, overt and flaring
radiance in contrast to the subtle, magical light of the moon.
Although there of course many exceptions, male deities are
often lustful and judgmental, and/or warlike and ferocious.
There are goddesses who share the bellicose qualities, such as
Andraste, a Celtic goddess of war, but these are in the
minority of female deities. If the goddess is vicious it
generally refers to natural disasters and catastrophic weather.
Femininity frequently equates to the earth mother, nurturing
deities or goddesses of love, whereas gods tend to possess a
sterner aspect. The mother goddess has her consorts, who are
deities of nature, but she takes prominence. The Green Man
and the Horned God have a threatening side to their nature –
they represent the wild forest and its creatures. Beautiful
young gods, as in the dying and resurrecting deities of nature,
such as Adonis and Attis, are usually boys, or men who are
newly adult. They are not represented as father gods of
nature. In organised religion, a father god is generally an
unbending individual with a bible of rules to follow.

In Khemet, male *neteru* could be gentle paternal deities of
nature, who were peaceful and benevolent – such as Osiris
and early versions of Geb. The moon was also personified
as male in the *neteru* Khonsu, Iah (who eventually merged
with Osiris) and Thoth. Even the original imagining of Set
was not hostile or dangerous as he's now typically

perceived. Later in Khemetic history, perceptions shifted slightly. In the myths, some male *neteru* eventually took on a more belligerent aspect. Geb is an example of such modification as explored later in this book. This was partly if not entirely due to the influence of the Greeks, through Alexander the Great, who conquered Khemet around the 7th Century BC. The Greeks, and later the Romans, ruled Khemet for centuries, bringing their culture and beliefs with them. The most prominent of the Khemetic *neteru* were adapted to be more like the Greek and Roman gods of whom they were considered counterparts.

In early Khemetic mythology, it was not uncommon for female *neteru* to be far more ferocious than the males – such as in the Eyes of Ra: leonine-headed deities like Pakhet and Sekhmet. Both Tefnut and Sekhmet have myths associated with them in which they go on the rampage and slaughter humans indiscriminately in a lust for blood. Yet Osiris, regarded as one of the most powerful *neteru* in Khemetic lore, is portrayed in the story of his kingship as unfailingly kind and gentle; he is virile, yet he possesses feminine qualities. The land and its people prosper during his reign. Eventually, he becomes a passive victim of his envious brother Set, while Isis is the *neter* who gets things done, using guile, magic and trickery when necessary to achieve her aims – not least rescuing and reviving Osiris.

And yet I find no discernible gender bias in these myths. *Neteru* who are gentle and peaceful are not weaker than more forceful and assertive peers. The *neteru* are what they are, true to their functions. I think it's interesting to consider this in the light of how these things are perceived in the modern world. Some drawn to pagan belief systems might be used to communing with a gentle, nurturing mother goddess of nature. In Khemetic magic, they will meet the gentle, nurturing father god of the earth.

Evolving Ancient Deities

In creating this system, I drew upon the knowledge and experience I've gained over decades of working with the Khemetic *neteru*. When you interact consistently with particular gods and goddesses you build up a relationship with them – they become alive to you because you put your own energy and desires into them. They might have seen you through difficult phases in your life and comforted you in times of sadness and grief. You might have called upon them in dire need and had your circumstances improve. You might have celebrated with them when success and triumph manifested in your life. They are, ultimately, aspects of our selves – our higher selves – but they also take on a kind of independent existence because we invest them with our hopes and fears, our beliefs.

Exploring the *neteru* in depth for this book, and performing the new rituals I wrote for them, I began to flesh out the individual characters in my mind. I saw them as part of a living family, fraught with friction at certain times, as any family is. Each *neter* differs from any other if they have their own personality, even when they share common qualities.

Most of the myths that bring dramatic realism to the lives of the *neteru* derive from quite late in Khemetic history, and I've expanded these with the impressions I've acquired from visualisation and ritual, similar to how the Greeks and Romans embellished the old myths. I've also drawn upon the experiences and ideas of those with whom I work magically and who have contributed to this system. Therefore, you should appreciate that in this work ancient myth is mixed with modern interpretation. The *neteru* within these pages have been adapted and expanded to be more relevant for our times and the aspects of life that most concern us.

The Creation Myth of Heliopolis

In the mythology of Khemet that remains to us, there is more than one version of how the world came to be. Temple complexes throughout the country had different groups of *neteru* associated with such stories, but the Heliopolitan version is the story that gives the most detail – possibly because it was expanded by other cultures, later in Egyptian history. Heliopolis is the Greek and Roman name for this city. In earlier times, it was known as Iunu or Awanu; its ruins lie beneath the suburbs of modern north-eastern Cairo. The myths associated with this area are commonly referred to nowadays as Heliopolitan.

The *neteru* associated with the Heliopolitan myth are known collectively as the Ennead, which means a group of nine. However, when you count the creator *neter* Atum and his descendants, the family comprises ten members, but generally Horus the Elder, Atum's third grandson, is not included within the Ennead, possibly being due to the story having different versions, and a second Horus being included later on as the son of Isis and Osiris. Within this system, I've kept Horus the Younger as the sole Horus of the Ennead to avoid confusion.

The story of the creation of the world begins with the Nun, the primal waters from which the Primal Mound of Creation emerged, also called Iunu. Although the Nun was not worshipped as a *neter*, it was often represented in temples as a sacred lake, (such as in Karnak and Abydos), and there would have been a shrine dedicated to this primal force within the temples. It symbolised the timelessness and formlessness before order and form came to the world. According to the myth, before the world was created there existed only a state of chaos and elements in flux.

Then, from the waters of the Nun, arose the first *neter*, Atum. An ancient document called *The Pyramid Texts* relate that the Primal Mound was called the 'High Hill in Iunu', and that it was actually a form of Atum. Only when he – or rather *they*, as Atum should be regarded as beyond specific gender – appeared as, or on, this High Hill did the first light break over the eternal darkness of the Nun.

Atum was androgynous since they 'gave birth' to all the other *neteru*. This is an aspect they share with other, later *neteru*, such as Neith, the creator goddess of Sais, who also produced offspring by herself.

One of Atum's epithets was 'Lord to the Limit of the Sky'. Their first action was to develop themself into a being. They stood upon the Primal Mound of Iunu, which then evolved into the Benben, a pyramid-shaped stone. This was an important part of Khemetic myth and was seen as the abode of the sun himself. Atum was the supreme being, master of the forces of the universe.

> *'O Atum! When you came into being,*
> *you rose up as a High Hill,*
> *You shone as the Benben Stone*
> *in the Temple of the Benu in Heliopolis.'*

From *The Pyramid Texts*

The Benu referred to in this quote is a mythical fantastical bird, the Egyptian prototype of the later Greek phoenix. Like Atum, the Benu was self-created, and also an aspect of the creator god. The cry of the Benu announced the coming of life and existence and broke the endless silence of the night and darkness before creation. In Egyptian art, the Benu was depicted as bird similar to a large grey heron.

*'All manifestations came into being after I developed...no sky
existed, no earth existed... I created on my own every being... my fist
became my spouse... I copulated with my hand...I sneezed out Shu...
I spat out Tefnut... Next Shu and Tefnut produced Geb and Nut...
Geb and Nut then gave birth to Osiris... Set, Isis, and Nephthys...
ultimately they produced the population of this land.'*

Atum's words from the *Papyrus Brehmer-Rhind*

With no consort to help them create the *neteru*, Atum
masturbated, (as indicated in the quote above 'my fist
became my spouse') and produced from their seed their
first children, Shu and Tefnut, the primal male and female.
Shu was associated with heat and dryness, for his name
means 'dry, parched and empty', while Tefnut was a *neter*
of moisture, in particular the moistness of the sky. Another
version of the myth suggests that Atum consumed
'moisture' they spat from their mouth, (which some say
indicates they consumed their own seed), and this became
Tefnut. The air they breathed from their nose became Shu.

Atum can be regarded as a version of another prominent
creator *neter*, Amun, who is often referred to as being a part
of the sun god, Ra. In an ancient hymn, it is said:

*'Oh Amun-Ra, the gods have gone from thee. What flowed forth
from thee became Shu, and that which was emitted by thee
became Tefnut; thou didst create the nine gods at the beginning
of all things, and thou wast the Lion God of the Twin Lion Gods.'*

The 'Twin Lion Gods' were Shu and Tefnut. Collectively,
they could be known as the Aker gods, the lions of
yesterday and today, each facing away from one another.
Tefnut represented the setting sun, while Shu represented
the rising sun. Shu can be depicted as a lion, or a lion-
headed man, but his usual form is that of a man wearing
upon his head one, two or four feathers. The symbol of the

feather is the hieroglyph for his name. The Khemetu believed he was the space that existed between sky and earth, and he was therefore shown in sculptures and reliefs as a figure kneeling upon one knee, lifting up with two hands the disk of the sun. Sometimes, he is shown without feathers on his head, but in their place will be found a decoration that represents the hind quarters of a lion. As well as personifying dryness, or dry heat, or air, Shu was a *neter* of light. He was light personified, who manifested in the rays of the sun by day and the beams of the moon at night. Shu was also regarded as life itself, because of the life-breath of the creator who gave rise to him.

Like her brother, Tefnut can be shown in pure animal form as a lioness, or as a full human, but is most often depicted as a lioness-headed woman. She wears a solar disk on her head, frequently decorated with a uraeus serpent, and carries an ankh and a sceptre. Generally, she appears very similar to Sekhmet, but some sources cite that Sekhmet always has rounded ears, while Tefnut's tend to be squared off.

In one version of the story, Atum created Shu and Tefnut in the waters of the Nun, before the Iunu came into being. After their 'birth', Shu and Tefnut became separated from their creator and were lost in the Nun. Atum sent their eye to look for their children, and once the offspring were found, they were named Shu as Life and Tefnut as Order, powerful natural forces. Shu and Tefnut lay entwined with their creator in the Nun, where they were kept safe from harm.

But eventually Atum tired of this inert existence and asked the Nun how they could create a more congenial resting place. The Nun said, *'Kiss your daughter, Order, put her to your nose; so will your heart live. Never let her leave you. Let*

Order, who is your daughter, be with your son, Shu, who is Life.'
Atum then asked Shu to support them while they held
Tefnut 'to their nose', which we can suppose is a
euphemism for kissing her, or perhaps something more.
From this act, the Iunu came into being and Atum was able
to rest comfortably upon it.

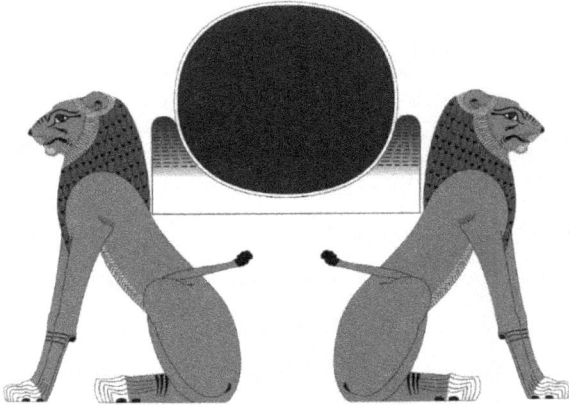

The Aker Lions

Shu and Tefnut became lovers and produced two children,
Geb, the earth, and Nut, the sky. We can discern from this
myth how the Khemetu imagined the creation of the earth.
First there was air (Shu) and moisture (Tefnut), and when
these elements came together the world came into being
creating earth and sky.

The Khemetu often represented the universe by showing
Shu standing with his arms raised to support the
outstretched body of a woman. The woman is Nut, his
daughter the sky, and she usually wears a long dress
covered with stars. A man lies prone at Shu's feet and this is
Geb, his son the earth. Shu separated earth from sky, which
in the legend created problems. One story relates that while
still in the womb, Nut had been in conflict with her mother,

Tefnut, and when the time came to be born, freed herself violently. As Shu and Tefnut had done before them, Geb and Nut became lovers. Nut placed herself on top of the earth god Geb, and there are representations of this act in Egyptian art. Geb is generally shown prone, sometimes with an erect phallus, while Nut arches over him.

Shu lifting Nut above the body of Geb

Nut fell pregnant, but once this occurred, their father Shu became jealous. He put one foot on Geb, pinning him down on his back, while he lifted Nut aloft with his arms. He tore them apart, and through this act, the earth became separated from the sky by air.

Eventually Nut gave birth to her and Geb's children, who were the sun, the stars and the planets. She placed them on her belly to protect them, perhaps so that Shu could not reach them. Shu, however, was incensed that his cherished daughter had born children to her brother Geb. He decreed that she could never again be delivered of a child in any month in any year.

Nut was naturally furious about this and decided she must do something about it. Atum had been occupied with acts of creation while this family drama was acted out and had created further *neteru*. The legend says that Nut had another lover, the *neter* Thoth, who among his other attributes was associated with time. She challenged him to a game of dice, which she won. She demanded from Thoth five extra days, which were separate from the normal year. This part of the myth shows how the Khemetu explained away the five extra, or epagomenal days, which they added to their calendar of three hundred and sixty days. On these days, as they were not part of the normal year, Nut was able to give birth again. It was said that on the first day, she bore Osiris, on the second, Horus (the elder), on the third Set, on the fourth Isis, and on the fifth Nephthys. Eventually, Osiris became the husband of his sister Isis, and Set paired with Nephthys. Thus Atum, their children and grandchildren (discounting Horus the Elder, who doesn't appear in all versions of the myth) became the nine gods known as the Great Ennead of Iunu.

It is tempting to think that the ancient story of the Ennead was partly based upon truth, not in the sense of supernatural beings performing supernatural acts, but that the story might be based on a dim memory of an early dynasty of kings and queens. The legend goes on to relate that Shu became king of Egypt, where he ruled for many years. As he grew older, he lost his power, becoming weak in his body and his eyes. (This suggests a human man rather than a god.) As he was no longer able to exert control, his followers began to fight amongst themselves. More importantly, now that his father had lost his strength, Geb was able to exact a revenge for the time when Shu had separated him from his beloved, the *neter* of the sky. In some versions of the story, Geb also envied his father's kingship.

Perhaps seeking sanctuary from his warring people and his hostile son, Shu departed to a heavenly realm, along with those of his followers still loyal to him. Once he had left the earth darkness fell upon it, and a terrible howling wind sprang up. For nine days, it was so dark that no-one could even see one another. Then, after this time, the wind died down and the light returned. Geb chose this moment to ascend to the throne of his father and everyone in the royal palace bowed down before him. He became king of Khemet, while Shu took his place among the *neteru* as an attendant of Atum or Amun-Ra.

Another legend continues the story of this royal/divine family and is probably of later origin than the original myth, most likely with Greek influences. It was said that once Shu had left Khemet, but before Geb became king, Geb 'fell in love' with Tefnut, his mother. He went to where she lived in the palace at Memphis, and here forced himself upon her. The story goes that he raped her with great violence but was not punished for it by man or *neter*. He simply became king in Shu's place. By taking the king's wife for himself, Geb could become king. To him, it was apparently irrelevant that the woman concerned was his mother, and the part of the story that tells us he 'fell in love with Tefnut' does not exactly ring true.

At this point, the story ends. Nothing remains to tell us what happened to Tefnut after this. However, there is another, very early surviving legend about her. This story departs from the strict narrative of the Ennead, as it takes place in a time when the sun *neter* Ra ruled on Earth as King of Khemet. Tefnut was known as the 'Eye of Ra', just as Sekhmet, Bast and Hathor would later on. This story is very similar to a legend of Sekhmet rampaging against humankind.

For some reason, which was not recorded, Tefnut became estranged from her father, Ra, and fled into Nubia. In this land, she transformed herself into a lioness. She raged through the countryside, emitting flames from her eyes and nostrils. Viciously, she drank the blood and fed on the flesh of both animals and humans. It is conceivable that this legend speaks of a time of drought in Khemet, when moisture went away and was replaced by cruel, murderous heat. It was up to the other gods to persuade the goddess of moisture to return.

As time went on, Ra missed his Eye, and longed to see her again. He summoned Shu to him, along with Thoth, who was the scribe of the *neteru* and famous for his eloquence. Ra must have known he'd need the powers of persuasion to draw Tefnut back to him. Ra issued the command that Shu and Thoth must go to Nubia and bring back his recalcitrant daughter. Before they set off on their journey Shu and Thoth disguised themselves as baboons. The baboon is an animal sacred to Thoth.

Eventually, Thoth and Shu found Tefnut in Nubia. Thoth began at once to try and persuade her to return to Khemet. Tefnut, however, wasn't interested. She liked hunting in the desert and was perfectly happy where she was. Thoth would not give up though and wove stories to depict to her how gloom had descended upon Khemet since she had left. The people clearly needed her. Thoth also promised that the game animals she loved hunting so much would be piled high for her on the altars in Khemet. She would not have to hunt for herself again. The Khemetu would do anything for her if she'd just return home. Ultimately, wooed by Thoth's promises, Tefnut relented and returned to Khemet accompanied by the two baboons. All the way there, Thoth kept her entertained with stories. Tefnut made a triumphant entry back into the homeland, accompanied by a host of Nubian musicians, dancers and baboons. She went from city to city, amid great rejoicing, until finally she was reunited with her father, and restored to her rightful position as his Eye.

A common fear in many ancient cultures was that when the sun disappeared at night it might never return. Similarly, when it lost its heat in winter, the people hadn't the scientific knowledge to be assured of its return. Consequently, they constructed myths to help them understand these frightening processes. The return of Tefnut to Khemet symbolised the miraculous return of the sun, auguring a period of warmth and light after a period of darkness or a season of lifelessness.

In *The Pyramid Texts*, Tefnut is credited with creating pure water for the king's feet from her vagina. She was responsible for the pharaoh's Delta residence and there created a pool for him. One of her titles is 'The Lady of Heaven', while another is 'The Distant One', which refers to the period she was in Nubia. According to the writer E.A. Budge, Tefnut was originally a *neter* of gentle rain and soft wind, and later became identified with other female *neteru*, of whom some if not all were associated with lionesses, such as Nehemauit at Hermopolis; Menhit at Latopolis, Sekhmet in Memphis and Apsit in Nubia.

Shu and Tefnut generally have to be regarded as one entity, as they were reputed to share a soul. Dendera was known as Per-Shu, which means 'the house of Shu', The city Apolloninus Magna was called Hinu-en-Shu-nefer, Edfu was 'the seat of Shu' and one name for Memphis was 'Palace of Shu'. A part of Dendera was also known as 'the House of Tefnut'. It's not known whether there were statues of Shu and Tefnut in these cities, but it is probable that they were worshipped throughout the land in the form of lions. The people of Heliopolis kept sacred lions in the temple of Helios.

Tefnut did not venture into Africa merely in legends. She became a popular goddess in Kush and Nubia, where she was credited with being the wife of local deities such as Apedemak and Arensnuphis. She was also known there as a wife of Thoth.

Some researchers now believe that the site of the sphinx in Giza is that of the first creation or the Primal Mound. At one time, it would have been surrounded by water, the sacred lake or Nun. Shu and Tefnut, as lions, guarded the eastern and western horizons. Shu, as lion of the eastern horizon, supervised the rising of the sun each morning, while Tefnut, as lion of the western horizon, guarded the sun by night. It has been suggested by the Egyptian writer Bassam El-Shammaa, with convincing conjecture, that at one time there were two sphinx. Shu looked out upon the east, and still remains to this day, but there was another sphinx that represented Tefnut looking out to the west, which has now been destroyed or buried.

For a modern practitioner of magic, Tefnut can be seen as a *neter* of knowledge, in that she has the wisdom of the source of creation. She is a teacher, who can lead the way along the path of development or initiation. She cannot really be seen as a lunar goddess, per se, even though she is associated with water and the sky at night. She is the setting sun, the evening, the guardian of the dark hours, the mistress of the primal waters. According to Lawrence Durdin-Robertson, in his book, '*Year of the Goddess*', the 21st May can be regarded as a feast day to Tefnut. This is because in the Dendera Zodiac, Gemini, the Twins, is represented by Shu and Tefnut.

Rituals and visualisations are included in this book for all the *neteru* with whom you'll work, except for Atum. As the prime creator, Atum remains a rather distant, inscrutable presence once Creation has been initiated. Atum's prime function was to fire the spark of life. Thereafter, this *neter* remains the first of the divine tribunal who judges the acts of other *neteru*. Atum's function has no correlation in human life experience. They represent the spark of life itself. Forms of the sun deity such as Ra or Amun, associated with Atum, are not included in this work. As this volume focuses upon the Ennead, you'll commune with the descendants of Atum, who are more approachable than their remote progenitor. However, you will perform a pathworking to experience the Creation itself.

Visualisation:
Witness to the Creation of Life

What follows is a pathworking for which you don't need to construct the sacred enclosure – although you can if you want to. Otherwise the procedure for creating lesser sacred space will suffice.

This visualisation explores the myth of the creation of Atum, Shu, Tefnut, Geb and Nut. The point of this working is simply to visualise the first moments of creation through the imagery of the myth and how this applies to your magical life. It is part of the Great Work and within this system the first step. The term Great Work derives from 'Magnum Opus', which was the goal of the early alchemists, who sought to transform themselves from base matter into gold, in a spiritual sense.

Construct your ritual space as you desire, then prepare yourself for visualisation. Charge the atmosphere with *heka.* Breathe deeply and slowly for a while to help alter your state of consciousness.

Now, imagine that you are sitting cross-legged, floating in absolute darkness, utter nothingness. It is neither hot nor cold. You feel relaxed and comfortable in this situation, set apart from mundane reality. Normal everyday cares have no meaning here. You are free and calm. Take some moment to bask in this feeling.

Gradually, you become aware of unseen activity around you. There is no sound, just a sense of movement. You realise that what you're perceiving is chaos in perpetual motion – what came before Creation. This is the building blocks of life. Raw potential. You feel a sense of imminence building up. Something is about to happen, but not to you. For this moment, you are simply a witness.

Now, your perception shifts, and you find yourself floating above an endless sea. It too is dark, as is the space above it, but you can perceive ripples within the depths. This is the Nun, the primal waters from which, in Khemetic myth, all life arose. There is no light in the accepted sense, but you're aware of shapes around you.

As you gaze upon the Nun, you see that something is rising from it in front of you – what appears to be an immense dark hill. This shape rises up and up, the dark water running from it. This is the god Atum in their earliest form, the High Hill in Iunu, the Primal Mound. As the *neter* rises from the waters, so the first light breaks over the limitless ocean. This is the first day. Rays of pale yellow and peach-coloured radiance dispel the eternal darkness. The sky becomes lighter, becomes dark blue, with the rising sun at the horizon, emitting a rosy light. This light reflects from the ripples in the Nun that spread out from the hill.

As the sun begins to rise – an immense golden globe – Atum, in a humanoid form, manifests upon the crown of the hill. They sit enthroned upon the Mound, the site of the first temple. As you watch, a white, pyramid forms around Atum, the original Benben stone.

Atum stands up and steps forth from the portal of the temple, a gigantic androgynous being, containing within them the potential for all life. Behind them, a great bird, like an enormous grey heron, flies out from the temple. This is the Benu bird, an aspect of Atum, which utters a piercing cry to shatter the eternal silence and herald the coming of life. The bird soars upon into the new sky, and its cry becomes a song, within which are words only for you to perceive, to hear.

This time is an Awakening. From this moment on, so your world is new and you recreate yourself within it. Contemplate how the moment of creation applies to you personally, your own evolution. Imagine it as the moment when 'the light' breaks over your own darkness, when you become aware of the mysteries of life.

You get to your feet and find you can walk across the water towards the Primal Mound. You walk up it. As you do so, the arms of Atum spread wide, as if cupping the rising sun behind the temple. You stand still, some yards away from Atum. Now the *neter* breathes out, and you experience this as a wave of cool, moist air. This becomes mist, which before your eyes gradually takes on a solid shape. Eventually, the neter Tefnut appears before you. She stands with closed eyes on the left side of her creator: she is a woman with the head of a lioness, her arms folded across her chest, her hands upon her shoulders.

Now Atum, breathes out again, and you experience this as a

gust of hot, dry air. This shimmers in front of you, like the heat haze that can be seen in air on a very hot summer's day. This shimmering air begins to take on a form, and gradually the neter Shu appears before you. He too stands with closed eyes, on the right side of his creator, with his arms in the same position as his sister's. He appears as a beautiful man wearing a head-dress of ostrich feathers.

Now Atum, utters a lilting song, which is like the fall of rain and the rush of a searing wind. Shu and Tefnut open their eyes and gaze upon you. They are the next creators, who will combine their own essences to create a fertile soup of potential. Heat and water combined.

The *neteru* stand before their creator and form a swirling mist of their breath. Within this mist, curled around each other, the forms of Nut and Geb begin to take shape. Eventually, they are fully formed and stand in front of their creators, a little further down the Primal Mound. They too are asleep at first. Nut has a dark body filled with points of light, while Geb's skin is brown and covered in moss and small plants.

Now Atum, Shu and Tefnut utter a new song together. This is the song of waking the earth and the sky, which as yet is empty of stars. Nut and Geb open their eyes and join with the song of creation.

There is a blaze of light and energy, which temporarily blinds you. When your sight clears, you find yourself in a new place, far from the Nun.

You stand upon the earth, the realm of Geb. It is night-time and, above, you see the spectral body of Nut stretched across the sky, filling it with stars. Some of the stars fill the air around you. Some of them touch the earth.

You see that the earth is the body of Geb. Within the hills and valleys, you perceive the image of the body of a man lying down. This land is green and lush with young plants and trees. Now Shu appears and with his hands separates the earth from the sky. He personifies the atmosphere, the air we breathe and the creatures that fly within it – the layer between earth and space. His sister Tefnut, strides across the young earth, bringing life to the oceans, lakes and rivers.

Shu, Tefnut, Nut and Geb together fashion the world, filling it with life. Nut populates the universe with stars, other worlds and suns. Her arching body protects the world from harmful powers beyond the sky. While all this takes form, Atum remains a benign, distant presence overseeing these acts of further creation. Their song inspires the *neteru*.

Spend some time experiencing this ancient scene. Use all of your senses to participate in it fully. Imagine how the attributes of the first *neteru* apply to you – what does heat and coolness, and dryness and moisture, mean to you? The physical world, the sky? The *neteru* are aspects of yourself. Find them within.

You hear the voice of Atum within your mind. '*So begins the Great Work,*' they tell you. '*This is the path of magic, the commitment to work towards the greater good, through self-evolution. Through stepping upon the path to ancient Khemet, through affirming it is your purpose to take up the Great Work, so the work is initiated. My blessings go with you. I open for you the gates of the sky.*'

Affirm what Atum has told you and thank them for revealing to you their mysteries – the creation of all. Bid farewell for now to Shu, Tefnut, Nut and Geb. You will be meeting with them again very soon.

When you are ready, close your eyes in the visualisation
and see the scene around you fading into a mist. Become
aware once more of physical reality around you. Come
back into the present moment in earthly reality. Breathe
deeply, bringing your consciousness back to your body.
Move your fingers and toes, and when you are ready, open
your eyes. Then record the results of your visualisation.

The Children of Atum

Tefnut – Neter of Moisture and Coolness

Attributes of Tefnut

Tefnut is the first of the female *neteru* and the first mother, since her creator Atum did not give birth to her in the traditional sense. She represents the realisation of the self, that moment when we recognise ourselves as individuals, different to all others. Tefnut is also our opportunity to grasp hold of self-responsibility, to liberate ourselves from limiting ideologies that ultimately disempower us. We *are* responsible for ourselves. We *are* the *neteru*. And to honour them we should regard it as part of the Great Work to rise above and cast off petty human weaknesses – boundaries that in some cases aren't even real.

Tefnut stands alone as the first female. There is no herd for her to follow. She forges her own way, bringing forth life as she moves across the newly created world. We can regard her as the physical expression of new creation – a child, a painting, a book, a building, a landscape. Her influence is cool and moist – the breath of water spray at the foot of a waterfall, the mist of early dawn, the finest rain filming your skin. Her moisture encourages growth, life itself.

The Magical Purpose of Tefnut

Every neter has a lesson – or several lessons – from which we may attain magical knowledge, and therefore knowledge of the self. Tefnut – and her brother Shu - represent the threshold to everything that comes after. They are the first components of the Work.

Tefnut possesses a kind of innocence, since in her world very little has yet taken place. She creates templates for future living creatures and events. As in the words of the Goddess, found in the Wiccan tradition, *'from me all things proceed...'* Tefnut can set you upon the path to full self-awareness and through her you begin to penetrate the Mysteries – the unfathomable depths of reality.

Symbols of Tefnut

Lioness

When working with Tefnut, pictures or ornaments representing lionesses can be placed upon the altar.

Sun Disk

A representation of the sun disk worn as a crown by Tefnut can be included in altar decoration. This need be no more than a red circle, or it could be flanked by serpents.

Epithets of Tefnut

When constructing your own invocations and addresses to Tefnut, you can draw upon this list of her epithets. These derive from both ancient times and modern magical practice.

Neter of Moisture and of Order
Daughter of Atum
Sister Consort of Shu
Lady in Repose
Lady of Heaven
The Distant One
Eye of Ra
Teacher of the Way
Lady of the First Dawn
Mistress of Yesterday

Offerings to Tefnut

Ritual foods appropriate to Tefnut are seafood, freshwater fish, or dishes made with watercress, cucumber and tzatziki. The drink should be white wine, or white grape juice. If necessary, substitute pale, quite bland or delicately flavoured alternatives, but preferably not anything made of bread or cake, which is more of the earth than Tefnut's realm. The food should have some moisture. Apples and apple juice would also be appropriate.

Visualisation:
Meeting the Primal Being

This is a pathworking for which you don't need to construct the sacred enclosure – although you can if you want to. Otherwise creating less formal sacred space will suffice.

Close your eyes and breathe deeply for a while to change your state of consciousness. Then, when you feel ready, visualise your environment gradually changing. A mist fills your enclosure, so that objects around you disappear within it. Presently, the mist begins to clear, and you see a new landscape appearing around you.

You find yourself upon the primal mound, rising from the waters of the Nun. It is night-time and yet the sun burns hot in the dark sky. Before you stands Tefnut, a tall, lioness-headed woman, dressed in a robe of turquoise and gold. She wears the sun disk upon her head to represent her progenitor – the first light that is beyond duality. The sun itself shines behind the disk, becoming part of it.

As you gaze upon Tefnut, you realise you have no body. You are merely a spark of consciousness floating before her. She begins to hum and chant in a low voice, breathing her moist breath onto you, her hands weaving upon the air, conjuring mists that swirl around her. Gradually, from these components, she creates a body for you. You stretch out your arms to look at your hands. You glance down at your feet. You are perfect, free from any blemish or defect. This is the idealised primal human form. You should visualise it as you will.

As your consciousness expands to occupy this vehicle of flesh, you become aware that all the thoughts and opinions you normally hold are missing. You are utterly free of these things, existing only as pure consciousness in a new vehicle. You are free of the conditioning that might have damaged you and held you back in life, free of all the negative emotions that are diseases of the soul – guilt, hate, fear, sorrow, disappointment, envy, jealousy, anger, greed, or the lust for revenge. In this state, you can consider all creatures with an unrestricted mind, having no desire to judge or criticise. All beings are what they are, even if they don't realise what that really entails and means.

While you are in this visualisation, you may experience complete freedom, outside of the past, the present and the future. Fully *be* in this moment. Bask in what it feels like to be so weightless, so unburdened, so *present*.

Then, conjure forth a memory – a situation, perhaps, or a person – and imagine it as a scene in the air before your eyes. You and Tefnut gaze impartially at this scene. It is like watching a play. View it objectively, from the outside, with no emotional engagement. Examine the components with a neutral state of mind, including the emotions and assumptions that might have driven it, fired it up. You can pick objects up from this scene as if they were children's toys. Turn them in your hands. A block of bilious yellow might represent a sour emotion, a pool of dull grey-green viscous liquid might be envy or jealousy. A misshapen spiky object of deep red might be anger or prejudice. A hole in reality so deeply black it cannot reflect light – in fact an utter absence of colour or *anything* – might be depression. In your visualisation, these are simply *things* that may be cleared away.

Talk about the scene with Tefnut. Listen to what she might tell you. Then begin to tidy up the situation before you. Remove the negativity, make things harmonious. Open up communication between the participants, freed of damaging, uncontrolled energy in their environment.

Be aware that even as you do this, it is only a visualisation, an ideal. But appreciate how stepping back – and not wallowing in subjective opinions and assumptions – grants greater clarity. You cannot look into the mind of another. You can only view the results – from your perspective – of their actions. Be aware of how different people may react very differently to the same stimuli. This demonstrates the fluidity of the concepts of right and wrong.

Think about how very few individuals (unless suffering from a mental illness) want to deliberately commit evil. They act from what they believe is right. 'But that is not *my* right', you might think. 'That is *wrong*.' Those whose views you oppose might say the same. Understand then, we live within the worlds *we* have created – like occupying different versions of the same physical reality. No wonder there is so much conflict in the world.

This is not the time or place to argue about what is right and just. This is simply the time to understand how differences of opinion and belief will inevitably, at some juncture, cause disharmony. While you might not be able to change the world, being able to step outside the construct of your personal reality to view situations impartially helps you resolve problems in your own life.

Tefnut holds out her hands to you and you take them. '*Seek me in my temple,*' she says, '*for we have work to do, you and I.*' She blinks, as a cat does when it shows you it is content. It is the smile of the lioness.

When you are ready, close your eyes in the visualisation and see the scene around you fading into a mist. Become aware once more of physical reality around you. Come back into the present moment in earthly reality. Breathe deeply, bringing your consciousness back to your body. Move your fingers and toes, and when you are ready, open your eyes. Then record the results of your visualisation.

Ritual:
Tefnut's Mysteries

In this full-length working, you'll meet Tefnut in her temple and ask for her teachings upon your magical path.

Place a representation of Tefnut on your altar. You may use either a picture or a statue. For the latter, a statue of seated

Sekhmet will suffice, since in statues from ancient times the two goddesses are almost indistinguishable in appearance. However, bear in mind the energies of Tefnut and Sekhmet are very different, so the statue should be consecrated before use and adorned in a way to signify Tefnut, such as with purple and silver feathers, beads or ribbons.

Equipment Required

- Altar gems should be amethyst and white quartz
- Purple or white candles.
- A fresh-scented incense, either a light flowery perfume, or else reminiscent of water/rain
- The altar cloth should be purple and/or silver
- The hieroglyph of Tefnut's name
- An appropriate feast

The Ritual

Following the instructions for these procedures already given, create your enclosure and enliven your altar statue with *heka*, if you have one. Light the altar candles and replenish your incense if necessary. Then sit down in the centre. Close your eyes and breathe deeply for a while to alter your state of consciousness. Visualise your environment gradually changing. A mist fills your enclosure, so that objects around you disappear within it. Presently, the mist begins to clear, and you see a new landscape appearing around you. You carry with you a satchel of offerings for Tefnut.

It is night-time and the sky is studded with brilliant stars. You stand between two immense pillars. Before you spreads a lake of silvery water, with a small jetty nearby, to which an open boat is moored. By the light of the moon, you can make out that there is a mound in the middle of the lake. You carry a bag containing offerings for Tefnut. Touch the columns one by one and ask for passageway to the primal mound to meet with the *neter* Tefnut.

When you are ready, step into the boat. It begins to glide across the lake. You see the mound looming up closer and closer, becoming less dense and dark. You can see a white pyramidal temple at the summit, which glows in the darkness. When you reach the mound, step out of boat. Mist pours from the temple's summit. Flowers and vines entwine this ancient structure. Their heady scent pulls you towards the pyramid's entrance. You begin to climb towards it.

At the summit, you enter the temple. You are in the outer hall, where a flame burns upon a high tripod and representations of Shu and Tefnut stand against the far wall. There are corridors leading off to either side. Take the left-hand corridor, which will lead you to Tefnut's shrine. The corridor curves before you. Follow it, noting anything upon the way.

When you reach the shrine, you are surrounded by a hazy light, muted by purple shadows. The air is misty, and you can hear the ripple of water. You see that the entire tiled floor is covered by water, like a shallow pool, and that a narrow bridge arcs over it, leading to a dais in the centre that rises from the water. Here, a statue of Tefnut sits enthroned. The goddess's head is covered by a veil.

The misty air enfolds you, fine tendrils weaving before your eyes. Your senses strain to make sense of this world that constantly shifts around you. At the foot of the dais, arrange the offerings you have brought for Tefnut. Say:

'Oh Tefnut, Neter of Moisture and of Order,
Daughter of Atum,

Sister Consort of Shu,
Lady in Repose.
Awaken to my presence.
I come before you in peace.
I come before you with reverence,
And ask that I might speak with you.'

Chant: *'Tefnut, qebh, tef-tef'* for a minute or so, while gently shaking the sistrum.

(Pronounced: Teff-nut, keb, teff-teff. Meaning (roughly): Tefnut, coolness, moistness.)

A beam of hazy light strikes the statue – a radiance filled with glistening metallic motes like miniature stars. This light fills the statue, makes it glow.

For a moment, without opening your eyes, cast your inner gaze back to the image of Tefnut in your enclosure in reality. Imagine it glowing with light, filled with *heka*. Tefnut is alive in both inner and outer realities and will communicate with you.

Return to the visualisation of Tefnut's shrine and see the statue start to come alive. The stone turns to dark, furred skin and the folds of her gown become soft and silvery grey. Her eyes glow behind her veil, which she now draws back to reveal her face. Her robes of silver and amethyst shimmer as mist oozes from her body. You remember that it is said her breath creates storms. Say:

'Oh, Tefnut, Teacher of the Way, hear my desires.
Reveal to me your mysteries.
Set me upon the path of learning and knowledge.
Awaken awareness within me.
Grant me rebirth in your waters
As a priest/ess of the neteru.'

Tefnut has heard your request and inclines her head in acknowledgement. You hear the chink of crystals wound into her hair.

Approach her. As you move closer, you find that it is not mist drifting from her at all, but her breath, her very essence. Its caress is cool and invigorating. At her feet there is a deeper pool. This water has collected from the mist she exudes, a gateway to the waters of life that collect beneath her island.

Now Tefnut points towards the pool at her feet. She says: *'Gaze into my waters, meruti.'* (Meruti is a Khemetic word meaning 'beloved'.)

You look into the pool and see, just beneath the shimmering surface, a swarm of strange glittering shapes that seem to beckon to you.

Tefnut says: *'Go deep, meruti. Immerse yourself in my waters.'* Without hesitation, you plunge into the pool. Feel the water rush over and around you. You swim down and down; the pool seems bottomless.

Eventually, you find yourself in an enormous crystal cavern. It is as if you have stepped into the heart of an immense underwater geode. You feel safe here and can breathe easily. Look above and below. Stalactites and stalagmites of crystal soar and plummet for thousands of feet. Far below, in the shadowy depths, there are niches, caverns and tunnels. You are in the waters of Nun. In this womb of darkness, there are only feelings; chaotic and half-formed, roiling like the primeval waters.

Then, a cool, refreshing current rushes past you, spiralling upwards. This is Tefnut, releasing her breath into the world. Follow that stream. Let it carry you. You can see light above.

Look into that light and let go. Feel it cut through layers of old fears, doubts, outmoded beliefs, prejudices and conditioning. Feel the water pulsing against your skin. Feel your body stretch, twist and flex as the process of change begins. Parts of yourself that are no longer needed, or are unhelpful and obstructive, fall away like dead skin. This reveals your potential self, which hangs as a mirror image before you, different to, but also a reflection of, yourself. What can this image teach you? Spend some time communing with it.

When you are ready to continue, move upwards through the water and break the surface. You are in Tefnut's shrine once more, surrounded by cool, moist air. Step out of the pool. Water streams from you. Bow to Tefnut and say:

'Oh, Tefnut, Mother of Nut and Geb,
Lady of the First Dawn.
I thank you for revealing to me your mysteries.
Through your wisdom, I will walk into my future
With a sense of wonder and anticipation.
I am open to all that the neteru will reveal to me.'

Commune with Tefnut for a few minutes. You may ask her questions about your experience. She may have other things to show you.

Then, when you are ready, take out the offerings and spread them before Tefnut. Now open your eyes and come out of the visualisation, whilst imagining part of you is still in Tefnut's temple. Say:

'Oh Tefnut, Eye of Ra, Mistress of Yesterday,
Who guards the boat of the sun on its nightly journey into the Duat

I have brought offerings to you,
As symbols of thanks and respect.
Through me, may you experience their pleasures.
As I eat this food, may you enjoy its flavours,
As I drink this wine, may you savour its fire.'

Now you will feast in Tefnut's honour. Consume the food and drink, concentrating on your body sharing the pleasure of doing so with Tefnut. Leave a small portion of everything you eat and drink. After this has been done, wrap the remains in paper and leave this parcel before the statue on your altar.

When you are ready, compose yourself and return to the visualisation. See your offerings around Tefnut, which she consumes with relish. Bow to Tefnut and say:

'Oh Tefnut, Teacher of the Way,
Continue to share with me your strength and your clear sight.
Grant me your understanding. Show me your wisdom.
Give me the courage to be all that I may be,
And the ability to know myself as you know me.'

Then bid farewell to her and prepare to leave.

Go back across the bridge and out to the entrance of the temple. Walk down the hill to your waiting boat. Sail back across the lake. When you alight upon the opposite shore, you see that there are no longer two columns on the shore, but a pair of lions sitting back to back. These are the Aker lions, the lions of yesterday and today. They also represent Tefnut and Shu.

The lion who faces the east is Shu. He welcomes the light of the sun and of life, the light of the dawn. See that sun rising up into the sky, moving across the heavens, as if the day has speeded up, arcing across to meet the gaze of the other lion, who is Tefnut. She will stand watch and guard over the setting sun, which represents the land of the dead in the west, Armenti. As the sun sets, it is a bloody red and darkness fills the sky.

Now imagine the scene turns to mist around you. Return to normal reality and dismantle your enclosure in the usual way. Record the results of your work and dispose of the remains of your offerings in an appropriate way.

Shu - Neter of Warm Air and Dryness

Attributes of Shu

As Tefnut was the first female, so Shu was the first male, the first father. His attributes are dryness, warm air and sunlight. As Tefnut wears a sun-disk on her head to represent the first spark of creation, Shu wears a circlet decorated with ostrich feathers, representing the breath of life. He is the *neter* of creatures of the air and of lightness of being. He is the air that exists between earth and sky.

Shu also stands alone for he too was the first of his kind. He is the potential of all possibilities, uncontaminated and pure. He represents clear thought, ideas and expression. Ideas fly like birds around him.

Our personalities evolve by the experiences we have and how we react to them. A young human is a fragile thing, so easily moulded by conflicting forces. Even before we become self-aware, we are already partly formed, the foundations set down. This is partly why in later life, should a person seek to evolve, they might find it very difficult to break free of negative early conditioning.

The Magical Purpose of Shu

Like his sister-wife, Shu may be called upon to assist with spring-cleaning of the heart and mind. He too allows you to experience moments of sheer, joyful freedom, in which ideas can form without restriction.

Shu can be regarded as the fount of all concepts, notions and thoughts – an ideal *neter* for those seeking creative inspiration or trying to free themselves from artistic blocks. He promotes inspired thinking that is helpful in any situation in life, in tandem with Tefnut's influence of clarity and objectivity.

Symbols of Shu

Ostrich Feather

Worn as a headdress by Shu, you could decorate your altar with ostrich feathers to represent the quality of air. You could also use the feathers to 'fan' incense smoke around your Sacred Enclosure.

Epithets of Shu

When constructing your own invocations and addresses to Shu, you can draw upon this list of his epithets. These derive from both ancient times and modern magical practice.

Neter of the Air and of Dryness
Son of Atum
Brother Consort of Tefnut
He Who Holds up the Sky
Lord of the Air
Lord of Light
He Who Mediates Between Earth and Sky
He Whose Bones are the Clouds

Offerings for Shu

As a ritual feast, the food appropriate to Shu should be light and associated with air – such as meringue that contains a lot of air, or wheat or potato snacks that are 'puffed'. The ritual drink should be fizzy and pale with a light flavour, even simply sparkling water.

Visualisation:
The Birds of Imagination

What follows is a pathworking for which you don't need to construct the sacred enclosure – although you can if you want to. Otherwise the procedure for creating lesser sacred space will suffice.

Close your eyes and breathe deeply for a while to change your state of consciousness. Then, when you feel ready, visualise your environment gradually changing. A mist fills your enclosure, so that objects around you disappear within it. Presently, the mist begins to clear, and you see a new landscape appearing around you.

You find yourself in the sky, among the clouds and become aware you are a birdlike creature with wings – perhaps a bird with a human head, which is how the Khemetu often depicted spirits. Your body seems to weigh nothing at all, and you can simply ride the air currents.

Spend a few moments enjoying the freedom this form gives you. As you swoop and glide, you see a vague shape appearing in the sky before you. As you draw closer, you see that this is the summit of a mountain and growing from the rock itself is a magnificent structure: a temple of crystal and air. It is surrounded by terraces of white marble, where a multitude of birds are resting and feeding. This seems to be a sacred place to them, and they are cared for here. The air smells of a light, delicate incense.

You alight upon one of the terraces, and as you do so, you transform into a more human form. A tall figure glides out from the temple interior. You know that this is Shu. He is radiantly beautiful, dressed in a short kilt with a plume upon his head, set into a circlet head-dress. His eyes are large and lined with kohl. He says to you: *'You are welcome here, meruti, to this temple between earth and sky.'* He summons you to him and says, *'Fly with me. Open your mind to all possibilities.'*

Shu holds out his hands to you, and you take them. They are warm and dry in your hold. You both rise up into the air and then he releases you. Once again, you are winged. At Shu's side, you fly away from the mountain temple, into the clouds and currents of warm air.

After a while, the sky clears, for you and Shu have risen above the clouds, which now lie beneath. You become aware of a multitude of iridescent shapes that flicker and soar around you. Shu tells you that these are potential ideas that you can pluck from the air itself, from his own breath. And yet, they are not his ideas, but yours alone. Through him, they have sprung from your own heart, mind and soul – untainted by the views and opinions of others.

Capture one of these shining thoughts in your hands. It rests there as if it is a delicate insect. It's uncontaminated by any negativity, any emotions from the physical world. It is pure and vibrant and a gift from Shu to you. Absorb that thought into yourself and gaze inwardly upon it. No other person can tell you what this thought might be and what it means. It is entirely personal to you.

After some moments, spread out your wings and hang upon the air, basking in the flickering patterns of all this fresh, dynamic energy. Feel it entering you, enlivening your mind, filling your heart with hope, eagerness and joy. Spend some time communing with Shu, for he may have further gifts and insights to give you.

When you are ready, bid farewell to Shu and close your eyes in the visualisation. The scene disappears into mist. Become aware of physical reality reforming around you. Breathe deeply, bringing your consciousness back to your body. Move your fingers and toes, and when you are ready, open your eyes. Then record the results of your visualisation.

Ritual:
The Quest for Self-Knowledge

Place a representation of Shu on your altar. You may use either a picture or a statue.

Equipment Required

- White feathers should be placed upon the altar
- White or pale blue altar candles
- A light, airy (or flowery) incense or burning-oil
- The altar cloth should be of the palest blue or white
- A picture of the hieroglyph of Shu's name
- An appropriate feast

The Ritual

Create your enclosure and enliven your altar statue with *heka*, if you have one. Light the altar candles and replenish your incense if necessary. Then sit down in the centre. Close your eyes and breathe deeply for a while to alter your state of consciousness. Visualise your environment gradually changing. A mist fills your enclosure, so that objects around you disappear within it. Presently, the mist begins to clear, and you see a new landscape appearing around you.

It is night-time but you can sense that dawn is not far off. There is faint yellowish glow on the eastern horizon. You stand between two immense pillars. Before you spreads a lake of dark water, with a small jetty nearby, to which an open boat is moored. You can make out that there is a mound in the middle of the lake. Touch the columns one by one and ask for passageway to the primal mound.

When you are ready, step into the boat. You carry a bag containing offerings for Shu. The boat begins to glide across the lake. The mound looms up closer and closer, becoming less dense and dark. You can see a white pyramidal temple at the summit. When you reach the mound, step out of the boat.

The air around the temple summit is hazy. Small, scented flowers grow upon its walls. Their light scent pulls you towards the pyramid's entrance. You begin to climb towards it.

At the summit, you enter the temple. You are in the outer hall, where a flame burns upon a high tripod and representations of Shu and Tefnut stand against the far wall. There are corridors leading off to either side. You are drawn to the smooth-walled corridor that curves away to the right, which will lead you to Shu's shrine. A pale light seems to beckon you forward. As you step into this corridor, you see it spirals upwards, as if towards the summit of the temple. The light is always just ahead of you, until you reach the radiant shrine. This is the court of Shu in the temple above Iunu, the primal mound.

A multitude of red marble columns stretches before you. When you look up, you can see that the centre of the temple is open to the sky. At the far end of the chamber, seated upon a marble throne, is a statue of Shu, the god of Light and Air. He is constructed of pale stone. Approach the throne and arrange the offerings you have brought before the *neter*. Say:

'Oh Shu, Neter of the Air and of Dryness
Son of Atum
Brother Consort of Tefnut,
Who holds up the sky,
Awaken to my presence.
I come before you in peace.
I come before you with reverence,
And ask that I might speak with you.'

Chant: *'Shu, rebhu, sesh-teh'* for a minute or so, while gently shaking the sistrum.

(Pronounced: Shoo Reb-oo, Sesh-tay. Meaning (roughly): Shu, warmth, dryness.)

The light within the chamber grows brighter and swirls around the statue, which appears to absorb the light, then throws it out in glittering motes.

For a moment, without opening your eyes, cast your inner gaze back to the image of Shu in your enclosure. Imagine it also glows with light, as it brims with *heka*. Shu is alive in both inner and outer realities and will communicate with you.

Return to the visualisation of Shu's shrine and see his statue start to come alive. The stone turns to reddish brown skin. His face is beautiful, his wide eyes lined with kohl. He wears a headdress of ostrich feathers and holds in one hand an ankh, in the other a staff. His arms are adorned with bracelets at the wrist and below the shoulder, as are his ankles. He wears a short kilt and his chest is bare but for an ornate pectoral that hangs around his shoulders. Say:

'Oh, Shu, Lord of the Air,
He who mediates between the realms of earth and sky,
Whose bones are clouds and fog,
Hear my desires.
Reveal to me your mysteries.
Bestow upon me the knowledge of the secrets of the air.
Grant me the gift of flight
That I may know true freedom of mind and spirit.'

Shu smiles at you in acknowledgement. He holds out his hands to you and you take hold of them. At once, you rise up, transforming into a creature of air, with no substance. As you rise, aware of warm, dry currents all around you, so a great lightness fills your being. It's as if you leave below all the heaviness of life's responsibilities and trials; they cannot follow you into these rare ethers.

Shu is suspended in the air before you, and in his gaze you see the simple truth. We choose to be laden, to be heavy and weary. At any time, we can choose also to rise above these things, to experience freedom. In this state, we may examine our dilemmas with greater clarity. Answers may come to us, freed from the burden of cares.

Shu is the air, the very thing that sustains us. He therefore is life, as all members of his family symbolise different aspects of existence. He is a *neter* of light and air, representing the space between the heavens and earth. He symbolises the rising sun and with his sister the constellation of Gemini.

He says to you: *'With me, meruti, your sky is always clear.'*

Birds begin to spiral and glide around you in complex formations, as if painting messages on the air with their wings. And you know you can seek Shu's wisdom in times when all seems dark and suffocating. You can ask for him to help dispel all that weighs you down.

If there is something now that you feel is holding you back, a great weight that restricts you, ask for Shu to release it, to resolve a situation, or change circumstances that will free you. Spend some time communing with Shu and see what he has to show you. He may take you on a journey or reveal secrets to you.

When you are ready to conclude this part of the visualisation, fly with Shu back down into his shrine within the temple at the top of the Primal Mound. Here, you indicate the offerings you have spread at the base of his throne. Open your eyes and come out of the visualisation, while imagining that part of you is still in Shu's temple. Say:

'Oh Shu, Lord of Light and Lightness of Being,
Whose feathers are the emptiness of the clear sky,
Whose bones are the clouds,
Who is the voice of the wind,
The Lord of Today,
I have brought offerings to you,
As symbols of thanks and respect.
Through me, may you experience their pleasures.
As I eat this food, may you enjoy its flavours,
As I drink this wine, may you savour its fire.'

Now you will feast in his honour. Consume the food and drink, concentrating on your body sharing the pleasure of doing so with Shu. Leave a small portion of everything you eat and drink. After this has been done, wrap the remains in paper and leave this parcel before the statue on your altar.

When you are ready, compose yourself and return to the visualisation. See your offerings around Shu, which he consumes with relish. Bow to Shu and say:

'Oh Shu, neter of Light and Air,
Continue to share with me your awareness and freedom.
Grant me your clarity.
Give me the liberty to be all that I may be,
And the honesty to know myself as you know me.'

Then bid farewell to him and prepare to leave. Return to the corridor that leads outside and pass through the entrance of the temple. Walk down the hill to your waiting boat. Sail back across the lake.

When you alight upon the opposite shore, you see that there are no longer two columns on the shore, but as before when you visited Tefnut, a pair of lions sitting back to back. You have now met both of the Aker lions and have experienced the different lessons they have to teach you.

Now imagine the scene turns to mist around you. Return to normal reality and dismantle your enclosure in the usual way. Then record the results of your work and dispose of the remains of your offerings as appropriate.

Wall Painting of Cat Hunting Birds

Nut from a Wall Painting at Dendera

The Children of Shu and Tefnut

Geb and Nut
Lady of Stars and Lord of the Earth

Shu and Tefnut created Geb and Nut: the earth and sky. We can imagine these divine offspring, in magical terms, as representing your mundane self that is centred in the earthly realm, and your visionary self that yearns for the stars. To be magical, some might think that we have to distance ourselves from earthly reality and strive for the rarefied realms of the inner landscape. But the accomplished practitioner seeks balance in themselves. Even small actions in the mundane world, can be as powerful as focusing intention with purpose during a formal ritual in sacred space.

To live magically, you should strive to keep a sense of wonder around you during all aspects of daily life. You can't be a perfect being, since you are human, and sometimes you will feel sad, angry, judgmental, fearful or envious. Negative feelings are as much a part of human makeup as love, joy, compassion and tolerance, but by being aware of when these feelings assail you, and acknowledging what they are, they lose power over you. The adept strives to break the chains that enslave them to extreme emotional reactions – when a person might strike out in resentment, fear or fury. When you react, you should work towards doing so with awareness – even if sometimes you might be pushed too far by something or someone and snap. These things will happen. All of us are only human.

In the later versions of the story of the Ennead, negative reactions abounded, in that Shu was jealous of Geb, Nut was in conflict with her mother Tefnut and injured her during birth, Shu tried to deny Nut having children, Geb violated his mother and so on. Yet these *neteru* are also supposed to embody the positive aspects of life – creation itself. They are gods and goddesses, divine creators, even if at times in their stories they squabbled and brawled like spiteful children. They, like us, are full of contradictions. There is something to be learned from that – not least that humankind has always possessed the tendency to shape gods and goddesses in their own likeness rather than the other way around. Knowing this, we can begin to shape our deities how we want them, to possess attributes that are strong, positive and useful.

Visualisation:
The Marriage of Earth and Sky

What follows is a pathworking for which you don't need to construct the sacred enclosure – although you can if you want to. Otherwise the procedure for creating lesser sacred space will suffice.

Imagine, in your mind's eye, that you are floating in blackness. Darkness lies over the earth, and the sky also is dark. You hang within this void as a spark of potential, shimmering with myriad possibilities.

Gradually the scene around you begins to lighten – at first the sky. You perceive pin pricks of light forming upon the velvet blackness, millions and millions of them, which you realise are stars. As you gaze upon this wondrous scene, you perceive a shape within the stars. It's as if the elongated body of a woman arches across the sky, filled with stars. She is emerging from the horizon, and her toes and fingers seem to touch the earth. This is Nut, *neter* of the sky. Her skin is deep blue. Say to her:

'Oh Nut, whose name is Sky,
She Who Holds a Thousand Souls,
She Who Protects and is the Coverer of the Sky
Reveal to me your mysteries.'

The light of the stars now illuminates the earth with a beautiful, almost spectral light. You catch glimpses of colour in this world – the deep blue of a lake reflecting the night sky, the rich green of trees and vegetation.

You perceive a giant figure reclining upon the earth – a male, with one knee raised, one arm curled above his head, which is turned to the side. He appears to be asleep. Say to him:

'Oh Geb, Neter of Earth
He whose laughter shakes the ground
He who causes the crops to grow
Reveal to me your mysteries.'

Nut in the sky glows above Geb on the earth, showering him with light. Now you see her immense form unbend and she steps down – or out of – the horizon, a towering, shimmering woman, her bare feet smoking with astral light upon the earth, as if the steam of distant galaxies trails from her.

She calls Geb to wakefulness, and so in symbolic form, the earth becomes aware of the sky – its immeasurable distances and mystery. Geb is black of skin, and trailing plants grow upon him as if from the earth itself. His black skin is furred with soft moss in places, and his night-dark hair like the swaying branches and leaves of willows. You can feel the attraction between Geb and Nut, which goes beyond mere physical desire or emotional love. It is an irresistible attraction, the drawing of one force towards another in order to create realities greater than the sum of their parts.

As the gigantic forms of the *neteru* embrace, think about what these symbols mean to you – how the infinite mystery of the universe turns within your own mind and spirit, how the power of the physical earth empowers your body, the vehicle you inhabit in this life. Creative thoughts might come to you from the stars but the power to realise them derives from the earth, your physical self. Contemplate how the marriage of earth and sky brings forth creation, the ability to manifest the secrets of the heavens into reality.

You are both Nut and Geb and contain their potential within you. Spend some time experiencing these *neteru*. Become the sky alight with stars. Become the earth itself. Become the sum of these parts, alive with possibility and the irrepressible urge to create.

When you are ready to end the visualisation, bid farewell to the *neteru*. See the scene before fade into a mist. Return to normal consciousness and open your eyes. Be aware you're still invigorated with the energy of earth and sky. Record your experiences.

A Neter Raising the Boat of the Sky

Geb - Lord of the Earth

Having experienced the creation of Geb and Nut and their coming together, you will next commune with them separately, beginning with Geb, *neter* of the living earth.

The Attributes of Geb

Originally named Seb or Keb in Khemetic, Geb is the Greek rendition of his name. As the *neter* of the earth he was associated with a number of animals, primarily the goose, but also bulls, crocodiles, rams and snakes. One of his epithets is 'Father of Snakes' (*Nehebkau*), and snakes were sometimes referred to in Khemet as 'sons of the earth'.

In art, Geb is generally depicted as a man wearing the false beard of a pharaoh with a goose on his head, although as in the illustration above, he was occasionally represented as having the head of a serpent. He could also be represented in art as a bull, crocodile or ram.

Geb symbolised the fecund earth, the rich dark soil – he was generally depicted with brown skin, but sometimes green. He was the lord of both Black and Red lands originally – before his sons, Osiris and Set, divided rulership of these regions between them. He also had connections with the dead and the Underworld, being able to release the deceased from their tombs, so they might seek the fabled Field of Reeds, the idealised afterlife. Or, if they were considered unworthy of attaining this paradise, Geb could prevent them from leaving their place of burial. Some writers have said that the staff he carries symbolises his connection with these duties and that it was used as a weapon against disreputable dead. This staff was also held by several other *neteru* in art and is known as the *was* sceptre. The head of the artefact is a stylised jackal's head and its 'tail' is forked.

As to why Geb is associated with the goose, this might only be because his name is the same as a type of goose that existed in Khemet. One of his epithets was 'the Great Cackler', perhaps referring to the call of a goose, and his laughter was said to cause earthquakes. Most writers on the subject agree the goose was a sacred creature of Geb. We can regard the goose as symbolising his connection with the Nile and its fertile land – it was a common bird in these areas.

Geb was originally associated with growth and vegetation, providing the fruits of the land for all people. The land was known as 'The Mansion of Geb' and it was said that the barley crop grew from his ribs. He was also connected with healing, in particular to assist with scorpion stings and snake bites. In his earliest form, he appears to lack the later aggressive aspects that resulted in his attack on Tefnut, his own mother, and seizing the throne of Egypt by force from his father, Shu. It's difficult to equate these hostile aspects of Geb with his role as the earth father. While there's no doubt that in legend violence occurred – Shu *did* separate earth from sky forcibly, either through his own volition or at the orders of Atum, and Geb did take the throne and his mother by force – the myths became embellished over time. The more theatrical elements most likely derive from Greek influence – as the Greeks clearly had a fondness for giving their gods and goddesses 'soap opera' life stories, full of murder, lust and revenge. I like to think that the original Khemetic idea of the *neteru* was simply a collection of metaphors for natural states, processes and conditions, rather than them being humanised players in a lurid melodrama of petty jealousy and a hunger for power. I don't deny the *neteru* a dark and/or dangerous side – as the most potent god forms often possess – but to me the very human traits of greed and spitefulness don't belong in a symbol with which we work to improve ourselves. Even though it's impossible to say for certain what the Khemetu believed the *neteru*'s 'life stories' to be, I prefer to interpret them as much as possible as symbols for the stages of creation as the Khemetu imagined these processes – their way of trying to understand the mysteries of life.

Adopting this view, we can appreciate the qualities of Shu and Tefnut made them rarefied creatures – *neteru* of nebulous air and moisture. Nut and Geb, their children, manifested the physical world and sky – the earth with its fertile land and the heavens full of stars. Shu, as the personification of air, separated the land from the heavens, as our atmosphere separates us from the airlessness of space. Geb became the ruler of the earth, because he *was* the earth. Under normal circumstances, Geb and Nut could never come together. In the myth, only by the intervention of magic was Nut able to manipulate reality and allow the five epagomenal days, extra to the normal calendar, during which she and Geb created their children.

Geb was associated with the growing of crops, a role taken on by his son Osiris once he came to the throne. After this, Geb became part of a divine tribunal, whose function was to act as judges among the *neteru*.

The Magical Purpose of Geb

If Shu and Tefnut represent your first steps upon the path of the Great Work, Geb represents 'grounding' the knowledge you've gained so far. He is the solid earth, the foundation, from which all future endeavours and experiences will manifest and grow. Through him you may put down roots deep into the earth.

Primarily, Geb facilitates connection with the earth, our home, of which we are an inextricable part. He may also be consulted in matters of healing the physical body or of calming the mind, so you might imagine yourself flowing serenely upon the eternal waters of the Nile – the spiritual river running through the idealised version of Khemet that the Khemetu believed lay waiting for them in the afterlife.

The Symbols of Geb

When performing rituals to Geb, you may decorate your altar with items that represent his sacred symbols.

Goose

You can use goose feathers as altar decorations, or else to 'fan' incense smoke around your enclosure. You could also include an ornament or picture of a goose on the altar.

Was Sceptre

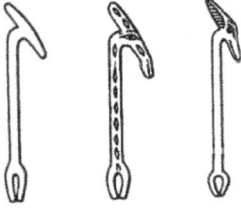

Similarly, a representation of the Was Sceptre, either as a picture or model may be laid across your altar.

Snake

A model, toy or picture of a snake or snakes would also be appropriate.

The Epithets of Geb

While not a great many epithets for Geb remain, in comparison to *neteru* such as Isis and Osiris, his functions can also be used as titles.

The Father of Snakes - Nehebkau
The Great Cackler
Lord of the Fertile Earth
Consort of the Sky
He From Whose Ribs the Barley Grows
Goose of the Nile

Offerings to Geb

Appropriate offerings to Geb would include cakes, biscuits and bread, eggs, fish or poultry, fruit and beer. If you are unable to consume any of these, you could substitute food cut into the shapes of a goose, fish or egg (to represent creatures of the Nile and the birds that live upon it) or a snake. Non alcoholic beer may be used if preferred.

Ritual:
Sinking into the Earth

For this ritual, place a representation of Geb on your altar. You may use either a picture or a statue.

Equipment Required

- A dish of the produce of the earth should be placed upon the altar – fruit and/or vegetables
- The altar cloth should be of deep green, black or brown, or a combination of these hues
- Green, brown or black altar candles
- A dark, heavy, earthy incense, such as Kyphi
- Flowers can be scattered upon the altar, and heads of cereal crops if the season permits that
- You can include the hieroglyph of Geb's name
- An appropriate feast

The Ritual

Create your enclosure and enliven your altar statue with *heka*, if you have one. Light the altar candles and replenish your incense if necessary. Then sit down in the centre. Close your eyes and breathe deeply for a while to alter your state of consciousness. Then visualise your environment gradually changing. A mist fills your enclosure, so that objects around you disappear within it. Presently, the mist begins to clear, and you see a new landscape appearing around you.

You find yourself in the fertile Nile Delta, early in the morning. You can smell the soil and the river. You can hear the call of geese from the water. You carry a satchel of offerings over your shoulder. You are here to commune with Geb, the *neter* of the earth. You will not seek him in a formal temple – he is all around you in the scents and sounds of the landscape. Walk along the bank of the Nile, your hands brushing through the tall papyrus reeds.

You see an island out in the water, not too far from shore. It is almost covered in reeds but there appears to be a wooden walkway to it. You can pass over this, although the cool water runs over your feet.

When you reach the island, stand for some moments with your eyes closed, absorbing the ambience of the site. This feels sacred to you. You're aware of creatures moving around you, the subtle sounds of snakes and crocodiles slipping through the water. You hear the call of geese nearby. The river ripples slowly. You can hear its sinuous movement. The wind hisses in the reeds. Hold out your arms and say:

'Oh Geb, Lord of the Earth,
Whose body is the fertile land,
From whose ribs the barley springs forth,
Come to my call.
Step forth from your abode in the earth
And speak with me.
Impart to me your mysteries
To illumine the path before me.'

Chant: *'Geb, tha-tenn'* for a minute or so, while gently shaking the sistrum.

(Pronounced: Geb, thar-ten. Meaning (roughly): Geb, male, earth god.)

For a moment, without opening your eyes, cast your inner gaze back to the image of Geb in your enclosure. Imagine it also glows with light, as it brims with *heka*. Geb is alive in both inner and outer realities and will communicate with you.

In the visualisation, you perceive a shimmer to the air ahead of you. It's as if something huge yet invisible is moving towards you. As it approaches, so the sounds and scents around you intensify. The reeds shake wildly as if in a strong wind, yet the air is calm.

Whatever approaches begins to manifest before you. You see a giant striding towards you with skin so dark a green it's almost black. Patches of moss and sprouting plants grow upon his skin. His hair is like swathes of dark reeds, rustling about him. His face is beautiful, serene. This, you know, is Geb, the Lord of the Earth and Guardian of the Nile in its earliest days. He will become the second King of Khemet, but that role is in the future. For now, he is a *neter* purely of the land and its crops and creatures.

By the time Geb reaches you, he has become no more than the height of a tall man. His dark eyes gaze upon you benevolently. You feel deep inside he is all that is good in nature – fertile earth, sleek, healthy creatures, abundant crops. Under his guardianship, all are happy and well-fed. The Khemetu appealed to Geb to keep nature in balance, to stave off a parched Nile, starving animals, withered crops and the plagues of insects that would accompany drought. Without Geb, all would be lost. His reason for being is to ensure the land thrives.

Geb sits down upon the ground and bids you to join him. He holds out his hands to you and you take them in yours. His palms are warm and slightly gritty, as if with soil. His body exudes a heady perfume of greenery and flowers. He says to you: *'Dream with me, meruti...'*

Close your eyes within the visualisation and breathe in

time with the *neter*'s breath. Feel yourself sinking into a pleasant, drowsy state. You are changing, becoming a green, lush papyrus plant. You can feel roots snaking down into the rich soil, aware of the nutrients you can take from it. In the dark earth, you're aware that all growing things are connected, and they are all part of Geb. You are not a separate, isolated entity but part of this immense thriving system.

Geb tells you that whenever you feel unsure or uncertain, or your situation in life seems precarious, you can commune with him. You can draw strength from his bones and flesh – the earth itself. Rooted to the land, you are strong. Geb is a potent yet quiet inexorable force, and you can take these qualities into yourself. You can examine your situation from a distance, perceiving the cycle of events, how relationships and circumstances ebb and flow. Whatever happens to you, whatever wild storms may howl across your world, you are rooted and grounded to the planet, your home. You will survive the hurricanes that will eventually pass. Contemplate these things for a few moments.

Now, speak with Geb for as long as you wish. He may take you on a journey with him or offer you a gift. If you have problems about which you'd like his counsel, tell him what concerns you. Ask for his serene influence to quell hostility, to allow peace and understanding to grow. Remember also, that as a *neter* of healing he can be called upon to help with matters of health, for yourself or others.

When you are ready to conclude this part of the visualisation, return to where you began, sitting upon an island in the Nile, surrounded by reeds. You notice that Geb's sacred animals have gathered around you, watching – serpents and geese. Now bring out the offerings you have brought and spread them before Geb. Open your eyes and come out of the visualisation, while imagining that part of you is still in Khemet with Geb. Say:

'Oh Geb, Grey Goose of the Nile
Father of Snakes,
Beauty of the Fertile Earth,
I have brought offerings to you,
As symbols of thanks and respect.
Through me, may you experience their pleasures.
As I eat this food, may you relish its flavours,
As I drink, may your thirst be quenched with enjoyment.'

Now you will feast in his honour. Consume the feast, concentrating on sharing the pleasure of doing so with Geb. Leave a small portion of everything you eat and drink. After this has been done, wrap the remains in paper and leave this parcel before the statue on your altar.

When you are ready, compose yourself and return to the visualisation. See your offerings around Geb, which he consumes with relish. Bow to Geb and say:

'Oh Geb, son of Shu and Tefnut,
Bounty of the Earth
Continue to share with me your strength and serenity.
Grant me your tranquil composure.
Give me the resolve to be all that I may be,
And the wisdom to know myself as you know me.'

Then bid farewell to him and prepare to leave. Get to your feet and walk back across the walkway. Pass into the tall reeds that hide the river from you. Come to a standstill. Imagine the scene turns to mist around you. Return to normal reality and dismantle your enclosure in the usual way. Then record the results of your work and dispose of the remains of your offerings.

Papyrus Marsh with Geese from a Khemetic Wall Painting

Nut - Mistress of the Sky

The Attributes of Nut

Nut's name (pronounced noot) means sky, and in early Khemetic she was known as Nuit, Nent or Nunut. She is often depicted as a gigantic woman filled with stars arching over the heavens – either naked or clad in a close-fitting long dress. Her skin can be dark blue or gold. She can also be represented as a human woman with golden skin, whose headdress is a clay pot. This symbol forms part of her name in hieroglyphs. Some writers have suggested it symbolises her womb. Originally personifying the sky at night, Nut eventually came to represent the sky itself. Occasionally, she was depicted as a white cow, known as the Sky Cow. The immense body of this creature formed the heavens.

Nut was believed to prevent the forces of chaos breaking through the sky, from some terrible, primeval realm beyond, and destroying the world below. She was not, then, imagined as the entire universe but what we can see above us in the night sky. She is the atmosphere that shields us from the radiation of the sun. She protects our world from above. In this aspect, she is a deity of order.

Thunder, which echoed around the sky inexplicably to the Khemetu, was described as the laughter of Nut. One myth describes her a swallowing the sun (or the *neter* of the sun) every night. He moves through her body during the dark hours and is reborn from her vulva in the morning. The red glow sometimes seen upon the horizon at dawn was known as 'the Daughter of Nut'.

Nut also has associations with the sycamore tree and the Underworld. In *The Book of the Dead*, there are depictions of her emerging from the trunk of a sycamore in the Duat. In this form, she enables the dead to breathe air again. She also offers them plentiful water and bread, reassuring them they will never go hungry or thirsty in the idealised version of Khemet found in the Field of Reeds. In one version of *The Book of the Dead,* Nut says, *'I am Nut, and I have come so that I may enfold and protect you from all things evil.'*

In a version of the Osiris myth, once he has been resurrected by Isis, the *neter* climbs a ladder (known as a *maqet*) into the sky, to find sanctuary in the body of his mother, Nut. He appeals to her, *'Oh, my mother Nut, stretch yourself over me, that I may be placed among the imperishable stars which are in you, that I may not die.'* After finding safety from Set in the sky, Osiris eventually goes on to become King of the Underworld.

In many mythologies, the Sky Father and the Earth Mother are responsible for creation. In Nut and Geb, we see a reversal of these roles.

The Magical Purpose of Nut

In a magical sense, Nut has several aspects. She represents the cosmos and its mysteries. She is the shield that protects the earth from unfathomable, chaotic influences beyond the sky. She safeguards humankind from what lies beyond our perception. As a deity of the dark hours, she can guard you from night terrors: you can find sanctuary in her body, the starry sky. Whenever you are afraid, you can call upon the immense power of Nut and her powers of protection. You can imagine her sky-spanning, arching body as a shield around you. Although, in art, it appears her hands and feet are close together, ancient texts reveal that the Khemetu believed Nut's extremities reached to each cardinal point of the sky. She can be visualised more like a dome or a canopy than an arch: the bowl of the heavens.

While Nut may be visited to ensure her protection in a general way, and to promote well-being free from fear, you could adapt the ritual in this section to deal with a specific threat. Nut also represents cosmic awareness, through which we can access the knowledge of creation. Merely by communing with Nut in meditation, intelligence of the mysteries of the cosmos may come to you.

Symbols of Nut

The Sky and Stars

You could arrange fairy lights over your altar to represent the night sky, or you could create a backdrop to place behind the altar representing a starry sky.

White Cow

You may place a model or toy of a white cow on your altar.

Round Pot

You could also place a receptable resembling the pot in Nut's hieroglyph on your altar, perhaps to hold the natron.

Epithets of Nut

When writing your own rituals to Nut, you can draw upon this list of her epithets. These derive from both ancient times and modern magical practice.

Lady of the Sky
The Sky Cow
Lady of the Sycamore Tree
She Who Offers Bread and Water in the Duat
She Who Holds a Thousand Souls
She Who Guards the Sun by Night
Coverer of the Sky
She Who Protects
Mistress of All
She Who Bore the *Neteru*

Offerings to Nut

A feast to Nut could include dark red wine or grape juice, sparkling drinks or milky drinks. For the food, you could have cakes or biscuits in the shape of stars.

Because of Nut's association with the Sky Cow, any dairy produce (or dairy substitute) such as cheese or puddings would be appropriate. You could also add edible glitter produced specifically to scatter on cakes or desserts. Some liqueurs contain gold flakes that sparkle when the bottle is shaken – this too would be a fitting ritual drink to Nut. You can purchase edible glitter to make drinks sparkle, so you may be creative in your ritual beverage! Edible flowers are also suitable as part of a cake, dessert or drink.

Ritual:
Rising to the Stars

For this ritual, place a representation of Nut on your altar. You may use either a picture or a statue. Place ornaments, table decorations or cut-out pictures of stars around the statue.

Equipment Required

- The main focus should be the starry night sky – any representation of stars is suitable
- The altar cloth should be black or very dark blue. If you can find such a cloth decorated with stars, all the better
- Dark blue or silver candles
- A heady, richly perfumed incense such as frankincense
- The hieroglyph of Nut's name
- An appropriate feast

The Ritual

Create your enclosure and enliven your altar statue with *heka*, if you have one. Light the altar candles and replenish your incense if necessary. Then sit down in the centre. Close your eyes and breathe deeply for a while to alter your state of consciousness. Visualise your environment gradually changing. A mist fills your enclosure, so that objects around you disappear within it. Presently, the mist begins to clear, and you see a new landscape appearing around you.

You find yourself in Khemet, out in the desert, in a deep rocky valley. Stark mountains rise all around you, sharp against the sky. It is night-time, and the sky blazes with the light of stars, although there is no moon. You are here to seek the mysteries of Nut and ask for her protection in your work. You carry a satchel of offerings for the *neter*.

Hold out your arms and throw back your head. Say,

'Oh Nut, Lady of the Blazing Stars,
She who carries the sun across the night in her body,
Until the rebirth of the light at dawn,
I call to you!
Nut, Mother of Osiris
Protector of all,
Let me ascend the maqet ladder to your body
Reveal to me your mysteries
And grant me your protection!'

Chant: *'Nut, hen-t, akhakh'* for a minute or so, while gently shaking the sistrum.

(Pronounced: Noot, hen-tay, ack-ack. Meaning (roughly): Great lady of the stars, the flowers of heaven.)

For a moment, without opening your eyes, cast your inner gaze back to the image of Nut in your enclosure. Imagine it also glows with light, as it brims with *heka*. Nut is alive in both inner and outer realities and will communicate with you.

As you gaze upon the sky, you begin to perceive the outline of Nut within it. The stars form the arching shape of a woman's body. As you focus upon it, so this form expands, spreading out over the whole sky like a canopy. You can see her limbs reaching down to the four compass directions.

You now perceive a faintly sparkling shape ahead and are drawn to examine it. You find a shimmering ladder in front of you, made of starlight. But when you place your hands upon it, it feels solid.

Nut's voice echoes over the sky, *'Climb to me, meruti! Find sanctuary in my body, which is the Temple of the Sky!'*

You begin to climb the ladder, which stretches high above you. Even though the top is so far away you can't see it, your journey is swift, as if Nut aids your climb.

Eventually you reach the head of the *maqet* ladder and step into a wondrous temple. Its columns are transparent like glass, filled with star shine. Its floor is polished obsidian yet glittering with flecks of quartz and veins of light. The air smells of night-scented flowers – a sensuous perfume. Yet breathing this air feels like taking sparkling wine into your lungs – not a liquid but fizzing ether, filling you with energy.

At the far end of the temple is a dais, and here a throne of light. Upon this throne sits Nut in her womanly form. She is adorned in a robe of dark blue decorated with stars, and upon her head she wears her strange crown in the form of a round pot. Her skin is golden now, and as you approach you can see it too is glittering. Approach her throne and bow to her. Say:

'Lady Nut, She Who Holds a Thousand Souls,
I thank you for allowing me ascension
To your mansion among the stars.
I ask that you extend your starry canopy over me,
To shield and protect me in my work.
I ask too that you reveal your mysteries to me,
To aid me in my quest for self-knowledge.'

(At this point, if you have a specific issue of protection you wish to ask Nut's help with, use your own words for what you require of her. Adapt the rest of the ritual as necessary.)

Nut gets to her feet and says, *'I am Nut. Come to me, meruti, so I may enfold you and protect you from all things evil.'*

You obey her request. Nut reaches out for you and takes you into her embrace. At once, you feel as if you are no longer a physical body but a creature of light yourself. You are able to travel through the heavens as a being of starlight. You see the constellations all around you, appearing like the starry outlines of beasts and *neteru*.

Nut transports you to the heart of her realm. Here, you feel entirely safe and comfortable. No worries or threats from the real world can touch you here. Nut stands before you and places a golden hand over your heart. As she gazes upon you, you see that her eyes are so dark they are almost completely black, but there are hints of shining blue within their depths, a hint of starshine. Her hand grows warm yet seems also cool. She says, *'So is my light in you for all time.'*

You experience her power as a warm current of energy that slowly fills your being. You can perceive a body of starlight forming around the essence of your soul. Like Nut in sky-covering form, you transform into an immense creature filled with stars. Nut says: *'Take on this form to fight evil and to protect those needful of shelter.'*

She shows you how to create a shield of starlight around those in need of protection, which you may forge with your will and intention. You can use this also to strengthen yourself in difficult situations. You can use it to banish fear.

When you are ready to conclude this part of the visualisation, return to where you began, in the Mansion of Nut among the stars. Now bring out the offerings you have brought and spread them before Nut. Open your eyes and come out of the visualisation, while imagining part of your is still in the temple of Nut. Say:

'Oh Nut, She Who Offers Bread and Water in the Duat
Mistress of All
Who Bore the Neteru,
I have brought offerings to you,
As symbols of thanks and respect.
Through me, may you experience their pleasures.
As I eat this food, may you relish its flavours,
As I drink, may your thirst be quenched with enjoyment.'

Now you will feast in her honour. Consume the feast, concentrating on sharing the pleasure of doing so with Nut. Leave a small portion of everything you eat and drink. After this has been done, wrap the remains in paper and leave this parcel before the statue on your altar.

When you are ready to end the ritual, compose yourself and return to the visualisation. See your offerings around Nut, which she consumes with relish. Bow to Nut and say:

'Oh Nut, Lady of the Sycamore Tree,
Coverer of the Sky,
Protectress of Osiris
Continue to share with me your starfire of protection.
Grant me your compassion.
Give me the means to intuit all that I may be,
And the wisdom to know myself as you know me.'

Then bid farewell to her and prepare to leave. Return to the *maqet* ladder and climb back down to the Red Land of the Khemetic desert. Here, imagine the scene turns to mist around you.

Return to normal reality and dismantle your enclosure in the usual way. Record the results of your work and dispose of the remains of your offerings.

The Children of Nut and Geb

Isis - Great of Magic

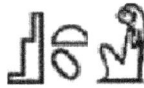

Her name and title shiver with power and majesty. Of all the female *neteru* of Khemet, Isis was well known in the modern Western world long before neo-paganism got a hold from the 60s onwards, and *neteru* such as Bast, Sekhmet and Hathor became widely revered. This is partly because Isis was quite an important goddess to the Romans, who adopted her after conquering Egypt and brought her cult into other parts of Europe and Britain. There are temple remains to Isis at various sites around Europe. Part of The Thames, the river that runs through London, is known as the Isis. The Romans also evolved their own form of Isis, known as Isis Urania.

Isis had many temples dedicated to her in the ancient world, the best known of which is probably at Philae. Part of the hieroglyph of her name depicts a throne, because she was intrinsic to the passing on of sovereignty to the pharaohs. She is always represented as a regal woman, and wears upon her head various symbols, such as the throne, a crown of cow horns and/or the solar disk.

A symbol that is particularly sacred to Isis is the *tyet*, a knot representing the cord used to tie her garment. This might also represent the ankh, symbol of life and divine power. The *tyet* was red in colour, perhaps to symbolise the *neter*'s blood. As an amulet it's ideally fashioned from red jasper.

Isis occasionally took on an animal form, such as a white sow, when she was known as 'the Great White Sow of Heliopolis'. Sometimes, like Nut and Hathor, she was represented as a divine cow: in this form she gave birth to the sacred bull at Memphis. Because she could sometimes manifest as a kite, which is a bird of prey, she is often shown as having spreading wings.

Isis is also one of the few Khemetic goddesses to have a rich mythology behind her. The stories of her family are so vivid, it's tempting to believe they might be embellished memories of a very early dynasty of pharaohs.

The Romance of the Divine Siblings

According to the creation myth devised by the priests of Heliopolis, Isis and her siblings (Osiris, Set and Nephthys – and in some versions a fifth sibling, Horus the Elder) were the children of the sky *neter* Nut and her brother/consort Geb, *neter* of the earth. Part of the myth relates how this divine royal family descended from the heavenly realms to govern Khemet, as if they were a human royal family. Isis assisted Osiris to rule and was greatly loved by him. However, Osiris had a rival, in the form of their brother Set, a deity of chaotic forces. Set coveted Osiris's crown and eventually tricked and murdered him. Isis and Nephthys mourned their brother deeply, each in the form of a bird of prey, the kite.

Documented versions of the story describe Isis's terrible grief for her beloved in great detail. She searched the world until she found Osiris's body, which was hidden inside the trunk of a tree that had become part of a palace in Byblos. But once the body was recovered, Set then dismembered it and scattered it in fourteen pieces throughout Egypt. Again, Isis relentlessly tracked down the parts and reassembled them (although one version of the story says she buried them where she found them). The only part that was missing was his phallus, but Isis was clever enough to replace this. In one version of the legend she fashioned a new one for him, while in another she eventually recovered the missing organ, which had been eaten by a Nile fish. There are some powerful representations in Egyptian art of Isis hovering as a kite over the prone body of Osiris, who has an erect phallus. In this manner, they were supposed to have conceived Horus the Younger, who would later be responsible for overthrowing the usurper Set.

Another story relates that in order to revitalise Osiris, Isis had to have powerful magic indeed, and the only way she could accomplish the task was by making the sun deity Ra (a form of, or *neter* similar to, Atum) reveal to her his secret name, which is the ultimate word of power. This feat earned her the epithet 'More Clever Than a Million *Neteru*'.

Initially Ra resisted all her attempts to wrest this name from him. Considering what happened to Osiris, and the lingering threat to her son, Horus, Isis could be said to have had some justification for seeking this means to protect herself and her family. Eventually, taking matters into her own hands, she managed to get hold of some of Ra's saliva, which she mixed with soil and moulded into the shape of a serpent. She left the magical creature in a place where she knew Ra would pass, and when he did so, the serpent bit and poisoned him. His body was wracked with pain and he became feverish. Isis told Ra she could cure him, but in return he must give her his secret name. Ra attempted to fool her by reciting a number of false names, but Isis was too clever for him, and refused to help him until he revealed his true, secret name. She made matters worse by causing the poison to hurt him even more. Eventually Ra gave in and revealed to Isis the knowledge she craved, thus granting her another epithet 'Mistress of the *Neteru*, who Knows Ra by His Own Name'. Ra also allowed Isis to impart this powerful information to her son Horus, thus ensuring his own future as a *neter* of immense power.

In all the myths, Isis comes across as an extremely determined and powerful woman, who is not beyond taking extreme measures if a situation merits it.

The Attributes of Isis

Isis is a Hellenised version of her name, which was used after the Greeks conquered Egypt and sought to amalgamate the gods of that country into their own pantheon. Isis's proper name is Aset, or Ast, as that of her brother Osiris is Asar or Wasir. It's thought that both Isis and Aset mean the same as the English word 'throne'.

Isis represented a puzzle to the Greeks, whose deities all had clearly defined roles within their belief system. Isis was a source of power for the pharaohs, and passed on divine sovereignty, so in this sense she was a deity of the earthly realm, but in addition she had a celestial aspect, deriving from the star Sirius (or Sothis, Sopdet or Sept as it was known in the ancient world), which was believed to be her home. She also possessed an otherworldly aspect, in that she had power in the Duat. The Greeks had separate goddesses for earth, sky and underworld, so in order to ignore the conundrum of Isis's complexity, they simply discarded some of her aspects and concentrated mainly on her as a symbol of divine wife and mother, renowned for her unstinting loyalty. She acquired a lunar aspect during Greek rule, which might have derived from the fact that sailors navigated by her star when travelling.

There has been a tendency in modern times to concentrate

mainly on her role as a mother deity, but this overlooks some of her most potent attributes. While there's no doubt that the myths surrounding her present her as a determinedly protective wife and mother, she is also portrayed as intelligent, resourceful, uncompromising and occasionally fierce. She has knowledge of the Underworld, as well as the celestial regions and the realm of earth, and is at home in any of these environments.

The Magical Purpose of Isis

Primarily, Isis is *weret hekau*, which means 'great in magic'. And *ur heka*, or the words of power, play an important part in her rituals. She is a *neter* who can be approached in respect of many matters, but perhaps most importantly in the search for wisdom and knowledge. Isis embodies loyalty and determination, as well as powerful magical abilities and a certain amount of craftiness. In several stories – some of which will be explored in the section on Horus – Isis deceives other *neteru*, particularly her brother Set following the murder of Osiris.

Isis is also in some respects a *neter* of healing, particularly of children, since she hid Horus in the dangerous swamplands in order to keep him safe from Set. Through this, she became associated with cures for scorpion stings and other hazards encountered during childhood.

Isis may be approached to help you with your magical training. You can ask for her wisdom and expertise to be bestowed upon you. She is also a *neter* to appeal to in matters of justice, especially when unfairness or lies are involved. She protects the weak and can be ruthless when the occasion demands it. When building your own relationship with Isis, you will know when the time is right to call upon her different powers.

The Symbols of Isis

When you create an altar dedicated to Isis, you may incorporate her symbolic items, along with all the usual equipment, such as incense, altar candles and *neter* image.

The *Tyet*

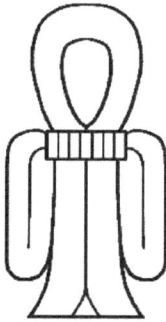

This is the knot of Isis and is red in colour. You can make one of these from red ribbon or thread, or else fashion one from modelling clay and paint it red or make a drawing of it. Whenever you perform a rite to Isis, have a representation of the *tyet* on your altar, or even wear a piece of jewellery in its shape if you can find or make one.

The Mirror

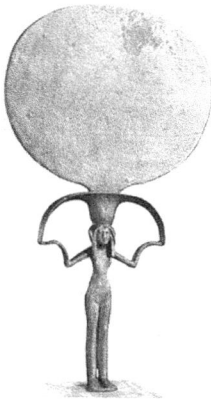

There was a particular kind of mirror used in the magic of Isis that had the same name as the word for life, i.e. 'ankh'. It is also symbolic of the solar disk. The picture here is of an authentic Khemetic hand mirror, but modern copies are very easy to acquire online. The ankh mirror does not necessarily have to incorporate a representation of an ankh, but if you can acquire a small cosmetic mirror, you could decorate it with modelling clay or set it into the 'eye' of an ankh you've made yourself. Otherwise, any small plain mirror will suffice.

The Sacred Lamp

When you perform a ritual to Isis, you should have a representation of a sacred lamp upon your altar. Although you might be able to find a ready-made Egyptian style lamp at magical suppliers or gift shops, you could substitute any lantern or candle holder with a tea light inside it.

Epithets of Isis

When writing your own rituals to Isis, you can draw upon this list of her epithets. These derive from both ancient times and modern magical practice.

Queen of the Heavens
Mut Netjer, Mother of the *Neteru*
The One Who is All
Lady of Green Crops
The Brilliant One in the Sky
Her Latin name was Stella Maris, or Star of the Sea
Great Lady of Magic
Lady of Fertility, Nature and Motherhood
Underworld Mistress of the House of Life
She Who Knows How to Make Right Use of the Heart
Light-Giver of the Heavens
Lady of the Words of Power

Offerings to Isis

Foods appropriate for Isis include dates, honey, raisins and melons. When you work with her darker aspects, you should use red wine or a dark fruit juice. In her stellar aspect, white wine and pale coloured juices should be used. Isis as mother deity would require cakes, honey and milk. In general, and for any aspect, have meat such as chicken, goose and turkey (poultry was a common food in Khemet.)

Visualisation:
The Dawn Rite of Isis

What follows is a pathworking for which you don't need to construct the sacred enclosure – although you can if you want to. Otherwise the procedure for creating lesser sacred space will suffice. You will need a candle or tealight and ideally you should perform it in a place where the light of the rising sun will fall upon you.

It might not always be easy or practical to undertake this short rite exactly at the moment of sunrise, but you should endeavour to do so at least once at the correct time, simply to experience the energies of that moment. Otherwise, regard it as a morning observance, which you perform as often as feels appropriate for you.

Sit down in the centre of your sacred space and meditate for a few minutes. Let your mind become empty, your body relaxed. When you feel the moment is right, open your eyes and light the candle or tealight. This represents the return of sunlight to the darkened world. It is the moment of the sun's triumph, after it has spent the night hours traversing the Duat. Now, it re-emerges in the east to begin its daily journey once more.

Stare into the flame. Imagine it as the first rays of sunlight breaking across the land, as the morning sun begins to light your ritual space. Now close your eyes, and visualise you are standing upon the banks of the Nile at dawn. As you gaze into the east, where the sun rises in a rose-yellow glow, the form of Isis begins to appear in the sky. She is immense, holding out her arms, and her face is veiled. She is both Mistress of Life and of the Duat and has the power to create and destroy. Say to her:

'Oh Isis, Queen of the Heavens
Who wears a luminous veil.
You conceal the bright darkness of your face.
May your power come to me in the dawn rays.
Fill my being with your light.'

You hear the sound of a clarion that rings across the sky. As this occurs, so the sun rises higher above the horizon and grows brighter. Isis lifts her veil to reveal her face, and even though she stands with her back to the light, she is illumined with her own radiance, a *neter* of indescribable loveliness. She begins to chant in a low, musical voice that fills the air. This wordless song of life flows over you, into you.

Spend some minutes meditating now. Let your mind become restful, empty, allowing the power and wisdom of Isis to enter into you. See what she might reveal to you.

Now the sun has risen above the horizon and day has come. Isis becomes a being of pure light and disappears into the sunshine. Sit for a moment to experience the feelings her presence has left within you.

When you are ready to conclude the visualisation, return to normal consciousness and open your eyes. Turn your face to the sun, and then meditate in the early morning light for a while.

The candle should ideally be left alight until it has burnt away, but in the interests of safety you may snuff it out, if necessary.

Ritual:
The Teachings of Isis

For this ritual, place a representation of Isis on your altar. You may use either a picture or a statue. As part of this rite, you will recite an adaptation of a traditional hymn to Isis, which derives from her temple now situated at Philae. (The complex was moved following the flooding of the sixth cataract of the Nile after the construction of the Aswan Dam.) While you are doing this, gently shake your sistrum rhythmically. Speak liltingly, or preferably sing these words. They are among the most ancient of *ur heka*.

Equipment Required

- A sistrum
- The altar cloth should be white or gold or both
- Fresh flowers of white and yellow
- White or yellow candles
- The hieroglyph of Isis's name
- An appropriate feast

The Ritual

Create your enclosure and enliven your altar statue with *heka*, if you have one. Light the altar candles and replenish your incense if necessary. Then sit down in the centre. Close your eyes and breathe deeply for a while to alter your state of consciousness. Visualise your environment gradually changing. A mist fills your enclosure, so that objects around you disappear within it. Presently, the mist begins to clear, and you see a new landscape appearing around you.

You find yourself travelling in a small boat along the River Nile in Upper Khemet. It is night-time and the sky is brilliant with stars. You see ahead of you a temple complex on the banks of the river, which you know is dedicated to Isis. You can see that ahead the river grows lively as you approach the sixth cataract, one of the rapids of the Nile. Avoiding this potential danger, your boat turns and glides towards the temple, as if drawn by an invisible hand. The vessel comes to rest gently against the riverbank and you climb out of it onto solid ground, taking with you a satchel of offerings.

The temple ahead rears tall, silent and majestic and you walk towards it. You pass beneath the imposing pylon gate and enter the outer court. The moon shines down brightly upon you. You enter between the stately columns of the temple and make your way by instinct to the scented inner sanctum. When you reach it, this chamber is softly lit, and a statue of Isis sits upon a throne at the far end of it. She wears a long robe and a crown in the shape of a throne upon her head. Behind her, carved wings spread out to either side of her from her chair. Approach Isis, bow to her, and say:

'Oh Isis, Mistress of the House of Life,
Great Lady of Magic,
Queen of the Heavens
I call to you!
Isis, Beloved of Osiris
Come to me, your humble student!
Reveal to me your mysteries
And grant to me your knowledge of ur heka,
That I may work for the good of all.'

Chant: *'Isis, wheret, heka'* for a minute or so, while gently shaking the sistrum.

(Pronounced: Isis, weh-ret, hekk-aah. Meaning (roughly): Isis, great lady of magic.)

Before your eyes, the granite statue transforms into a living woman, who wears a long white robe. She gazes benignly upon you.

For a moment, cast your inner gaze back to the image of Isis in your enclosure. Imagine it glows with light, as it brims with *heka*. Isis is alive in both inner and outer realities and will communicate with you. Now recite the hymn to Isis:

'Ra is in celebration,
The heart exults in joy,
For your heart is soft and sweet, oh Isis,
Queen of the World.
And your son Horus,
He is king upon the throne of his father,
Governing both poles.
The seat of Geb is in your possession.
The function of Atum is in your hand.
The strength of Mentu[1] is in your grasp.
The divinity who produces the beginning
And fills the sky and earth with your perfection.
This crown that is bright in gold appears.
August is your sign,
Lives in the house divine,
Sovereign of the neteru of the sky,
Queen of the neteru of the earth,
and of the neteru of the Duat.
The Mistress of Bright Glory,
It is by your order that the temple is blessed.
With the return of your brother,
Your name is pronounced,
And the world is loyal to you.'

Now open yourself to the presence of Isis. Connect with her different aspects and meditate upon them. She is the bestower of divine sovereignty, meaning that she endows those who care for the earth with her power and protection. She is *neter* of the words of power, granting knowledge of the greatest of magics. She is mistress of the Duat and of the fertile earth. She is the mother of Horus, and the protector of the young and the vulnerable. She is the grieving wife of Osiris, who died so that he might become what he was meant to be. Feel her great love for Osiris and Horus, and experience what this means in terms of spiritual symbolism, what each of the three represent. After some minutes, say:

'Isis, Mistress of Magic,
I am here before you
to ask for your aid in my spiritual journey.
Open my mind, oh queen!
Open my heart, oh Aset!
Open my inner eyes, oh beloved of Asar!
I come before you, in the sight of Maat,
In all honesty and integrity.
Reward my work with your strength and wisdom.
Teach me, oh Gold of the Neteru!
I will follow where you lead me, oh Isis.'

Now spend a few minutes communing with Isis. She may offer a symbolic gift to you or have things she wishes to show you. Speak to her about your magical path and your aims upon it. Ask her to grant you knowledge and to empower your work.

When you are ready, lay out your offerings before her. Then open your eyes and come out of the visualisation, while imagining that part of you is still in the temple of Isis. Say:

'Oh Isis, Mistress of the House of Life,
Lady of the Words of Power,
The One Who is All,
I have brought offerings to you,

As symbols of thanks and respect.
Through me, may you experience their pleasures.
As I eat this food, may you relish its flavours,
As I drink, may your thirst be quenched with enjoyment.'

Consume the feast, concentrating on sharing the pleasure of doing so with Isis. Leave a small portion of everything you eat and drink. After this has been done, wrap the remains in paper and leave this parcel before the image of Isis on your altar.

When you are ready, compose yourself and return to the visualisation. See your offerings around Isis, which she consumes with relish. Bow to Isis and say:

'Oh Isis, Great Lady of Magic,
Queen of Heaven,
Consort of Osiris,
Continue to share with me your great power.
Grant me your courage and tenacity.
Give me the means to realise all that I may be,
And the wisdom to know myself as you know me.'

Then bid farewell to her and prepare to leave. Imagine the scene turns to mist around you. Return to normal reality and dismantle your enclosure in the usual way. Then record the results of your work and dispose of the remains of your offerings appropriately.

1. Mentu, known also as Montu, was a falcon-headed *neter* of war, who also represented the conquering strength of the pharaoh.

Temple of Isis, Philae

Osiris - Neter of Growth, The Afterlife and Rebirth

Attributes of Osiris

The son of the earth deity Geb and the sky *neter* Nut, Osiris presided over the cycle of life, death and rebirth. His myth involves his own murder at the hands of his brother, Set, a *neter* associated with the chaos of the elements. His name in Khemet was Asar or Wasir.

Osiris was the brother-husband of Isis, and one of his epithets was 'The One Who Continues to be Perfect' (or *Wenen Nefer* – pronounced wen-nen neff-er). He was regarded as having great beauty, remaining forever youthful and was always benign. He was the deity of the afterlife, the Duat and of rebirth. He was a judge of the dead and yet he also gave life. He represented the inundation of the Nile and the fecund growth of vegetation following the flood. He was also connected to the heliacal rising of the stars of Sirius and Orion at the start of the Khemetic New Year, which coincided with the inundation of the sacred river. Orion was believed to be one of his homes.

Despite his connections with death and the afterlife, Osiris was given the epithet 'King of the Living' most likely referring to his rulership of the blessed dead, whom the Khemetu sometimes called 'The Living Ones' – presumably denoting their 'true' life following the purification of death and rebirth.

In appearance Osiris resembles a mummified pharaoh, as he wears the wrappings of a mummy and the false beard that was adopted by sovereigns of Khemet (including, in some cases, female kings). His head is adorned with a crown known as the *atef* crown, which is the White Crown of Upper Khemet, decorated on either side by ostrich feathers. His face is beautiful, and his skin is depicted as either green or black. Green represents rebirth, while black represents the rich, fertile soil of the Nile delta. He carries symbolic weapons – a crook and a flail – which some writers believe connect him with the shepherding of animals. It's easy to appreciate how the crook is associated with this occupation, but the symbolism of the flail is less clear. It could refer to a whisk to dispel flies or a whip used by shepherds to help control their livestock. A flail was also used by farmers to separate grain from chaff.

According to the myth – and there are several versions of it, from both early Egyptian sources and later Greek writers – Osiris's brother Set became extremely envious of him, to the point of murderous rage. One reason given for this is that Set represented the desert landscape and the ferocity of its storms. He was elemental chaos itself. Another interpretation of the myth suggests that because he *was* the desert, he was infertile. Osiris, by contrast, was the neter of the Nile and its fecund lands, and therefore innately fertile. Although, Set was married to his sister Nephthys, they could not produce children. Set was also said to have desired Osiris's throne, his power.

The story of the death and resurrection of Osiris has already been described in the previous section on Isis. Suffice to say, neither her magic nor her love could keep him alive on earth forever, and after Horus was conceived Osiris died once more. After ascending to his mother Nut through the agency of the *maqet* ladder, Osiris eventually became King of the

Dead and the Underworld. He lived on in the Fields of Aaru, (the Field of Reeds), over which he reigned supreme. One of his epithets, *Khenti Amenti*, means 'the Foremost of the Westerners', the West referring to the Land of the Dead. He was also known as 'The Lord of Silence'. After Osiris left the earthly realm, Horus became the ruler of the black fertile Delta, taking on his father's role as king.

As a *neter* of nature, Osiris was closely linked with the germination of crops, particularly wheat. Annual ceremonies performed in his honour centred around fertility rites connected with the soil and the growth of plants. Grain was planted to represent Osiris in death and its eventual sprouting represented his rebirth – a continual cycle. The festivals dedicated to Osiris could also involve 'Osiris Beds', receptacles formed into the shape of the *neter*, which were filled with soil and planted with grain seeds.

Osiris festivals could also involve public dramas, or mystery plays, in which his murder and dismemberment was re-enacted, followed by Isis's search for the parts of the body. Ultimately, Osiris would be resurrected, and after that his son Horus would defeat Set – the latter being a later part of the story which will be examined in more detail in the section focusing upon Horus. During the re-enactment, participants were reported to have injured themselves by cutting their own bodies – we must assume these were only superficial injuries rather than actual dismemberments. Greek writers also revealed that the priesthood held private rites within the temples, attended only by privileged initiates. The rites – both public and esoteric – typically took place over several days. One of the main sites associated with Osiris is Abydos, where his funeral rites were enacted during the last stages of the inundation in the Khemetic springtime. There is a temple structure here known as the Osireion, whose ruins remain to this day, partly flooded.

The Magical Purpose of Osiris

Osiris, being a neter associated with fertility and growth, can be approached about matters associated with creativity, expansion, fecundity of any kind, and preserving the natural order. As a wise judge, his illumination may be sought when the mind is clouded and confused, or not enough information is known about a situation to allow informed action. Osiris has no tricky side to his nature as his sister-wife Isis does. He is always gentle, concerned more with the inexorable power of the natural world, righting wrongs rather than using guile to obtain a result.

No one can stand before Osiris and lie, for he will see through all deceits. You can ask him to reveal truths, when lies and falsehoods cause injustice. But when seeking his justice, remember we are often influenced, if not blinded, by our own ideologies and opinions – these may be subjective rather than 'fact' or 'truth'. Osiris does not accommodate revenge. He will only expose it for what it is.

In terms of magical training, Osiris grants the ability to be fair and objective, to see all sides of an argument and discern the truth. He also presides over initiations – rites of passage and the rebirth of the self through magical progression. He can be called upon to plant seeds of self-development within you that will flourish and grow beneath his influence.

Symbols of Osiris

When creating an altar to Osiris, you can include objects to represent his symbols. You can make these yourself by fashioning the crook, the flail and the *djed* pillar from modelling clay, or else you can use pictures of them.

The Crook

This represents his role as king, it is a symbol of royal power. It's also said to have some reference to Osiris's role as a shepherd deith.

The Flail

This whisk-like object could represent a whisk to repel insects, or an instrument to help separate the grain from the chaff after the harvest. From a magical perspective, it can represent your intention to separate 'the wheat from the chaff' within yourself, discarding notions, beliefs and conditioning that impede self-evolution.

Djed Column

This is a symbol in Khemetic mythology particularly associated with Osiris, and also the creator deity Ptah in the belief system of the city of Memphis. This object symbolises stability and allegedly represents the spine of Osiris. Another meaning is that it represents the pillar from the version of the myth in which Osiris's body was hidden in the palace of Byblos in Lebanon.

Ostrich Feathers

Long, curling ostrich feathers adorn the *atef* crown of Osiris. You can decorate your altar with these, which are easily obtained from craft stores.

Epithets of Osiris

When writing your own rituals to Osiris, you can draw upon this list of his epithets. These derive from both ancient times and modern magical practice.

The Mighty One
Lord of the Perfect Black
Wennefer – the Beautiful One
The Lord of Love
Slain and Resurrected King
Khenti Amenti -Foremost of the Westerners
He Who Dwells in Orion With a Season in the Sky and a
Season on the Earth
Lord of the Duat
He Who Presides Over Rostau*
The Lord of Silence
Lord of the Living
Ruler of Eternity
Lord of the Two Plumes
He Who is Everlastingly Perfect
He Who is in the Grain of the *Neteru*

the entrance to the Duat – pronounced ross-tow (as in owl)

Offerings to Osiris

A feast for Osiris could include cakes, biscuits, bread, (all preferably homemade), fruit and salads. He is not particularly associated with any kind of meat. The ritual drink should be fruit cordials, white wine or wheat beer. Non-alcoholic alternatives may be used if preferred.

Visualisation:
Purification in the Fields of Aaru

What follows is a pathworking for which you don't need to construct the sacred enclosure – although you can if you want to. Otherwise the procedure for creating lesser sacred space will suffice.

This pathworking will take you into the idealised version of Khemet as found in the Duat. You will not be experiencing death and rebirth, but rather Osiris will allow you into his realm – his private estate within the Duat – in order to learn his mysteries. This visualisation would be especially beneficial if you have recently endured a difficult period in your life or are still going through one. Osiris helps you 'rise up' from conflict, grief or disaster.

Prepare yourself for visualisation and charge the atmosphere with *heka*. Imagine that the everyday world fades away around you, replaced by a floating mist. Gradually the mist begins to clear, and you find yourself in a new landscape.

You are standing upon the Giza plateau, with the pyramids around you. This is not modern Egypt but Khemet in ancient times, when the pyramids were new. They are perfect, clad in smooth, glittering stone. The sun is going down in the west as a huge red globe. Before you, a hole opens in the ground, and you see steps leading down. This, you realise, is the Road to Rostau, the path to Osiris' realm in the Duat.

A figure climbs up the steps to meet you. This appears to be a young priest with a shaven head and a white robe that leaves one shoulder bare. His eyes are thickly lined with kohl. He bows to you and tells you that Osiris has sent him to accompany you, to guide you to his realm, avoiding areas not appropriate to your visit. You realise then that this guide must be a lesser *neter* of the Duat, of which there are thousands.

Thank the guide for his assistance and follow him below the ground. At first, there are steps, worn smooth as if by many feet, but eventually the well-chiselled stairway becomes a rough tunnel with a sloping path leading downwards.

Eventually, you emerge into a dark temple, but your guide tells you not to linger here. It is the Hall of Judgment where the hearts of the dead are weighed. The guide draws a series of symbols upon the air and a side corridor appears within the wall. You presume these signs are hieroglyphs that can open doorways.

The guide tells you that this journey is not the one that the dead experience. As a living guest of Osiris, your path to meet him is different. The corridor leads you to open air. When you emerge from it, there seems to be sky, as if you are once again above ground. You mention this to your guide, but he only smiles and says *'This is the Lake of Lilies, which we must cross to reach the Mansion of Osiris in the Fields of Aaru. This is a realm of the Duat, where all is perfection.'* And you see that before you a vast body of shining water stretches away to the West.

The guide utters sounds and draws symbols on the air, which summon a small boat. You both climb into this, and then, without the agency of oars, the boat begins to travel swiftly across the lake. You gaze around you, wondering at the beauty of the landscape. Birds and other wildlife abound. The papyrus reeds growing around the edge of the lake are of the deepest most glorious green you have ever seen. The water of the lake is like liquid crystal, with brightly coloured fish swimming within it. The air is delicately scented with the aroma of flowers.

The lake seems endless, like a sea, but eventually you perceive land ahead. As you draw closer, you see this is the idealised version of Khemet you've heard about. You see fields of grain stretching for miles, full of plump produce. All of the crops are of extraordinary height and lushness. The trees are heavy with ripe and succulent fruit. Animals are all sleek and healthy. Presently, you see a town ahead, nestling on the lakeside. The boat heads towards it and comes to a halt at the docks, where a woman comes to help your guide secure the vessel. As you disembark you see that the town is very busy. Everyone around you appears vigorous and extremely healthy. Some are simply sitting together, laughing and talking. Others are fishing or undertaking tasks they might have undertaken in life. No one is unhappy. People are accompanied by the pets who died before them and have been waiting for them. You see huge families working together or playing together, clearly comprising many generations.

If you were weighed down by cares before you began this journey, now you feel light of heart. The very air of the Fields of Aaru dispels darkness and misery. Those who are already content feel madly joyous in this place. Life is full of hope, excitement, adventure and desire.

Your guide directs you to follow him, although the inhabitants of the Fields of Aaru are curious about you, inviting you to their homes, wanting to show you their possessions, wares or produce. They constantly seek to distract you, but with no ill intent. They are genuinely proud of their homes and accomplishments and want to share them with you. Patiently, the guide allows you to speak with people briefly before moving on. He is clearly known to them, as everyone you meet greets him cheerfully.

Eventually, you reach the edge of the town, and here there is a complex of decorative canals and islands. In the centre is an immense palace of pale, glittering stone, fronted by many columns. This is the Mansion of Osiris. You follow your guide along a pathway between the canals and gardens to the entrance of the mansion. Beyond the initial gateway is a courtyard, a walled garden with pools, streams, lawns, many flowers and trees. Here, Osiris holds court. He does not sit upon a throne, or act in a lordly way. He is seated on cushions on the ground, surrounded by others, both the blessed dead and other *neteru* and spirits of the Duat. He is not bound in his 'official costume' of mummy wrappings and tall crown, but in a plain robe similar to that worn by your guide. He wears a long wig and his skin is golden-brown, yet faintly tinged by green. You have never seen a more beautiful man. He is the epitome of kindness and gentleness, yet you can see he is also strong. When circumstances demand it, he can make severe judgements.

Osiris notices you approach and beckons to you, smiling widely. He says, *'Welcome, honoured guest. If anything burdens you, discard it here. Be free of care in my house.'*

Any remaining incumbrance of troubles or worries you might have had now fall away from you like ancient dust, which sinks into the ground. Osiris gets to his feet and asks you to walk alone with him. He seems very young yet extremely old. Compassion and love for humankind streams from his being. It is easy to talk to him.

Spend some time now talking with Osiris. If you have issues you wish him to help you resolve, tell him about them. He will give you wise counsel. He might have a gift for you or suggest ritual actions you might take.

As you walk around his wondrous home, Osiris tells you that the Fields of Aaru comprise the ka or soul of the Nile Delta on earth. He tells you about his role as judge in the Duat, but that he does not expect people to live up to impossible ideals. No human is without moments of weakness, and while they might strive to be what are thought of as 'good people' they will sometimes experience times of anger, fear and distrust. In the Duat, Osiris weighs the heart of the dead against the Feather of Maat, the symbol of truth and justice. If the heart is heavier than the feather, filled with the consequences of evil and cruelty, the deceased is denied entrance to the afterlife, their soul devoured by the monstrous creature named Ammit. Osiris says each heart is weighed against its own actions – to reach the Fields of Aaru, a person's positive acts and thoughts in life must outweigh the negative, but sadness and sickness do not count as negative. No soul can be truly without blemish unless natural human impulses and drives are repressed, which in itself is a negation of life.

'Do not judge yourself harshly,' Osiris says. He smiles and adds, *'for that is my task and I am very lenient with those I love.'* Osiris then leads you to a feast, where he serves you food and drink himself.

Spend as much time as you like exploring this domain. You may bathe in the waters of the garden, further freeing yourself from everything that might weigh you down.

When you are ready, thank Osiris for his hospitality and tell him you are ready to leave. He embraces you in farewell, and murmurs one final message to you. The priest who guided you here reappears and once again uses symbols to open a portal. When you pass through it, you are back upon the Giza plateau where the sun continues to sink. No time has passed at all. The priest says that when you wish to visit Osiris again, he will meet you at this spot and guide you once more. Thank him and say farewell. The scene before you now fades into mist, bringing you back to the present time, and earthly reality.

Return to normal consciousness and open your eyes. Be aware you're still invigorated with the power and love of Osiris. Record your experiences.

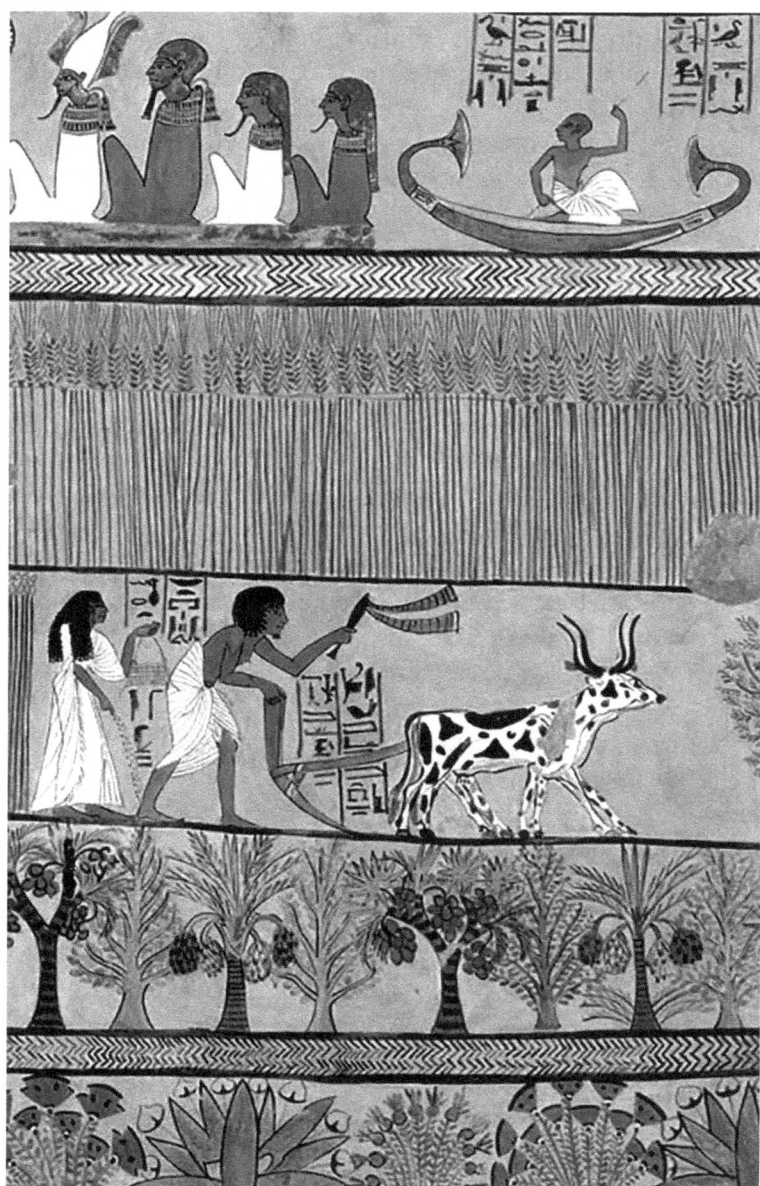

In the Fields of Aaru, Khemetic Papyrus Painting

The Flourishing Grain

For this ritual, place a representation of Osiris on your altar. You may use either a picture or a statue. You will plant seeds to represent your own growth, so have the equipment for this placed on the altar or near to hand.

Equipment Required

- Seeds of any kind and a container filled with soil to plant them in
- Place fresh flowers upon the altar, or growing grain crops if the season permits it
- The altar cloth should be green or black decorated with green and strewn with petals, preferably scented
- Green, white, gold or yellow candles
- A light flowery or fruity incense
- The hieroglyph of Osiris's name
- An appropriate feast

The Ritual

Create your enclosure and enliven your altar statue with *heka*, if you have one. Light the altar candles and replenish your incense if necessary. Then sit down in the centre. Close your eyes and breathe deeply for a while to alter your state of consciousness. Visualise your environment gradually changing. A mist fills your enclosure, so that objects around you disappear within it. Presently, the mist begins to clear, and you see a new landscape appearing around you.

You find yourself at dawn in Abydos (or Abtu as it was known in Khemet), on the day of the Festival of Osiris. Amid the temple complex next to the Nile, people are busy preparing for the celebrations ahead. You are among the temple staff and join in to help them. People are converging from towns and villages to take part in the festival.

Once the sun has risen higher in the sky, everyone is ready. The crowd falls quiet in the outer courtyard of the temple. Presently, the priests bring out the cult statue of Osiris from within. The statue has been dressed in a new robe; its stone skin anointed with oil. In a cloud of incense, the impassive face of the king of the *neteru* stares out towards the river.

The statue is placed carefully within the courtyard and now prayers will be chanted over it. Now open your eyes and come out of the visualisation, while imagining that part of you remains in the temple. Recite this adaptation of an ancient prayer to Osiris.

'Glory be to you, Osiris Wennefer,
the great one who dwells within Abtu,
King of Eternity,
Lord of Everlastingness,
Who passes through millions of years.
You are the eldest son of the womb of Nut,
Engendered by Geb, the Ancestor.
Let your heart, O Osiris,
Who is in the Mountain of Amentet, be content
For your son Horus is established upon your throne.
You endure for ever in your name of Wennefer.
Homage be to you, Oh King of Kings,
Lord of Lords,
Who from the womb of Nut
Has ruled the world and the Fields of Aaru.
Praise be to you, Osiris, Lord of Eternity,
Wennefer-Heru-Khuti,
Whose forms are manifold,

And whose attributes are majestic.
You are the guide of the Duat,
Whom the neteru glorify
When you set in the night sky of Nut.
The dead who have lain down rise up to look upon you.
They breathe the air and they look upon your face,
When the disk rises on the horizon.
Their hearts are at peace when they behold you,
Oh Osiris, who is Eternity and Everlastingness.'

Adapted from 'Hymn to Osiris'
The Book of the Dead (c.1400 BC)

Chant: *'Osiris, tha nefer tchetu'* for a minute or so, while gently shaking the sistrum.

(Pronounced: Osiris, thar neffer chet-oo. Meaning (roughly): Osiris, beautiful *neter* of the crops.)

Now close your eyes and return to the visualisation. For a moment, once the prayer is complete, there is silence. A sense of immanence fills the air. Osiris is with you. The celebrations will now begin.

Actors and musicians appear, who begin to perform the mystery plays of Osiris, re-enacting his life and death. You see people dressed as Isis, Set, Nephthys and Horus. They wear masks and elaborate costumes. The crowd clearly loves this performance with its dramatic twists and turns. The plays go on for some time, with pauses for refreshment. In the early afternoon, another rite begins.

The priests bring out from the temple a series of objects that look like shallow open sarcophagi. These are laid out in the courtyard and you can see that they are filled with the black soil of the Nile.

The priests beckon you to them so you may enact the rite with them. They recognise you as a guest of Osiris. One of them hands a bag of grain seeds to you, which you will plant in one of the receptacles that resemble the shape of Osiris's sarcophagus. The planting-box is a representation of his body, which is the land itself. It symbolises his fertility.

Now open your eyes and come out of the visualisation. Plant the seeds you have ready into the container of soil. As you do so, with great care, imagine these are the seeds of your future. They may represent hopes and ideas but also more tangible things like progress in a project or learning a new skill. Put your intention into the soil as you pat it down over the seeds. Finally, pour a little water over them, imagining this is from the Nile. When the task is complete, raise your arms and say:

'Osiris, Lord of the Perfect Black,
He Who Wears the Crown of Two Plumes,
I plant seeds to represent your gift to the land.
As these seeds flourish, conjure growth within me.
Let my mind be open to all possibilities.
Let my work grow strong and true.
Let my ambitions come to fruition.
I ask this in your name, Oh Beautiful One,
Lord of the Fields of Aaru.'

Now close your eyes and return to the visualisation. The priests have planted seeds within the receptacles prepared for them. They too now water the seeds with water from the Nile.

You see then that the actor who played Osiris earlier is walking towards you. He is very beautiful, his skin painted green, dressed in a white robe. He wears upon his head the tall *atef* crown, flanked by curling ostrich feathers. As he draws nearer, and you gaze into his eyes, you have an uncanny feeling. Is this person before you now only an actor or the *neter* himself? He smiles to you, raises a finger to his lips as if to bid you to be silent. He says *'Where I lay my hands, so growth begins.'* He leans down to place his hands upon the soil. As he does this, the skin of his hands turns black, like the land. Small shoots already begin to poke through the earth.

An image forms in your mind, as if you are looking down at the whole land of Khemet from above. You see the Nile and the land around it, a narrow band running north to south. As you focus upon this sight, you perceive the nebulous figure of Osiris stretched over the Black Land. His body is its dark soil, the earth that sustains life in Khemet. He *is* the Black Land.

Now your perception returns to the temple courtyard, where you find the mysterious actor has left you. He now sits upon a throne nearby. The priests lay a feast out in front of him and you approach. Now open your eyes and come out of the visualisation, imagining that a part of remains in Khemet at the temple. Say:

'Oh Osiris, Lord of Love,
Slain and Resurrected King,
Firstborn Son of the Earth and the Sky
I have brought offerings to you,
As symbols of thanks and respect.
Through me, may you experience their pleasures.
As I eat this food, may you relish its flavours,
As I drink, may your thirst be quenched with enjoyment.'

Now you will feast in Osiris' honour. Consume the offerings you have prepared, concentrating on sharing the pleasure of doing so with Osiris. Leave a small portion of everything you eat and drink. Then wrap the remains in paper and leave this parcel before the image of Osiris on your altar. When you are ready, compose yourself and return to the visualisation. You see that Osiris is consuming the feast with relish.

Time has moved on and now the sun begins to sink. The statue of Osiris is carried back into the precincts of the temple, and the crowds move away, back to their homes. The actor-Osiris rises from his throne. No one is paying attention to him now. He beckons to you to walk with him, so you may spend some time with the *neter* alone. You may ask him for help with creative projects or any other aspect of life you feel Osiris can help you with.

When you are ready to conclude the ritual, thank Osiris for his help and bow to him. Say:

'Oh Osiris, Khenti Amenti,
Foremost of the Westerners
He Who Dwells in Orion
With a Season in the Sky and a Season on the Earth,
Consort of Isis,
Continue to share with me your eternal compassion.
Grant me your strength and positivity.
Give me the means to accomplish all that I may be,
And the wisdom to know myself as you know me.'

Then bid farewell to him and prepare to leave. Imagine the scene turns to mist around you. Return to normal reality and dismantle your enclosure in the usual way. Then record the results of your work and dispose of the remains of your offerings.

From a Khemetic Wall Painting

Nephthys - Lady of Night

"Ascend and descend; descend with Nephthys, sink into darkness with the Night Barque. Ascend and descend; ascend with Isis, rise with the Day Barque."

From *The Pyramid Texts*

Attributes of Nephthys

The original Khemetic name of Nephthys (pronounced Nep-thiss or Neff-thiss) was Nebthet or Nebet-Het. As with many *neteru*, the hieroglyph of her name includes symbols for her epithets, which were often included in the crowns they wore. In Nephthys's case, this was a symbol for a house or temple enclosure, surmounted by a basket. This name means literally 'Lady of the House', but this does not refer to a domestic role. The title refers to Nephthys's position as a functionary either of the sacred enclosure or within the mansion of Osiris. In this role she can be regarded as a priestess of Osiris. Nephthys was highly regarded throughout Khemet, her image found in countless temple paintings and carvings, but she has been somewhat overshadowed in modern times by her more 'famous' sister. Nephthys holds a prominent role within the Ennead myths, even if only as the prime supporting actress.

In the stories, Nephthys enjoyed a close relationship with

her sister Isis, often assisting her or taking on responsibility for the care of Horus when Isis had business elsewhere. She was said to be a wet nurse for Horus. When Isis grieved for Osiris, Nephthys grieved too, and she assisted Isis in recovering Osiris's body. This might be because she had a very close relationship with Osiris herself. Some versions of the Ennead story relate that because Nephthys was unable to conceive a child with Set, she disguised herself as Isis and seduced Osiris. From their union, Anubis was conceived. Some renditions of the myth claim Isis colluded in this plan, suggesting she had no jealousy where Osiris and her sister were concerned. They worked together, suffered together, triumphed together.

In late Khemetic temple texts, Nephthys was regarded as a *neter* of protection and guardianship, and her part in the story of the Ennead certainly suggests these traits. She attempted to help Isis hide the body of Osiris from Set, which unfortunately was not a successful venture. She accompanies her sister as a funerary deity; statues of the pair are often found protecting the tombs of kings and queens. Upon earth, Nephthys was given the protective role as the nurse of the pharaoh. She was able to take on a ferocious aspect and smite the pharaoh's enemies with fiery breath. She was also a *neter* who helped guide the newly-dead through the Duat, another role she shared with Isis. Between them, their magical spells could protect those travelling through the Underworld from its monsters and demons. Both *neteru* was known as *weret hekau* – great of magic.

Nephthys was often depicted as having the wings of a bird, in particular those of a kite or a falcon, another attribute she shared with Isis. The call of the kite is a forlorn and mournful sound, which could be said to sound like a lament for the dead. This is perhaps one reason why

Nephthys – and also Isis for that matter – is connected with this bird. When the wings are outspread, they represent an enfolding gesture of protection.

Healing was also an attribute of Nephthys, predominantly assisting with childbirth. At Edfu, revealed by bas reliefs depicting her, she's associated with festivities, and particularly with beer. A scene shows the pharaoh offering copious amounts of this beverage to her, which she promises to return, along with the assurance the pharaoh can drink his fill without suffering a hangover. As such, she's earned the reputation as a '*neter* of beer'.

Her relationship with Set, he of the bad reputation, can be problematical for some modern pagans. Some writers claim Set abused her, but I have found no evidence for this in the original myths. Perhaps, for some practitioners, if she is portrayed as a hapless victim of an undesired marriage, they are able to reconcile in their minds how a benign protective deity could be the consort of a violent aggressor and remain with him. Some writers have gone so far as to suggest that the Nephthys and Set who were husband and wife were different from the *neteru* featuring in the myths of the Ennead. This is not entirely unlikely, as there are so many contradictory stories within Khemetic mythology. The Set and Nephthys of early Khemetic history no doubt differ greatly from their later forms, and there might have been several versions of them in all eras. In some early tales, Set and Horus work together as protectors of the pharaoh without conflict. Also, Set did have a role as helping the Ra, *neter* of the sun, as he travelled through the Duat every night – Set destroyed the serpent Apep who threatened Ra – the darkness that devours the day. In texts describing this role, there's no hint of Set's unsavoury aspects. But however people in ancient times might have regarded Set, and Nephthys's relationship with him, there's very little surviving description of it, other than she was his wife, their relationship endured, and they had no children. The reason for the lack of offspring has already been discussed in the section on Osiris, in that Set was the *neter* of the barren Red Land – the desert.

While I'll examine how we can perceive Set in a modern context in the section devoted to him, we can't escape the fact he *was* a neter personifying chaotic forces – primarily to do with the weather, which is uncontrollable. His violent acts are metaphors for these raging forces. Set had his function and sometimes when fulfilling his predestined role, he was responsible for bad things. In the stories, Nephthys clearly took Isis's, and by default Osiris's, side when Set murdered Osiris and later when he threatened Horus. So that does not exactly suggest a harmonious household in the realm of the desert. But, in the later myths, Nephthys does to a large degree represent loyalty, so perhaps we can regard her as being aware of the difficult role Set has to play in the scheme of things – the storm that can devastate a landscape, killing thousands – but nonetheless remaining his consort. Set is what he is – and cannot help but remain true to his nature: disruption. Because no evidence remains, (or the details of the story might not even have existed in the first place), I believe it is up to us to decide how we interpret Nephthys and Set and the nature of their relationship. We can attach our own narratives to them, which can be *based* on what they might have meant to people in ancient times, but for us to interact with these *neteru* meaningfully, they should have relevance to our own lives. They are symbols, after all. From the viewpoint of a writer of fiction, the mysteries and questions surrounding these early deities offer fertile ground for some interesting stories and interpretations.

There is one aspect of Nephthys, not widely discussed, which most clearly gives her a separate identity from other *neteru* of the Ennead: she was sometimes referred to as a *neter* of darkness, who prevailed over the eerie hinterland between the desert and the fertile Delta. She was therefore a *neter* of the boundary between the zones of barrenness and fecundity – mirrored in the story of her affair with Osiris. Bas reliefs at the Edfu temple complex provide the information that she possessed the ability to enable the pharaoh to see 'that which is hidden by moonlight'. That phrase alone can be interpreted to have subtly different meanings.

From all the fragmented evidence, we can discern a pattern of opposites in Isis and Nephthys. They are inseparable and complement each other. From this we can draw the following correspondences: Isis is the day, while Nephthys is the night. Isis symbolises all that is visible in the world, while Nephthys represents the unseen and hidden, all things connected with the dark. Isis was the consort of the Black Land, while Nephthys was the consort of the Red Land. In some accounts, Nephthys was connected with the cat and its apparent associations with the moon. Occasionally, she was shown in the form of a cat.

In this system of magic, Nephthys takes on her own prominent position within the Ennead. She's not simply the wife of Set and the obliging faithful sister of Isis. She becomes the *neter* of the night and her sacred animal is the cat.

The Magical Purpose of Nephthys

If you look at the myths, Nephthys's traits are loyalty, steadfastness, protectiveness and helpfulness. These are all qualities you would no doubt wish to nurture within yourself. They are virtues associated with her position within the Ennead and the role she took in the myths. However, outside of those duties, she had her own somewhat secret attributes, which enables her to take on a unique personality beyond responsibilities to her family and the dead in the Duat.

As a night deity, a *neter* of the dark, Nephthys reveals that which is hidden. She can therefore be regarded as a *neter* of divination, of instinct and intuition. While not strictly a *neter* of the moon – there are others who personify that as their main role in Khemetic tradition – her environment is moonlight and starlight. What lies hidden in moonlight? That within the shadows.

Nephthys's influence is also appropriate for the magical practitioner who seeks self-knowledge in order to move forward in their spiritual work, as well as for solving problems within magical groups – revealing that which we ourselves hide.

The dark can be frightening simply because it offers hiding places. We lack the ability to see what threatens us and are therefore at a disadvantage. Things not seen in daylight prowl at night. Nephthys is no stranger to threat. She was the consort of chaos and risked his rage to help her family. The myth depicts clearly what Set is capable of. Nephthys then is fearless and can impart this quality to you. Fear often holds us back – fear of the unknown, the darkness and unpredictable outcomes. Nephthys personifies qualities of both The Moon and The High Priestess in the Tarot.

Nephthys's urge is to make things better, to effect repairs. In this way she is a healer, and her energy can be particularly useful to help with confronting emotional problems or restrictions caused by early life conditioning. Her role as midwife applies not only to the delivery of children but to all kinds of birth, including those connected with creativity. She can help you rise from a dark place after a creative block.

Divination is an appropriate component of rituals to Nephthys. Invoking her influence brings clarity to matters of foretelling. She can be asked to clear the shadows, to reveal what is hidden. She can also be approached to dispel fear and, because she is so closely associated with guardianship and protection, to shield you (or others) from those who wish to do harm.

Another quality can be drawn from her myth – the ability to deflect or even quell rage and violence. There's no direct evidence for this, and yet the myth never speaks of Set taking revenge on Nephthys, even though she remains loyal to Osiris and Horus, who invoke Set's jealous fury and its bloody consequences. One interpretation of this is simply that Set *cannot* harm Nephthys. She hides in shadow. She is slippery as starlight. This, then, gives her attribute of protection even greater strength.

Symbols of Nephthys

The House

Nephthys's prime symbol is the oblong shape representing 'the House'. This is a symbolic representation of a building or part of a building and not something found easily to place upon your altar. However, you can make one, or include house-shaped cakes or biscuits as part of the feast.

The Kite

You can include a picture or ornament of a bird of prey. It's also appropriate to decorate the altar with feathers, particularly of birds of prey if you can find any.

The Basket

Any shallow bowl or basket can represent this symbol of Nephthys. You can place a part of your ritual feast in it.

Dark Moon Disc

While not a symbol for Nephthys deriving from ancient times, a representation of the dark moon is appropriate for her workings. You can make the disk from cardboard or paper or use a round, black scrying mirror.

The Cat

This animal is a symbol of Nephthys in her aspect of neter of the night. You can place pictures of Khemetic cats, or small statuettes on your altar.

Epithets of Nephthys

When writing your own rituals to Nephthys, you can draw upon this list of her epithets. These derive from both ancient times and modern magical practice.

Lady of the House
Lady of the Temple Enclosure
The Excellent *Neter*
Nephthys of the Bed of Life
Queen of the Embalmer's Chamber
She Who Reveals That Which is Hidden by Moonlight
Protectress of the Benu Bird
Mistress of the Mansion of the Sistrum

Offerings to Nephthys

Foods appropriate for Nephthys include most of those deemed suitable for her sister Isis: dates, honey and raisins and cakes. You could cut small cakes or biscuits into the shape of her House symbol, the dark moon disc, birds of prey or cats, and decorate them with black icing. The markings within the House oblong could be drawn with red icing. This part of the feast could be placed on the altar in a basket or shallow bowl, another of her symbols. You could also include chicken, duck or turkey snacks as part of the feast. The ritual drink should be beer or a non-alcoholic alternative. As with all other feasts, make substitutions according to dietary requirements.

Visualisation: Eyes in the Dark

What follows is a pathworking for which you don't need to construct the sacred enclosure – although you can if you want to. Otherwise the procedure for creating lesser sacred space will suffice.

This visualisation may be used to confront parts of yourself you either don't understand or which worry you. This can also help to gain clarity concerning situations and the actions of other people, which are affecting you but that you lack information about. Another purpose for this pathworking is to face aspects of yourself that might be blocking your creativity or holding you back in life. Nephthys helps you discard such blocks. To discover what lies in the darkness you need to be able to see without light, using your instincts. Nephthys is a guide through the Duat, so is familiar with the dark places. She will protect you. One of her functions is to reveal what is hidden. She can sharpen your intuition.

Prepare yourself for visualisation and charge the atmosphere with *heka*. Imagine that the everyday world fades away around you, replaced by a floating mist. Gradually the mist begins to clear, and you find yourself in a new landscape.

You are in Khemet, standing on the banks of the Nile, raised higher than the water. It is night-time, and you can see the thinnest sliver of the old moon in the sky amid a blaze of stars. As you gaze upon the crescent of light it gradually grows thinner, until it disappears completely. And yet the moon is still visible, a dark orb surrounded by a very faintly glowing greyish-white nimbus. You are able to see quite clearly because of the starshine, but you become aware that even the stars are growing gradually dimmer, until they disappear completely.

You gaze out over the river, down across the reed beds, although all you can perceive is indistinct outlines of reeds and water. The Nile flows slowly, silkily through the dark. You hear a faint rustling sound and see that the reeds are moving slightly. Then you see the glow of eyes shining from them. Round unblinking eyes, gleaming as if with residual moonlight. They are completely greenish-white, with no pupil. But even so, you realise these are the eyes of a multitude of cats hiding in the reeds. You notice that one pair of eyes is larger than the others and almond-shaped. Slowly, a shape emerges from the reeds, growing taller as you watch, until you can make out it is the form of a woman. She exudes a faint glow of her own. Has she been crouching in the reeds and is now standing up? Or was she a cat only moments before?

The woman parts the reeds with her hands and steps up the bank towards you. You can see this is no ordinary woman. Her long black wig is formed into plaits, and hung with amethyst crystals, which chime together as she moves. She wears a dark garment and even the faience collar around her neck is fashioned of obsidian beads and black metal. Her skin too is very dark and strangely unreflecting, with a matt velvet sheen to it. Upon her head is a crown in a strange shape, an oblong capped by a hollow bowl. You realise this is Nephthys, wearing the crown of the sacred enclosure coupled with an offering basket. This is the dark sister of Isis. She says: *'You have come seeking that which is hidden in moonlight.'*

And you reply, *'Yes, I seek what lies in shadow.'*

Nephthys smiles and raises her arms towards the sky. She makes a swift gesture and then the sky goes completely black. The dim moon is gone. The only illumination comes from Nephthys's eyes where moonlight lingers, and the eyes of the cats who have crept out of the reeds to sit around you.

Now, if you have a specific purpose to visit Nephthys, tell her what your difficulty is and that you want her assistance in resolving it. You are aware you will have to face what lies in the dark, but you can feel Nephthys's strength around you, and also her compassion. Her instinct is to protect, and you know that nothing bad can happen to you in her company.

If you are here simply to hone your perception and intuition, then tell Nephthys you wish to learn her mysteries and also how to reveal what lies hidden in darkness. Listen to what Nephthys has to tell you. If you need help with a problem, she may suggest action you can take in the physical world. She may disclose information you lacked before.

After speaking for a few minutes with Nephthys, she gestures for you to follow her. She and the cats lead you away from the river. You can't see what lies around you but think you must be entering crop fields. The ground feels soft beneath your feet like fertile soil. Ahead you see a weirdly shimmering shape in the air, like a tall, oval doorway. There is no light, and it is in fact darker than the darkness itself, but still you can perceive it, like a hole in reality.

Nephthys says to you, '*If you wish to visit the Realm of Shadows, I will take you there. In this place all that is hidden is revealed. Your shadow self can be confronted here. This shadow represents your deepest fears, your conditioning, your disappointments and sorrows. It can block your creativity, weigh you down with feelings of inadequacy. You can control the shadow, but you should only take this step if you feel ready to do so. If not, then I will lead you back to the river and the light's return. You may visit again, at any time, if you so wish.*'

Now, you must decide whether to face your dark self, or whether what Nephthys has already revealed to you is enough to help you deal with your dilemmas or blocks at the current time. If you choose to conclude the visualisation here on this occasion proceed to the end, thanking Nephthys for her help and asking her to take you back to where you started. Return to normal consciousness in the usual manner. Should you choose to enter the Realm of Shadows, tell Nephthys your decision. She takes hold of your hand and leads you through the black portal.

At once you are enveloped in a void, your senses quelled, although you can still feel Nephthys's cool, soothing hand in yours. But you cannot see, cannot hear, cannot smell. Even the gasp of your own breath is silenced. Nephthys will now guide you the through the darkness of your own psyche, so you may study all that is hidden. You will confront your shadow self and by knowing it and seeing it, its hold over you will be loosened. Nephthys will show you what is holding you back in your life.

What happens next cannot be predicted. This will be personal to you. Spend some time in the Shadow Realm with Nephthys, aware always that she will guide and protect you from harm.

When you feel ready to end this part of the visualisation, tell Nephthys you are ready to do so. At once, she takes you back to the world of Khemet. Once again you can smell, hear and see the world around you. Even in darkness, it appears crystal clear, beautiful. The night air smells wonderful. The croaks and cries of the river creatures sound like a song of the earth. As you walk to the river, you see the stars once more begin to appear in the heavens. You're aware of how much lighter you feel and when you look up at the starry sky you see that the first sliver of the new moon is visible. This is the seed of your renewed creativity, your liberation from the past. The cats who are Nephthys's companions trot alongside you. At the river's edge, bid farewell to Nephthys and thank her for her help. She smiles at you and walks away with her retinue of cats.

The scene before you now fades into mist, bringing you back to the present time, and earthly reality. Return to normal consciousness and open your eyes. Be aware your senses are still enlivened by the power and protection of Nephthys. Record your experiences.

Ritual:
Revealing That Which is Hidden

For this ritual, place a representation of Nephthys on your altar. You may use either a picture or a statue. You will need a Tarot deck, or some other cards used for divination. The purpose of the ritual is to scry in the presence of the *neter*, to penetrate situations and people which might mystify you, or simply to gain magical knowledge and expertise in divination. This is not a simple reading but a working with Nephthys to reveal the deepest secrets and the true meaning of what symbols might come to you.

Equipment Required

- You can create a dark moon – a large black disk of paper or cardboard – or use a black scrying mirror. Place this behind the image of Nephthys
- A Tarot deck or some other cards for divination
- The altar cloth should be black. You may decorate it with moonstones or a few white crystals
- Black candles
- A heavy, dark incense
- The hieroglyph of Nephthys's name
- An appropriate feast

The Ritual

Create your enclosure and enliven your altar statue with *heka*, if you have one. Light the altar candles and replenish your incense if necessary. Then sit down in the centre. Close your eyes and breathe deeply for a while to alter your state of consciousness.

Before you start the visualisation, take up the Tarot deck and hold it in both hands against your heart. Imagine it filling with *heka* to become a tool of magic (unless you are using a deck you've already permanently infused with *heka*). Put your intention into the deck that it will reveal information to you about what you seek to illumine.

With closed eyes, draw three cards from the pack and lay them face down upon your altar. (If more than one person is taking part, each should take three cards and place them face down on the floor in front of them.) Set the rest of the deck on the altar before the image of Nephthys.

Now settle yourself again and close your eyes. Visualise your environment gradually changing. A mist fills your enclosure, so that objects around you disappear within it. Presently, the mist begins to clear, and you see a new landscape appearing around you.

You find yourself in the Red Land of Khemet, in the outer precincts of a great temple in the desert. The place feels deserted. It isn't ruined, but you feel that no one is around. It is night-time, and the sky glitters with the light of stars, although the moon is dark. You know that this is a secret temple to Nephthys, and that people come to this place to look into the future and gain insight into current situations that mystify them. But the temple can't always be found. It appears in the desert only in the dark phase of the moon. You are here to seek the mysteries of Nephthys and to scry in her presence. You carry a satchel of offerings for the *neter*. Hold out your arms and say:

'Oh Nephthys, Lady of the Temple Enclosure,
She Who Reveals That Which is Hidden by Moonlight,
I call to you!
Nephthys, Most Excellent,
She Who Sees All,
Come to me in your hidden temple.

Reveal to me your mysteries
And grant me insight into all things!'

Chant: *'Nephthys, repit kamen'* for a minute or so, while gently shaking the sistrum.

(Pronounced: Nep-thiss, rep-it, kah-men. Meaning (roughly): Nephthys, great lady of the dark.)

For a moment, without opening your eyes, cast your inner gaze back to the image of Nephthys in your enclosure. Imagine it glows with soft light, as it brims with *heka*. Nephthys is alive in both inner and outer realities and will communicate with you.

You hear a whispering voice in your head, which says, *'Then come seek me in the shadows of my sanctuary.'*

Returning to the visualisation, you climb the steps to the inner courts of the temple. Now you can hear the hissing rattle of sistri. Thick incense fills the air the further you venture into the complex. Eventually you come to a shrine, the entrance to which is simply a dense black oblong, much like the shape of Nephthys's crown.

A dark woman dressed in black emerges from the shrine. This is Nephthys and the chamber she has stepped out of is her most sacred inner sanctum. She wears an elaborate collar of moonstones, as well as bracelets of silver around her upper arms and wrists. Her slender feet are bare. Approach the *neter* and bow to her. Say:

'Most Glorious Nephthys of the Bed of Life,
I thank you for allowing me to visit your secret temple,
Visible only in the dark of the moon.
I ask you to sharpen within me the gift of foretelling,
The insight to penetrate that which is hidden.

Let the silent symbols speak,
Let the marks upon the stone walk.'

Nephthys inclines her head to you. *'Then let us see what is to be known, meruti.'*

At this point, come out of the visualisation, whilst imagining that part of you remains in the temple with Nephthys. In silence, turn over the three cards and gaze upon them. Have no thoughts or judgement about what you see; simply absorb the images.

After a few moments, resume the visualisation. You are now sitting with Nephthys in the inner sanctum, which is lit only by the dim glow of an oil lamp on the floor. The cards you drew are laid out in a row before Nephthys and she is studying them. She tells you what they can mean for you, and what action they suggest you can take. They might reveal a secret. Nephthys then asks you to tell her what the cards have said to you. Talk about your thoughts with Nephthys and see if any further insight comes to you. After this discussion, Nephthys invites you to explore her temple with you. She may show you some of its concealed rooms and the secrets within.

When you are ready to conclude this part of the visualisation, return to the shrine of Nephthys. Bring out the offerings you have brought and spread them before the *neter*. Open your eyes and come out of the visualisation, while imagining that part of you is still in the shrine of Nephthys. Say:

'Oh Nephthys, Neter of the Darkness
Yet Mistress of Festivity,
Lady of the Mansion of the Sistrum
I have brought offerings to you,
As symbols of thanks and respect.

Through me, may you experience their pleasures.
As I eat this food, may you relish its flavours,
As I drink, may your thirst be quenched with enjoyment.'

Now you will feast in her honour. Consume the offerings, concentrating on sharing the pleasure of doing so with Nephthys. Leave a small portion of everything you eat and drink. After this has been done, wrap the remains in paper and leave this parcel before the statue on your altar.

When you are ready, compose yourself and return to the visualisation. See your offerings around Nephthys, which she consumes with relish. Bow to her and say:

'Oh Nephthys, Daughter of the Earth and Sky,
Sister of Osiris, Isis and Set,
Continue to share with me the ability to see that which is hidden
Grant me your instinctive vision.
Give me the means to become all the good things I foretell,
And the wisdom to know myself as you know me.'

Then bid farewell to her and prepare to leave. Depart from the temple, back out into the Red Land of the Khemetic desert. Here, imagine the scene turns to mist around you. Return to normal reality and dismantle your enclosure in the usual way. Then record the results of your work and dispose of the remains of your feast appropriately.

From a Khemetic Bas Relief

Set - Lord of Chaos

Attributes of Set

Set is one of the most complex *neteru* in Khemetic lore, since there are so many variations of his myths. His name in Khemet could be Seth, Setekh, Setesh, Suty or Sutekh – and there are further variants. There's little doubt he's one of the most ancient *neteru* of Khemet. He was originally associated with the south of the country, and his celestial home was thought to be in the northern part of the sky, in a star known at Khepesh that's part of the Great Bear. His sacred animal is

an enigma, known only as the *sha*, or else the 'Set animal'. In appearance, this beast resembles a slim hunting dog, like a greyhound, but with a strange curving snout, almost like a bird's beak, and long squared-off ears like fins. Its tail ended in a fork, as represented in the base of the *was* sceptre often carried by Set. It's speculated that the *sha* was based on a real animal that has become extinct, but seems more likely it is, and always was, a mythical creature. Set was usually depicted as having the head of a *sha* and was only rarely shown as having a fully human form.

In the earliest period of Khemetic history, Set was a benign *neter*, associated with virility, growth and fecundity – much like his brother Osiris, and just as beautiful. He was a *neter* of love, invoked for success in love spells.

Set was the favourite of a number of pharaohs, such as Seti I and Rameses II, who regarded him as their patron *neter*. He was believed to accompany the Ra every night on his journey through the Duat in order to slay the serpent Apep, whose eternal aim was to devour and put out the sun. In one myth, Horus and Set, as twin deities, help Osiris to ascend to heaven by providing him with a ladder. The pair are also shown together, in a bas relief at Thebes, teaching Thothmes III in the art of using weapons - a bow and a staff. Another story describes Horus as *Neter* of the Sky by Day and Set as *Neter* of the Sky by Night. There are representations of Horus-Set having the body of a man with two heads – a falcon and a *sha*. E. A. Wallis Budge suggests in *The Gods of the Egyptians* that Horus and Set represented opposites: Day and Night, Light and Darkness, the Cosmos and Chaos, Life and Death, Good and Evil. Set's wife Nephthys remained by him in all his different aspects; they shared temples and worshippers throughout Khemetic history. Few of these attributes and stories seem pertinent to the vicious *neter* we find in the myths of the Ennead.

Set's association with weather was given some explanation by the German Egyptologist, Dr. Heinrich R Brugsch. He claimed that Set represented the descent of the sun in the lower hemisphere, in a southerly direction. This linked him with the fierce heat of summertime. As the days grew shorter after the summer solstice it was thought that this was down to Set stealing the light from Ra (or Horus). Similarly, the light of the new moon, which was brought to the earth by Thoth, was also eventually stolen by Set over the course of a month, resulting in the dark of the moon. Set was believed to be responsible for all bad weather – mists, thunder, lightning, hurricanes, the searing, sand-filled windstorm known as the *khamsin*, and even eclipses and earthquakes – and thereby took on a fiery aspect, through his association with the unrelenting desert sun and intense heat. He was the *neter* who could overturn the natural order of things, disrupting harmony, bringing chaos and darkness.

These attributes could either have been added to Set over time, or else applied to him only in certain areas of the country. However, as these traits clearly symbolise natural states – good and bad weather, light and dark – it doesn't mean that Set was regarded as the personification of evil: the personification of potentially *harmful states*, yes, but Set as a purely malevolent *neter*, estranged from Horus, came later in Khemetic history – at least in some parts of Khemet. As I said at the start of this book, trying to fit a linear narrative onto the myths of the *neteru* is often difficult.

Hadad:
Storm God of the Hyksos

At some point, Set became demonised, and various reasons have been given for this. Because of the jumble of conflicting stories involving the same characters, it's difficult to pinpoint precisely what took place. But at one time Set was the presiding *neter* of Upper Khemet, while Horus (perhaps Horus the Elder) was the *neter* of Lower Khemet. At this time, Set was not exclusively a *neter* of the desert (Red Land) or of violent weather. He was a powerful, benign *neter* of kings and a virile symbol of the land. Eventually, invasion by an Asiatic people known as the Hyksos into the eastern Delta around 1600BC changed the course of Set's destiny in spiritual lore. The Hyksos associated Set with Hadad, their god of rain, thunderstorms and hurricanes, and adopted him as their own. Set became known as the '*neter* of foreigners' at some point, probably after being embraced by the Hyksos. But however the various versions of Set might have developed over time and location, he eventually took his place in the Ennead myth as an aggressor. He was the lord of desert storms, of the chaotic elements. His domain was the desolate, barren wastes of the desert and of unknown lands beyond Khemet itself. His case is a clear example of how gods are subject to the whims of humankind, rather than the other way around. Set was changed, because people's beliefs and political circumstances changed.

Set was said to have had red hair, and this was a colour regarded as unlucky or associated with harmful things. Any animal having red skin or fur, or that lived exclusively in the desert, was regarded as either a creature of Set or an incarnation of him. Red is the colour associated with the desert and fire – which of course are included in Set's attributes. He was also connected with creatures that lived in or near water, because the forces of water were supposed to resist light and order. This included fish, crocodiles, serpents and hippopotami. It was believed that even people with red hair were under the influence of Set.

Set had a trickster aspect, shown in one version of the murder of Osiris story. This has a distinctly fairy-tale ambience to it, similar to the tale of Cinderella and the glass slipper. According to the story, Set ordered a casket or chest to be made, the most beautifully crafted and decorated artefact of its kind, secretly created to the exact measurements of Osiris's body – the most perfectly-proportioned male form. Set threw a grand party, to which Osiris was invited. At this event, he presented the magnificent jewelled chest to his guests and declared that whoever fitted most perfectly inside it could take it home with them. The eager guests all tried the casket for fit, but it was the wrong size for them, until Osiris took his turn. The casket fit him perfectly, as Set intended. At once, Set slammed the casket shut, and threw it into the Nile. Osiris suffocated within the chest, which floated down the river until it came to rest near Byblos, where it became absorbed by a tamarisk tree growing beside the water, an area where Isis later found it. There are slight variations of this myth, in which Set acted with accomplices rather than alone, or describing how he murdered Osiris in the casket before slamming the lid on him.

Historian Andrew Collins has proposed that Set's trickster aspect is similar to that found in the Norse god Loki (according to some writers, Loki too was red-haired and associated with fire). He suggests that Loki and Set derived from the same origin, in the area that eventually became Siberia, with the cult of the trickster god dispersing into different lands and taking on a variety of faces as his journey through history and landscapes progressed. Collins hypothesises that Osiris in effect stole Set's role as a deity of virility and fertility from him, relegating Set to the role of adversary, the despised and exiled one. Yet even when Set, as a trickster, might take actions that seem destructive, through time they are eventually seen to have initiated change for the greater good. Collins suggests that Horus might never have been created but for Set's actions in the myth of the Ennead – and Horus ultimately united Khemet, bringing in an era of prosperity. The aims of the trickster are not always clear, and in fact largely misunderstood. The trickster is often the scapegoat.

It's important to keep in mind that the Khemetu were not squeamish about the *neteru* having dark sides. Acts that are repellent and horrific to us were entirely acceptable to them, indeed a part of everyday life. They loved their pets and were reunited joyfully with beloved animal companions in the afterlife, yet in the temples they could sacrifice cats and falcons in their thousands, if not millions over the centuries, so that their spirits could act as messengers, taking human requests to the *neteru*. At certain festivals connected with Set, people would stamp birds and fish to death, because they represented qualities of Set. This wholesale ritual slaughter was conducted with apparently no consideration of – what to us is – its barbaric cruelty. The Khemetu acted this way because they believed it was right to do so, ensured the continuity of life and pleased the *neteru*. Times have changed. In the Western world, such practices are abhorrent, but that is down to the way ethics and morals have developed in our society.

Elsewhere in the world, animal sacrifice still continues and is considered sacred and/or magical.

Set is a *neter* of mystery and contradictions, spontaneous and ungoverned like the weather, able to lash out in anger, yet capable of causing positive change. The weather is an essential system in the world, even though it may wreak havoc.

The Magical Purpose of Set

Set is not a *neter* who lends himself to self-evolution through serene reflection in gentle pathworkings. He is wild, unpredictable and ungovernable. You might wonder what part of Set you'd want in your magical development and what positive lessons he might teach you.

However, consider the idea that you can find omens in the random events of the physical world – the wind may be full of messages, half-heard voices, the feverish shaking of leaves and branches, the hiss of the rain among the reeds beside a pool. The leaves might be torn by wind from the trees to land in a certain shape that has meaning. Patterns can also form (and constantly change) in the fall of raindrops on the surface of water. Like gazing at a stereogram (which looks at first like nothing more than a jumble of coloured shapes) to perceive the picture hidden within it, you just have to look at the world in the right kind of way to see the signs hidden in plain sight. Randomness possesses its own magic and is studied by chaos magicians, who divine meaningful patterns within chance and probability. Therefore, like his sister-wife Nephthys, Set has a connection with divination, the interpretation of omens and signs. He, like her, is also associated with the night. If you are prepared to face the screaming desert storm in the depths of darkness, messages might come to you.

One way in which I see Set as differing from Nephthys is that I don't feel he's concerned with facing the shadow self. His expression can be regarded as towards outward movement, to chaotic influences around you and understanding them. If his domain is inhospitable and dangerous beneath the fierce light of the sun, at night he is more approachable – his fire burns low, his ferocity subsides.

Another lesson I believe we can learn from Set is acceptance and tolerance. While you might not approve of Set's place in the Ennead story and the actions he takes, you can choose to appreciate he is part of the whole, and the story could not happen without his participation. The Khemetu believed in Maat – cosmic order and balance. To them chaos and disorder were as much an essential part of creation as order and harmony. Neither can exist without the other. Set is a component of the metaphor for life upon earth. Disruption and disharmony make you appreciate pleasurable periods of peace and tranquillity far more keenly, because you have the knowledge and experience to know there is a difference: the storm before the calm.

As far as a pathworking is concerned, the power of Set's windstorms can be used to clear your life of 'dead wood' to allow for new growth and new starts. Walking through a storm can be invigorating and refreshing, even if you get blown about and soaked through. You may visit Set for divination, but not through using cards as you did with Nephthys. Set's powers of divination come from the elements and the natural world.

Symbols of Set

Set has few symbols exclusively associated with him, but the following can be included in altar decoration.

The Was Sceptre

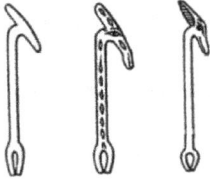

As with Geb, a representation of the Was Sceptre, either as a picture or model may be laid across your altar.

The Sha

The hieroglyph for this creature of Set can be part of altar decoration, or else you can make a model of the animal or draw/paint a picture of it.

Epithets of Set

When writing your own rituals to Set, you can draw upon this list of his epithets, as well as creating your own. The titles below derive from both ancient times and modern magical practice.

King of the Red Land
Lord of the Desert
Ruler of the South
King of the Sands
Triumphant and Victorious One
Mighty One of the Two-fold Strength
Lord of the Forces of the Water
He Who Lives in the Windstorm
He Who Abides in Khepesh
Lord of Disorder

He Who Shakes the Sky
Great Set, Who Stands Within the Boat of Ra
Slayer of the Serpent Apep
He Whose Devastating Storms Allow New Growth

Offerings to Set

Foods appropriate for Set include hot and fiery flavours. You can have bread or cakes spiced with ginger or chilli, as well as spicy wheat or potato snacks. Fruit drinks should also be laced with ginger, or you can include a fiery liqueur. As with most neteru, beverages such as beer and red wine are appropriate for Set, or non-alcoholic substitutes. As with all other feasts, make substitutions according to dietary requirements. If you're unable to eat spicy foods, for example, you can have food coloured red instead.

Visualisation:
Signs in the Storm

What follows is a pathworking for which you don't need to construct the sacred enclosure – although you can if you want to. Otherwise the procedure for creating lesser sacred space will suffice.

This visit to Set will take you into his realm of the desert to search for omens and signs that will help you look into your possible futures. It will also be an invigorating journey into whirling elements in order to blow unwanted aspects of the past away. This time, you are not seeking your shadow self, but what is outside you – information regarding circumstances and people. Set will show you truths that might be uncomfortable, for we rarely know precisely how we are viewed by others. People might talk behind our backs but are not prone to tell us what they think to our faces. Set has no such reticence. He's not concerned about your feelings or what you might think of him in return. But, if you are prepared to face the consequences, gazing into the mirror of others might fill in the gaps in your knowledge about what holds you back or obstructs you.

Prepare yourself for visualisation and charge the atmosphere with *heka*. Imagine that the everyday world fades away around you, replaced by a floating mist. Gradually the mist begins to clear, and you find yourself in a new landscape.

It is night-time, and you are in a mountainous area of the Khemetic desert, deep in the Red Land. You are standing in a gorge with rocks rising all around you. The air is hot and close, and you know that a storm is approaching. You have a sense that all the desert creatures, even those who hunt by night, have sought cover. The land around you feels empty and desolate.

You hear a low rumbling sound and, peering ahead, you see that a whirling dust storm is billowing down the gorge towards you. You know it is full of stinging sand and that the most sensible thing to do would be to mimic the animals and seek shelter, but you are here to commune with Set, so must endure his element.

The sound of the approaching chaos is deafening, roaring like a maddened crowd. You brace yourself as the storm engulfs you. As you are not in your physical body, you're able to keep your eyes open for the sand cannot hurt them. You can see whirling patterns in the storm, as if swarms of tiny insects are performing an elaborate dance. Sometimes you glimpse strange faces and hear the cackle of laughter and whispering voices in the wind.

Raise your arms and, with your hair and garments flapping around you, cry, *'Oh Mighty Set, who lives in the windstorm, come to me! Reveal to me that which is hidden from my sight!'*

At first nothing changes, and then you perceive an immense figure forming before you, within the flying sand and grit. This is Set as the embodiment of chaos. The eyes of his *sha* head glow like dull red suns. His skin is red too. He wears only a short kilt and carries a *was* sceptre. This is no ceremonial ornament, but an instrument to inflict pain, to damage. It has a stylised jackal head as a blunt weapon, and a viciously sharp forked blade at its other end. He grips this across his body with both hands, which are not like human hands. They are unnaturally long, and his fingers terminate in curving claws like scimitars. His weirdly curved snout hangs open, revealing a scarlet maw, which drips fire or blood, or a combination of both. You see he has a very long black forked tail that whips back and forth behind him. This is no friendly creature, willing to help you, yet you steel your resolve, because you are aware Set only appears to you as monstrous because he's testing your courage.

Say to him: *'I do not fear you, King of the Red Land. I am prepared to face truths in the spirit of Ma'at, of which you are a part.'*

Set then stands up straight and places the base of the *was* on the ground. He leans upon it and beckons you closer with a claw. As you approach the *neter*, he shrinks to the size of a tall man. The wildness of the storm dies down around your immediate vicinity, as if you are caught in the eye of it. Set says, *'You seek my counsel, little thing? How do you know what I reveal is true?'*

You say: *'Because I shall hold you by the tail. In that way, all tricksters must speak true.'* At this point, you must reach out and grab hold of the long, whipping tail. You must hold on to it.

Set might first try to escape, but your grip is firm. You know that if you falter you will not be able to communicate with Set, for he respects strength. But he is bound by Maat and is obliged to abide by its rules. Eventually, he ceases to struggle and laughs. *'So be it, brave little thing. I grant you true sight in the place where no one can see.'*

He strikes the *was* against the ground, and the storm presses in once more. You hold onto Set's tail tightly but presently notice that he appears to be helping you. The end of the tail has curled about your lower arm. That, or if you displease him, he'll squeeze you so tight he'll cut off your limb. Both things could be true with Set.

Now visualise that which you wish to know more about, so that Set can see your requirements. Tell him about the situation if you wish. He won't offer advice, as other *neteru* tend – and want – to do, but he will send you images in the storm. It's up to you to interpret the signs.

If you have no current dilemma you need assistance with, ask Set to show you information from the past – whatever you wish to explore. This can extend to your magical work and finding out more about the more obscure *neteru*. You might know their names but little more. Ask Set to show you their purposes and functions, the titles by which they were known. Spend some minutes scrying in the storm, holding onto Set's tail.

When you are ready to conclude the visualisation, say: *'I thank you, Lord of the Sands, for complying with my wish. I now release you.'* Let go of his tail.

If you wish to spend further time with Set now he is no longer under obligation, you may do so, but remember that once you relinquished your grip of his tail he regained the ability to trick and deceive.

When you are ready to depart, bid Set farewell. He disappears into the storm, as if turning in a mass of whirling dark motes. And the storm rises up into the sky, heading towards the north, where eventually it dissipates. You realise the experience of the elements has refreshed you. You feel strong and renewed, and the information you have received will aid you to resolve difficult matters.

The scene before you now fades into mist, bringing you back to the present time, and earthly reality. Return to normal consciousness and open your eyes. Be aware your senses are still enlivened by the power of Set, which will remain with you for the days to come. Record your experiences.

Ritual:
What Lies Beneath the Mask

The point of performing this ritual is to look behind the mask – not just Set's but your own. We all construct masks to help us deal with life's events, whether to give the impression of strength in a challenging situation or merely to appear sociable when the last thing you feel like doing is socialising. We have all shaped a multitude of masks.

You should have a mask to wear for the first part of the ritual. This can be anything you feel is appropriate, whether an elaborate costume mask or a diaphanous veil worn over your head to cover your face. You can make your own mask if there is an aspect of yourself you want particularly to explore.

Equipment Required

- A mask
- The altar cloth should be red. You may decorate it with red stones and crystals
- Sistrum
- Red candles
- A fiery spicy incense
- The hieroglyph of Set's name
- An appropriate feast

The Ritual

Create your enclosure and enliven your altar statue with *heka*, if you have one. Light the altar candles and replenish your incense if necessary. Then sit down in the centre. Put on the mask. Close your eyes and breathe deeply for a while to alter your state of consciousness.

Visualise your environment gradually changing. A mist fills your enclosure, so that objects around you disappear within it. Presently, the mist begins to clear, and you see a new landscape appearing around you.

You find yourself outside a town on the River Nile. This is Sepermeru, and in this place are temples devoted to both Set and Nephthys, where they were worshipped in ancient times. As is customary in a ritual, you carry a satchel of offerings for the *neter* you will meet. You walk towards the town and see the temple complex ahead of you. You arrive at the immense pylons of the gateway and pass beneath them. Beyond is a courtyard where there is a pool with trees growing around it. Doorways lead off to shrines within the building. You are drawn to one particular entrance, because you're aware it leads to the shrine of Set. Beyond the doorway, it's dark, but there are lamps upon the floor that provide some illumination. The walls are beautifully decorated with paintings. Eventually you emerge into the shrine itself, where a life size statue of Set stands before you. Raise your arms and shake the sistrum gently while you speak. Say:

'Oh, Great Set, Most Powerful,
He Who Abides in Kepesh,
May your heka come into this stone.
May you live in this vessel
And speak with me.
Let me see beyond the mask,
Oh Lord of the Red Land.'

Continue to shake the sistrum and chant: *Set Sta-ur* for a minute or so.

(Pronounced: Set-star-er. Meaning: 'Set, Great Quaker' – referring to being neter of earthquakes and thunder.)

Then, without opening your eyes, cast your inner gaze back to the image of Set in your enclosure. Imagine it glows with soft light, as it brims with *heka*. Set is alive in both inner and outer realities and will communicate with you.

Focus upon the statue in the visualisation once more. As you gaze upon it, you see that the stone is gradually changing; it is turning into a living creature. Set comes alive before you and you realise that the strange animal head he wears is a mask enveloping his head. This is not the monstrous creature you met in the visualisation, but more like a man. Bow to him and say:

Oh Set, Triumphant and Victorious One,
I thank you for your presence,

I am here to know your different faces
And ask that you reveal to me your mysteries.'

Set steps towards you and lifts the *sha* mask from his head.
You see beneath it the face of a snarling demon with bared
fangs and can't help stepping back in surprise. Then you
realise this too is a mask. Set lifts it from him. Beneath is
the face of a man but a face twisted with bitterness and
anger. Gradually this face becomes like carved wood – a
mask – and Set removes this too. What you see now is a
face that is the twin of Osiris, but a reddish-brown in colour
as opposed to Osiris's colours of green or black. Set's hair
is long and red, worn naturally and not covered by a
formal wig. He is, you realise, very beautiful. This is the Set
of the most ancient times, the *neter* of love and fertility
before other aspects were applied to him. He smiles at you
and there is a sense of wistfulness about him. He knows
himself and that his role in maintaining the balance of Maat
decrees what he must be – ostracised, alone, exiled.

(If you are working alone, you may temporarily open your
eyes and read the words of Set simultaneously imagining
him saying them to you. Then recite your response. Return
to the visualisation thereafter.)

He says to you: *'I am storms and the destruction within the*
hurricane. I am the shout of thunder in the heavens. I am the
flood that drowns the fields, the dark that banished light, the
brother who slew his brother. I am the Black Sun and the Hidden
Moon. I am Chaos. I am Darkness.'

You consider these words, then say: *'These things are true.*
But it is you who contains the desert storms and protects the
Black Land from their devastation. You hold back the searing
winds and the scouring sands, shielding the fertile soil from
drought. You are the Red Land. It is you who slays the serpent

who would devour the sun. You are the adversary of Horus and the making of Horus. You are the complement of Osiris in the eyes of Maat. By your nature, you ensure balance. You are essential. You were love once, and fertility and virility. And these are part of you forever. You are Set.'

Set bows his head to you. He goes to the side of the shrine where ritual items are displayed. From these he lifts a mirror of polished gold. He returns to you, holds the mirror at chest height, then says, *'Reveal what lies behind your mask.'*

Without opening your eyes, remove the mask you're wearing in reality and in the visualisation. Be conscious that for a moment, this action makes you feel vulnerable because it reveals truths. As to what lies beneath, that is between you, the mirror and Set. There might be more than one mask to take off. They represent the defences you utilise in life to deal with all situations. Most will be beneficial, not to be discarded but acknowledged for what they are. Sometimes it might be necessary to wear a forbidding mask that allows you to be harsh, to make difficult choices. But perhaps there are other masks which are not helpful. Be honest as you look into the mirror. Talk with Set about what is revealed. Ultimately, the essence of Set and the essence of you will face one another, free of artifice of any kind, good or bad.

Spend some time now in free visualisation. Set may take you somewhere or give you a gift – perhaps even a new mask that will be useful to you.

When you are ready to conclude this part of the visualisation, return to the shrine of Set. Bring out the offerings you have brought and spread them before the *neter.* Open your eyes and come out of the visualisation, while imagining that part of you is still in the shrine of Set. Say:

'Oh Set, Mighty One of the Two-Fold Strength,
Who rides in the barque of Ra by night,
I have brought offerings to you,
As symbols of thanks and respect.
Through me, may you experience their pleasures.
As I eat this food, may you relish its flavours,
As I drink, may your thirst be quenched with enjoyment.'

Now you will feast in his honour. Consume the offerings, concentrating on sharing the pleasure of doing so with Set. Leave a small portion of everything you eat and drink. After this has been done, wrap the remains in paper and leave this parcel before the statue on your altar.

When you are ready, compose yourself and return to the visualisation. See your offerings around Set, which he consumes with relish. Bow to him and say:

'Oh Set, He Whose Storms Allow New Growth,
Bother of Osiris, Isis and Nephthys,
Continue to share with me the truth behind the masks
Grant me your uncompromising vision.
Give me the means to be in balance,
Aware of my own dark suns and hidden moons,
Yet free of judgment.
Grant me the honesty to know myself as you know me.'

Then bid farewell to Set and prepare to leave. Depart from the temple, back out into the Red Land of the Khemetic desert. Here, imagine the scene turns to mist around you.

Return to normal reality and dismantle your enclosure in the usual way. Then record the results of your work and dispose of the remains of your offerings appropriately.

The Sons of Osiris
And Their Families

Horus - Boy King of Khemet

Attributes of Horus

Horus's name was Heru in Khemetic. He is generally depicted as a man with the head of a falcon, wearing the double crown of Upper and Lower Khemet. His annual festival was the winter solstice, presumably as he represented the sun, and this is the time when the days start to grow longer. He eventually took on his father's role as a king and *neter* of the land itself – representing fertility, fecundity and the welfare of crops and animals. In addition, he was a *neter* of sovereignty and the sky. But this legacy didn't come easily. Set had claimed the throne of Egypt for himself and had no intention of relinquishing it to its rightful heir. After Osiris's murder, resurrection and consequent instatement as a *neter* of the dead, Horus had to fight for the crown, both in law and physical combat, culminating in a court case, hotly contested by Set, before the tribunal of the *neteru*. In his story we find the concluding chapters of the volatile history of the Ennead.

There are two major *neteru* named Horus – Horus the Elder, who is sometimes included in the myths as a brother of Set and Osiris, and Horus the Younger, who is the son of Isis and Osiris. In this work, I've omitted Horus the Elder, as I see him as somewhat separate from the core myths of the Ennead, and one Horus to represent both can comfortably fulfil the required roles at different stages of his life. Horus the Younger fits more neatly into the narrative as a whole. There are several other versions of this *neter* cropping up in various regions of Khemet and at different times in history, so again it's beneficial to take a few artistic liberties with the myths to give them a coherent timeline.

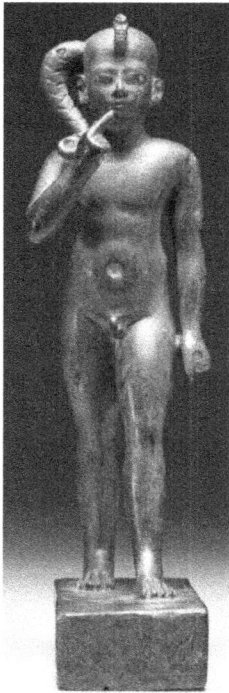

Horus as the son of Isis and Osiris is sometimes depicted as a child, called Harpocrates by the Greeks, or Heru-Pa-Khered in Khemetic. He is often shown with his mother Isis and is represented as a young, naked boy with a finger to his lips, his shaven head sporting a single 'youth lock' of hair. This image in Khemet was simply to emphasise that he was a child, but the Greeks interpreted the young *neter*'s hand gesture differently, associating him with silence and secrecy. As Horus took on this aspect permanently under the Greeks, it became part of him, so it's not inappropriate to see Horus Harpocrates representing these qualities. But primarily, Horus the Younger represents the rising sun at dawn, the reborn light at the winter solstice and the first shoots of growing crops. Later, in his adult role, he takes on the attributes of the sky *neter*, with his eyes representing the sun and the moon. But before he could become the supreme *neter* of the Heliopolitan royal family, Horus had to deal with Set.

Isis gave birth to Horus after Osiris had taken up residence in the Fields of Aaru to perform his new role as *neter* of the dead and the afterlife. Set was threatened by the idea of Horus from the start and was intent on hunting him down and destroying him. Isis had to hide Horus from his uncle throughout his childhood, aided by the loyal Nephthys – who by this point, as Set's consort, was technically queen of Khemet, and also by the scorpion *neter* Serket. Isis told her son that his duty would be to protect Khemet from Set and also to avenge his father.

When Horus became adult, he declared that he was the rightful ruler of Khemet. Predictably, Set did not agree with this claim. The case was brought to Atum and the divine tribunal. Isis took up the cause and began to fight for her son's legacy, employing other *neteru* as allies. The majority of the Ennead supported Isis and Horus, but Atum, the first *neter* and progenitor of the Ennead, felt that Horus was too young to be king, and that Set had in fact proved himself to be a competent leader, if rather chaotic in nature. Atum's view then appears to be that Set should be king for at least until Horus had gained more experience of life. But no doubt feelings ran high over the fate of Osiris, and some of the Ennead and their allies wanted Set removed from power immediately. With strong *neteru* like Isis behind him, Horus was capable of becoming king; he would have a team of wise and reliable advisors to aid him. But Atum didn't see it that way. The debate went on for eighty years, during which time Set and Horus fought for dominance continually, both physically and before the tribunal. In some versions of the story, their combat was part of the legal process – seen almost as sporting contests to determine which *neter* was more suitable to be king. But this was more brutal than sport. Both were said to have suffered severe injuries – Horus lost an eye while Set was partially castrated.

There are many stories associated with this stage of the Ennead's history, invented and embellished over time – enough probably to fill a book themselves. There are even differing versions of the episodes I've chosen to include in this book.

One of the most prominent tales concerns Set's seduction of Horus, another of his plays for power. The story goes that somehow Set was able to subdue the conflict for a while in order to seduce his nephew. This was not an act of desire or affection, merely part of a plan to secure his position; he'd clearly given up on winning any other way. By law, if Set could prove he had dominance over Horus, even in a sexual sense, (taking the active role), then he was rightfully king. The Ennead could perform a rite to prove that Horus's body contained Set's semen, which would provide irrefutable proof that Set should rule. However, Horus was wise to this plan and although he went along with the liaison, he contrived to catch Set's semen with his hands, which he then threw into the Nile. Confident he'd got Horus where he wanted him, Set demanded his nephew be brought before the tribunal. If the Ennead could call Set's semen forth from Horus's body, there would be no doubt who should be king. However, when the call was made, Set's seed answered from the river. Therefore, his claim was invalidated. After this, Horus went on the offensive. Using the guile he inherited from his mother Isis, he scattered his own seed over a crop of lettuces, which happened to be Set's favourite food. (In one version, it is in fact Isis who adulterates the lettuce with her son's semen.) The lettuce was presented to Set, who devoured it, and then Horus and Isis called in the judgement of the Ennead. This time, when the seed was summoned, it answered from within Set's body. Horus was thus proved to have dominance and the kingship was awarded to him.

There are many disparate stories of how Horus eventually achieved power, but another I feel should be mentioned (and which I think fits best into the narrative) involves the guile of Isis. Again, there are multiple variations of this story in Khemetic texts. In this version, the conflict between Set and Horus seems interminable. Atum insists that Horus has yet to prove his capability to be king, and neither of the contending *neteru* are able to defeat the other. In addition, Set is frustrated by the support that Isis has been drumming up among the *neteru*. Stubbornly, he states he won't cooperate with the tribunal of the Ennead if she continues to be present when the case is being discussed. Therefore, and no doubt with some reluctance, the tribunal agrees she should be banned from attending. They move the tribunal to an island on the Nile, and the ferryman is ordered not to allow Isis to cross the water. Tiring of this situation, Isis takes matters into her own hands. First, she tricks the ferryman by taking on the appearance of an old human woman, who claims she has food to deliver to a boy caring for the cattle on the island. Once Isis reaches her destination, she alters her disguise to appear as a lovely *young* woman. She takes up a position outside the court where the tribunal is meeting and begins to weep and wail, no doubt using her magic to make sure this lamentation reaches the right ears. Eventually, Set himself ventures outside to see what the commotion is. He asks the woman what troubles her. She tells him that she has suffered from the actions of an evil man, her husband's own brother. This man has murdered her husband to take their land, and now hunts her son to kill him too. She's been banished to the swamps where her only companions are scorpions. She's lost everything. Set declares he is outraged by this sad and dreadful story and that the wicked brother must be punished severely. For his evil, this villain deserves to die. Set vows he will hunt down the miscreant himself, slay him, and reinstate the woman and her son to their rightful position. They will have their land restored to them. Triumphantly, Isis then reveals her true self, which is unfortunate for Set as other members of the tribunal have come outside to see what's going on. They've heard all that's been said. Horrified, Set realises the tribunal have gathered behind him. He has condemned himself with his own words. Atum then has to agree that Horus should be king, and Set is banished to the desert.

In another version of this story, Neith, who is considered the wisest of the *neteru*, (and is often asked to mediate in disputes), is called upon to make the final judgement. She decrees that Khemet should be divided between Horus and Set, but because of Set's actions he will be given dominion of the harsh Red Land and foreign lands beyond, while Horus will rule the fertile Black Land. In yet another version, Geb is the judge who divides the land between Horus and Set, only later revising his judgement – in the light of Set's actions – to give Horus sole control. In either tale, it appears that once the judgement has been made, and order has been restored, and – we assume – everyone is happy with the arrangement or at least accepts it, Set and Horus make peace with each other. There's no further mention of conflict between them.

The story in which Isis makes Set confront his own behaviour, which even he judges wrong, seems the best finale of the drama to me – at least in terms of narrative and symbolism. Once Set accepts his actions were not only illegal but immoral, he has no choice but to accept the judgement of his peers. The chaotic sandstorms are confined to the desert and, under the counsel of his mother and the other *neteru*, Horus rules benevolently over the fertile Delta, bringing abundance and prosperity to all – just like his father did before Set overturned the natural order of things.

As a storyteller, I find it odd that Osiris, as one of the Ennead, isn't given a voice in the final act of the story. Of course, he dwells somewhat apart from his family in the Fields of Aaru, although it isn't as if he no longer interacts with them. He continues to be depicted in art with Isis and Nephthys, for example, in his own realm and beyond. Yet he remains aloof, even when his son's future is at stake. Given his gentle and benevolent nature, I interpret this to mean that Osiris knows it's unnecessary for him to get involved: Maat will triumph, regardless. He's aware that what Horus goes through will be a rite of passage, experiences to make him wiser and stronger, more capable of being a fair and competent king. Set's explosive nature was bound to be his undoing at some point.

We can't leave the story of Horus without exploring further what happened to his eye during his conflict with Set, and how this organ became one of major symbols of Khemetic belief. During the battle for sovereignty, Set put out the left eye of Horus (or both eyes, according to different versions of the story). His sight was later restored by either Thoth or Hathor – the latter using gazelle's milk to heal the wound. The Eye of Horus became known as the *Udjat* and had properties of healing and restoration. It could avert 'the evil eye', dark magic that could be inflicted by an enemy through no more than a glance. The Eye is always shown outlined in cosmetics that extend down onto the cheek, representing the facial markings of a falcon. In his role as *neter* of the sky, Horus's left eye represented the moon and his right eye the sun. In Khemetic magic it is a powerful symbol of protection and healing. In some texts, Horus is known as 'Horus of the Two Blue Eyes' and 'Horus of the Two Red Eyes', perhaps referring to his different aspects – the *neter* of the sky and the belligerent *neter* who fought Set.

There is one story in which Horus thought the power of his eye could bring his father Osiris back to the world of the living, but he could not go against what was ultimately Osiris's destiny. Osiris was meant to become the King of the Dead, which was an essential role in the Khemetic belief system. To become this, he had to die, and then someone else had to replace him, but that was not meant to be Set, who had his own role. Because of the way he'd developed, Set could not exclusively personify the fertility and bounty that the Black Land needed. It had to be someone more like Osiris before he died. Horus was created through magical means after the death of his father, which wouldn't have occurred without the conflict between Osiris and Set. When Horus triumphed over the *neter* of chaos, with the help of his mother and her allies, he ruled as his father did – with kindness and fairness. Aside from his conflict with Set, he was not habitually hot-headed or unpredictable as Set could be and therefore a more suitable ruler. In effect, Set helped create Horus, the *neter* who eventually got him under control. Balance and Maat was maintained.

I think it's also important – and interesting – to consider that in some ways Horus possesses attributes of both Osiris and Set, as well as Isis's deft use of cunning. While he has all the positive traits of his father, he's not beyond fighting when he needs to or using trickery as a means to an end. One story of the contention between Set and Horus relates how Horus had cornered Set and had chained him up, prior to despatching him. Isis, in a rare moment of sympathy for her brother, frees him from his restraints to prevent his death. Horus, caught up in the mindless rage of combat, beheads his mother without thinking. Isis then has to be reconstituted by Thoth. It's clear that within the Ennead myths, Horus is not – and was never meant to be – simply a younger version of Osiris. He has a dark side. I feel too that he always remained young, even after eighty years of fighting for his throne, so therefore retained a streak of impetuousness. To me, he remains the boy king of Khemet.

The Magical Purpose of Horus

Horus is a versatile *neter*. He shares many attributes with his father – protection, wise judgement, fairness, fertility and prosperity – and in some circumstances is more appropriate than Osiris for specific rituals, simply because he dwells in the world of the living rather than in the afterlife. You can use your own judgement over when Horus or Osiris is most relevant to a rite. However, Horus has additional traits that you can call upon for your magical work.

The child *neter*, Horus Harpocrates or Heru pa Khered, may be approached in respect of his attributes of silence and secrecy. He can quiet the tongues of gossips, who spread malicious lies and rumours. He can preserve secrecy when it's needed to avoid unnecessary discord and distress. Because his festival took place at the winter solstice, he's also an appropriate neter to commune with at this time. For this reason, the ritual to Horus in this work is a festival to celebrate the rebirth of the sun, and to think about the future, which is of course a rite Khemetic magic has in common with other traditions.

The adult Horus, when he becomes Heru-Haroeris, is concerned with matters of prosperity, promoting success, commitment to a cause, determination, courage, quick-wittedness, and the creation of complicated and perhaps lengthy plans to produce a result. Horus is no stranger to playing a long game, as his stories reveal. As a *neter* of the land he can be called upon to aid the growth of a garden or crops. His determination and courage may be invoked to aid new enterprises. His guile and quick wits may be useful when dealing with tricky problems.

He is also, in a more mature aspect, Ra-Harakhte. This is when he merges with Ra, *neter* of the sun, to become Horus of the Two Horizons, who rises at dawn in the eastern sky and sinks into the western horizon in the evening. The sun is a benevolent influence, whose rays can be visualised to augment any project, plan, event or cause.

Finally, Horus is also a mighty symbol of protection, a *neter* you may call upon at times when you need the strongest shield and guardian. But when this side of him is invoked, it isn't subtle, so rituals have to be worded carefully. Even when threatened, a practitioner of magic should not wish harm upon an adversary. They should work towards the hostility (and/or damaging self-interest) in a situation being dispelled.

Symbols of Horus

The Left Eye of Horus

The left eye represents the moon and is known as the *wedjat* eye.

The Right Eye of Horus

The right eye represents the sun and is known as the *udjat* eye.

Representations of the Eyes of Horus can be placed upon your altar, or you can paint them upon your body as part of preparing for a Horus ritual.

The Falcon

The falcon is sacred to Horus. Models or pictures of this creature may be placed upon the altar.

Sun Disk

If you are appealing to Horus in his neter of the sun aspect, then you could include a red or gold sun disk as part of the altar decorations.

Epithets of Horus

When writing your own rituals to Horus, you can draw upon this list of his epithets, as well as creating your own. The titles below derive from both ancient times and modern magical practice.

Horus Neferheru (the good Horus)
Lord of the Rising Sun and the Setting Sun
Ra-Harakhte
The Face of the Heavens
Lord of the Heavens
He Who Personifies Light
Heru-Khuti, Lord of the Two Horizons
Horus of the Two Eyes
Uniter of the Two Lands
The Great Protector
Heru-Sa-Aset-Sa-Asar (Horus, son of Isis and Osiris)

Offerings to Horus

Foods appropriate for Horus include those you'd present to his parents, Isis and Osiris, such as cakes, bread, honey, figs, dates, and other fruit. Offertory biscuits may be cut into the shape of the sun disk and sprinkled with edible glitter. Primarily, for his feasts, the colours of gold and yellow should predominate to represent the sun. Any yellow or orange fruit juice would be appropriate for the ritual drink, along with a light-coloured beer or white wine, or non-alcoholic substitutes. As with all other feasts, make substitutions according to dietary requirements.

Visualisation
The Trials of Horus

What follows is a pathworking for which you don't need to construct the sacred enclosure – although you can if you want to. Otherwise the procedure for creating lesser sacred space will suffice.

The experience of Horus can be a quest in which we have to use our wits to survive, be prepared to be patient and ultimately learn what is best for the future. In this visualisation, the life of Horus is depicted as a mystery play, such as would have been enacted at festivals. Through his trials, you can think about your own.

Prepare yourself for visualisation and charge the atmosphere with *heka*. Imagine that the everyday world fades away around you, replaced by a floating mist. Gradually the mist begins to clear, and you find yourself in a new landscape.

You find yourself at the edge of the swamplands of the Delta of Lower Khemet. Marshland stretches all around you, where high reeds grow. You can see fields of crops and tall palm trees. There is much for people to harvest in this fertile area. But further in, away from civilisation and farming, is the area where Isis hid from Set. This is where Horus was born, guarded by scorpions with the help of the scorpion *neter* Serket, under constant threat of discovery.

You're able to travel over the swamps without difficulty, as you assume the form of a falcon and can fly high above the land. Beneath you, the swamps of tall papyri and snaking rivulets spread out in a vast landscape. The papyrus plants wave in the breeze and sunlight glitters off the pools and streams. Eventually, you arrive at a small house hidden among a stand of palms. This is where Isis and Horus live, with Serket as a companion who cares for Horus when Isis is elsewhere. Outside this dwelling, a young man in his early teens is sitting upon the ground, who you know is Horus. His divine presence is unmistakable, even in one so young. Hovering above him, you discern that he's clad simply in a loin cloth and has a shaved head, but for the long lock of hair hanging over one shoulder, which identifies him as a youth. He has the beauty of both his parents, but his face is set in a disagreeable expression. He seems frustrated and angry. It's clear he's not aware of your presence.

Discreetly, you land behind him and take on the form of a traveller of Khemet, dressed in a plain robe and sandals and carrying a staff. You approach the young *neter*, and now he glances up at you, at once suspicious. This is not surprising since his mother and Serket will have drummed into him how careful he must be against attacks by his uncle, Set. Displaying your palms in a gesture of reassurance, you tell him you mean no harm and are a friend. He appears to accept this, but doesn't seem inclined to talk. You sense the burning dissatisfaction within him and ask what is wrong. Can you perhaps help? He tells you abruptly that you should ask instead what is right, and then he can tell you: nothing!

You sit beside him and say gently that the fertile land spreads out verdantly around him, where animals and birds are abundant. He is free to sit here and do nothing. You gesture at the wild landscape. What cares could he have in this place? The hardships of life have not yet begun. This idyll should be savoured.

Horus glances behind him at the house, no doubt where

Serket is. *'I am not free,'* he hisses in an undertone. *'Set will hunt me. One day I must fight him. I must kill him and avenge my father.'* Then he sighs, surveys the landscape. *'Yet I'm stuck here where nothing happens. I hide like a craven beast.'*

You can see then all the conflicting emotions of the young – a struggle for independence, uncertainty about the future, uncertainty about himself. Yet he is also sure he's correct in all his opinions and beliefs. Think back to when you were his age and how you felt about life. Some of the fears you had proved foolish, and some of the hopes you had never came to pass. But life is the anvil on which you were forged. The person you were would no doubt barely recognise themselves if they were to stand before the person you have become. Consider now how aspirations for the future you had when younger worked out.

The landscape you inhabit now melts away into swirling colours. You're aware of moving on through time to another point in Horus's story. A different vista unfurls before you. Now, you find yourself before a gracious palace upon a verdant island in the Nile. This is the abode of the tribunal of the *neteru*. You walk inside, into a large official-looking chamber. Here Horus stands before his forebears, who are seated on a curving dais before him: Horus is arguing with the tribunal. At the centre of a row of thrones sits Atum. They appear as a beatueous androgynous human in their 30s yet exudes the sense that they are wise and ancient. Although their countenance is neutral, they seem somewhat forbidding. On one side of Atum sits Tefnut and Shu, on the other Geb and Nut. They are accompanied by other respected *neteru*, who Atum has created since Shu and Tefnut. These include Neith and Thoth, *neteru* often called upon to make judgements and to aid the tribunal. They are all listening to Horus's complaints, how he should be king of Khemet as his father was, that he is the rightful heir and Set is a usurper.

Then, after the tribunal has conferred among themselves, Atum speaks. They tell Horus he is still young and should learn more of life before becoming king. Whatever Set has done in the past, he is capable of ruling Khemet until Horus is ready. *'But he murdered my father!'* Horus yells. *'None of you did anything. My father had no one to avenge him, no one to be his champion, but I will be that. Let me prove myself to you!'*

The tribunal confer again, then give their assent, but you sense they're not pleased to do so. Still, Horus is the son of Osiris and Isis, and they know Isis supports her son in his desires and she is not a *neter* to be denied.

Time shifts again, and the scene dissolves before you. Once again you take on the form of a falcon and take to the skies. You fly over different scenes depicting moments of Horus's life. You witness the conflicts of Horus and Set, the endless battles for dominance, the wounds, the despair, the lack of forward movement, with no end in sight. Sometimes you fly over the court of the tribunal and observe the bickering between Set and Horus before the elder *neteru*, who do not intervene. This is because Horus asked for this situation; the tribunal know he must get through it by himself. You see him, ultimately, lash out at his mother, who has done nothing but support him. She is his greatest ally, and if she prevented Set's death, it's because it was the right thing to do, because in slaughtering his bound uncle, Horus would be no better than Set. Horus can't see this. He's blinded by anger.

Now, you fly down to the desert lands and take on the form of a human once more. As you wander through the desolate landscape, think about situations in your own life that mirror the trials of Horus, albeit in a much less dramatic and bloodthirsty fashion. Other people don't always act the way you want them to. They obstruct you, and their opinions might seem stupid to you. It might seem you have fought constantly to progress in life. Perhaps you have already learned from this and can now look back fondly upon the person you once were. Or perhaps you're still caught up in what sometimes feels like conflict with everyone and everything.

As you're contemplating these things, you feel a cool, comforting touch upon your shoulder. You turn and gaze into the lovely face of Isis, who smiles at you. '*Ah, how we must prove ourselves,*' she murmurs. '*Yet we are fashioned by our sorrow and anger as much as by our happiness and love. This is the quest of life.*'

Talk with Isis for a few minutes now if you wish to. In this moment, she is in her mother aspect – nurturing, reassuring and encouraging. She had to watch Horus act unwisely, and although she sometimes intervened, in an effort to help, it didn't always work out well. What can this teach you about your own life?

When you are ready to move on, you once more take on the form of a falcon and fly to the island of the tribunal, to witness the moment when all the conflict and bickering has been resolved. Outside the building, you transform into a human again and walk discreetly inside.

Horus stands before the tribunal, his mother Isis beside him. Set and Nephthys stand nearby. You notice that Set is unusually subdued in his manner. He does not wear the mask of a *sha* now, but appears as a man, who has condemned himself.

For a moment, you see through the eyes of Horus. You can

hear his thoughts. He realises that becoming king wasn't facilitated by all the fighting and discord. What led to this moment was Maat; cosmic balance, truth. If Isis had confronted Set in this way at the start, how would things have turned out? Better, surely, and yet…? The experiences Horus has been through have strengthened him, toughened him. His trials are a metaphor for the lesser conflicts of life, the problems we face, the difficulties we must overcome. Our growth as individuals. Both you and he realise this together.

At this moment, Isis again touches you upon the shoulder, only this time you are a passenger in the body of her son. *'And so you become the sovereign of your own life, meruti,'* she says and kisses him fondly.

You move your consciousness out of Horus's body and become a witness once more. The Ennead stand united, and celebration will ensue. Even Osiris has joined them for this significant moment, appearing dressed in a plain robe of softest white linen, wearing no crown but a long black wig. You walk out with the *neteru* into the sunlight, where the people of Khemet are waiting. They cheer and clap as they see the Ennead appear before them.

Now the festivities begin. Spend as much time as you wish speaking to any members of the Ennead. The story is done, and what comes after begins a new story. Blank new pages waiting for a pen.

Ultimately, you seek out Horus, who has retreated into the great palace of the tribunal to be alone for some time. You find him sitting in a darkened inner chamber. He is king now, yet he seems melancholy. You can sense that the years have caught up with him to a degree. He's no longer an impulsive youth, even if he appears young. He's eighty years older and has endured decades of pain and conflict. Some things that have happened will never be forgotten, can never be undone. He must live with that. Spend some time now with Horus, talking about your own life and listening to whatever he has to tell you.

When you feel it's almost time to depart, you notice a shadow appear in the doorway. It comes into the chamber and you see it is Serket, the *neter* who will one day become his consort. She greets you cordially but tells Horus it is time for him to rejoin the gathering. He is king now and has responsibilities. She extends a hand to him and he takes hold of it.

Bid Horus farewell and thank him for his counsel. You watch him and Serket walk out of the dark chamber together, hand in hand. For a moment you too feel somewhat wistful, but then you think about how the future is before you, whatever it might bring, and the past has brought you to this moment. For a time, you can exist in this *now*, free of all cares.

The scene before you gradually fades into mist, bringing you back to the present time, and earthly reality. Return to normal consciousness and open your eyes. Record your experiences.

Ritual
Birth of the Sun

The winter solstice is traditionally the time of new beginnings. It is the new year, when the shortest day heralds the return of light and the sun will grow stronger. People celebrate this time, not just for what is to come but also the past year. It's a time for both reflection and looking forwards. A time to plant the seeds for the future.

Equipment Required

- A sistrum
- The altar cloth should be yellow or gold. You may decorate it with ornaments of gold or yellow stones and crystals and a string of golden fairy lights
- Yellow or gold candles
- The incense should be mainly of frankincense
- The hieroglyph of Horus's name
- An appropriate feast

The Ritual

Create your enclosure and enliven your altar statue with *heka*, if you have one. Light the altar candles and replenish your incense if necessary. Then sit down in the centre. Close your eyes and breathe deeply for a while to alter your state of consciousness.

Visualise your environment gradually changing. A mist fills your enclosure, so that objects around you disappear within it. Presently, the mist begins to clear, and you see a new landscape appearing around you.

You find yourself at the great temple of Horus in Edfu on the eve of the winter solstice, carrying a satchel of offerings for Horus. You see immense statues of falcons around you, standing guard. You walk along a path towards the temple itself and enter its inner courtyard.

Here, raise your arms and say:

'Oh Horus Harpocrates, King of the Two Horizons,
Lord of the Reborn Sun, I call to you!
Nefer-heru, He Who Personifies Light,
Come to me in your temple, at this time of rebirth.
Reveal to me your mysteries,
And grant me the pure light of your benevolence!'

Now shake the sistrum and chant: *Heru-peh-khart* for a minute or so.

(Pronounced: Heh-roo-peh-cart. Meaning: 'Horus the Child'.)

Then, without opening your eyes, cast your inner gaze back to the image of Horus in your enclosure. Imagine it glows with soft light, as it brims with *heka*. Horus is alive in both inner and outer realities and will communicate with you.

A figure emerges from the temple. You see it is a child, Horus in his youngest aspect, with the long youth lock of hair hanging over his shoulder. He has a finger to his lips. Bow to him and say:

Oh Horus, Face of the Heavens,
I thank you for your presence,
I am here to witness the rebirth of the sun
And to ask for your radiant influence in the new year.'

Horus nods and beckons for you to follow him. He heads back into the dark of the temple, always keeping a few feet ahead of you. You follow him down dark corridors, where lamps of burning oil provide a dim illumination. You pass by shrines, where the indistinct and shadowy figures of *neteru* statues stand in darkness. The atmosphere is still and silent. No one is around.

Horus now leads you upwards, following a flight of steps that lead high into the temple. At the head of the steps, the *neter* pauses. He turns to face you and lowers his hand from his face. He says: *'Are you ready to let go of the darkness and welcome the light?'*

You give your assent. Horus says: *'Then speak of what you will let remain in the old year and what you will take forward with you.'*

Think of the past year. What did you achieve? What things will you be glad to leave behind? This night is a time of beginnings. You need take with you only what is helpful to your own future. Tell Horus of these things.

The *neter* nods to you and bids you follow him outside. You emerge onto a high flat roof. Dawn is near for the light is becoming twilight. Horus says: *'What are your wishes in the light of the new sun?'*

Speak now of your aspirations and hopes for the forthcoming year. As you speak, so the sun begins to rise. It's as if its golden-pink rays illumine the words that come from your mouth. The pure light gives them wings like a flock of tiny birds. These birds fly from you, carrying the message of your hopes to the heavens.

The new light slants across the flat roof of the temple. Horus seems older now, not yet a man, but no longer a little child. He is new and perfect, as is the start of any new year, when anything seems possible and nothing has yet happened to sully that dream. For this moment, your life is in balance, and you must believe that the hopes that flew from you are already manifesting in reality. Horus smiles at you and inclines his head. He says, *'Your hopes become reality in my light.'*

Spend some time now communing with Horus in your own way. Talk about your future aims and what you wish to change in your life. Horus may take you to places of significance he wishes to show you. He may offer you a gift. When you are ready to conclude this part of the visualisation, return to the temple roof in Edfu. Bring out the offerings you have brought and spread them before the *neter*. Open your eyes and come out of the visualisation, while imagining that part of you is still on the roof at the temple of Horus. Say:

'Oh Horus, Heru-Sa-Aset-Sa-Asar
I have brought offerings to you,
As symbols of thanks and respect.
Through me, may you experience their pleasures.
As I eat this food, may you relish its flavours,
As I drink, may your thirst be quenched with enjoyment.'

Now you will feast in his honour. Consume the offerings, concentrating on sharing the pleasure of doing so with Horus. Leave a small portion of everything you eat and drink. After this has been done, wrap the remains in paper and leave this parcel before the statue on your altar.

When you are ready, compose yourself and return to the visualisation. See your offerings around Horus, which he consumes with relish. Bow to him and say:

'Oh Horus, of the black eye of the moon
And the white eye of the sun,
Uniter of the Two Lands
Continue to share with me the lessons of Maat
Fill me with your never-ending light.
Give me the means to grow as the seasons change,
Grant me the awareness to know myself as you know me.'

Then bid farewell to Horus and prepare to leave. Imagine the scene turns to mist around you. Return to normal reality and dismantle your enclosure in the usual way. Record the results of your work and dispose of the remains of your offerings appropriately.

The Temple at Edfu

Serket - Scorpion Queen

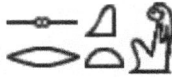

Attributes of Serket

The wife of Horus was known in Khemet as Serqet (with variations of Selket, Selqet or Selcisis). She is strongly connected to the scorpion, and her headdress is a representation of this creature with its tail raised threateningly to sting. Her most common representation is that of a woman with a scorpion crown, but occasionally she's depicted in a quite monstrous form: a scorpion with the head and arms of a woman.

Serket is associated with fertility and the natural world and its creatures, but her predominant attributes concern healing and using magic to effect cures, particularly of venomous stings and bites. She has the power to heal the effects of venom because she's also adept at using it to harm. One of her epithets is 'She Who Binds the Throat', which refers to how scorpion stings paralyse the throat, inhibiting – if not preventing – the ability to breathe. Yet, in the law of Maat, this means Serket is also 'She Who Causes the Throat to Breathe'.

Serket was called upon to smite enemies through poison and became the patron *neter* of several pharaohs, among them Scorpion I and Scorpion II, who reigned during one the early Khemetic dynasties, known as the Naqada III culture, which lasted from around 3200 to 3000BC. While Serket isn't known for having temples dedicated to her, there are records of her having numerous priests in the community. Like Set, she was sometimes credited with helping to vanquish the serpent Apep and was one of his guards when he was captured.

Serket's attributes led to her being associated with the dead, and in particular the fluids used in mummification that cause the corpse to stiffen. With her son Duamutef, she was the guardian of the canopic jar that housed the intestines of the deceased, since this jar was also associated with venom. She is known to have had four sons, the other three being Imsety, Qebehsenuef and Hapi, who became funerary *neteru* themselves and guardians of the four canopic jars used during mummification. (The canopic jars will be explored in full in the section devoted to the sons of Serket and Horus.) Serket had a role as protector, both for the dead themselves and the chambers of the embalmers.

No stories survive as to why and how she became the consort of Horus, although she does appear in one myth about him. During the childhood of Horus, Isis was obliged to protect him from Set, and one story relates how she was imprisoned in a house by Set while she was still pregnant. Thoth realised that the child would be in great danger once it was born. One night, he helped Isis escape her prison and advised her to travel to the papyrus swamplands and hide there. Disguising herself as a human beggar woman, Isis headed into the wilderness, accompanied by seven guardian scorpions called Befen, Tefen, Mestet, Mestetef, Thetet, Petet and Matet. It's thought the scorpions represented seven stars near to Isis's heavenly home of the star Sothis, found in the constellation Canis Major. They are also known as the Scorpions of Serket, indicating this *neter* aided in Isis's escape. In some versions of the story, Serket isn't mentioned at all, while in others she is a prominent character. In this rendition, she acts as a protector of Isis, and accompanies her on her travels. When it's time for Horus to be born, Serket helps with the delivery. This later led to her being a *neter* of protection during childbirth. Isis and her party settled near the town of Buto in the swamps. Here, Serket guarded Horus while Isis went out at night to look for food with the seven scorpions. The scorpions surrounded Isis to protect her from Set. Thetet, Petet and Matet led the way to make sure Set wasn't waiting in ambush, Mestet walked on one side of Isis, Mestetef on the other, and the most fierce and powerful among them, Tefen and Befen guarded Isis's back, alert for attack from behind.

One night, when out seeking food, Isis passed the house of a rich woman and asked for a meal and shelter. But on seeing her in her bedraggled disguise, with her retinue of scorpions, the woman refused to help and rudely denied Isis entrance to her house. The scorpions were furious about this, but Isis simply carried on walking. Eventually, they came to the house of a simple peasant woman, who gladly welcomed the party into her home. Even though she was poor and had little for herself, she offered her guests food and shelter. Serket, however, had been keeping an eye on proceedings from afar and, like the scorpions, she was incensed by the treatment Isis had received from the rich woman and felt she should be punished. Serket sent a message to Tefen, the leader of the scorpions, to deal with the situation and teach the woman a lesson. Tefen ordered his companions to give him all their poison. He then went back to the rich woman's house, crept inside and stung her son in his sleep with a venom six times its normal strength. On finding her son dying of the sting, his body wracked with pain, the rich woman ran out into the street, carrying her son in her arms. She screamed for someone to help her. Isis heard her cries and went to investigate. She realised what had happened and, instinctively empathising with the mother's sorrow, commanded the poisons of her scorpions to leave the boy's body:

> "And I, Isis, the Mistress of Magic, whose voice can awake the dead, I called aloud the Words of Power, the words that even the dead can hear. And I laid my arms upon the child that I might bring back life to the lifeless. Cold and still he lay, for the sevenfold poison of Tefen was in him. Then did I speak magical spells to the poison of the scorpions, saying, "O poison of Tefen, come out of him and fall upon the ground! Poison of Befen, advance not, penetrate no farther, come out of him, and fall upon the ground! For I am Isis, the great Enchantress, the Speaker of Spells. Fall down, O poison of Mestet! Hasten not, poison of Mestetef! Rise not, poison of Petet and Thetet! Approach not, poison of Matet! For I am Isis, the Great Enchantress, the Speaker of Spells. The child shall live, the poison shall die!"

> From 'Ancient Egyptian Legends', by M. A. Murray (1920)

The rich woman was humbled by Isis's compassion and forgiveness, and ashamed of the cold, imperious way in which she'd treated someone who had only sought her help. In her gratitude and chagrin, she offered all her wealth to Isis and to the peasant woman who had offered hospitality unreservedly. Serket, still observing from afar, bitterly regretted her impulsive act of harming an innocent boy. She vowed from that moment on to be a protector of children.

Serket is a *neter* who can heal with apparent compassion yet who is also capable of harm or murder and can act without thinking – much as Horus did when he lashed out in anger at his mother and cut off her head. In her positive aspect, Serket is a *neter* of healing, childbirth and a protector of children, but she is also potentially dangerous through the venom of her sacred creature. I visualise her, again like Horus, as perennially young and somewhat impetuous. She's not deliberately evil but can act impulsively to right what she perceives as a wrong. In this she seems the perfect match for Horus. She might have started off as his carer and protector when he was a child but eventually he must have seen her in a different light and asked her to be his wife. Or maybe it was Serket herself who came up with the idea. I like to think there are unwritten stories about her role in the conflict between Horus and Set.

The Magical Purpose of Serket

Serket can be a protector, but perhaps her most useful function, in a magical sense, is her ability to neutralise poison. As a metaphor, this applies to diverse situations. She may be invoked to calm down toxic incidents and circumstances and remove their 'sting'. In a healing sense she eliminates toxins from the body. If there is a situation in which you think poison is involved, in whatever sense, Serket is the *neter* you may approach for help.

From a personal development perspective, Serket helps you examine 'poisonous' situations and people and to expel any remaining 'venom', i.e. bad feeling, that might be affecting your life. Another interpretation of Serket's quality is that what might feel like a sting – and hurt very much – is actually a remedy, such as in painful truths.

However, you should not forget or overlook the *neter's* positive qualities. She is especially appropriate to invoke at the time of childbirth, when she is protective and helps avert infections in the mother resulting from the birth. She is a powerful guardian with her retinue of armoured scorpions, and she can assume the form of a scorpion herself – not many enemies or assailants would want to take such a group on. You can visualise her and her scorpions as a protective force around you when you feel threatened. As a protector of children and the vulnerable, she can be called upon to form a shield around those who need to be guarded.

Symbols of Serket

There is only one symbol associated with Serket in Khemetic mythology and that is the scorpion, her sacred creature. You could decorate your altar with images and motifs of scorpions. You could include the form of Serket as a scorpion with the head of a woman.

Epithets of Serket

When writing your own rituals to Serket, you can draw upon this list of her epithets, as well as creating your own. The titles below derive from both ancient times and modern magical practice.

She Who Tightens the Throat
She Who Causes the Throat to Breathe
Protector of Children

Lady of Scorpions
Wife of Heru
She Who Stings the Unrighteous
Protector Against Venom
She Who Gives Breath

Offerings to Serket

Foods appropriate for Serket should include those with sour and bitter flavours, which can be offset with sweetness to make them palatable. This could include fruit with a sour-sweet taste, dark bitter chocolate, or liqueurs and spirits with a bittersweet taste. Any green fruit or juice would be appropriate for the ritual drink, along with a tart white wine, or non-alcoholic substitute. Nuts with a slight bitterness to them such as walnuts or pecans would also be appropriate. As with all other feasts, make substitutions according to dietary requirements.

Visualisation: The Venom That Purifies

What follows is a pathworking for which you don't need to construct the sacred enclosure – although you can if you want to. Otherwise the procedure for creating lesser sacred space will suffice. In meeting Serket, you will seek the cleansing fire of her poison. What wounds also heals. This can help you free yourself from lingering hurts and resentments that have hung around you for far too long. They can sap your energy and blight your ability to feel happiness and joy. This visualisation can also be adapted to be a healing rite.

Prepare yourself for visualisation and charge the atmosphere with *heka*. Imagine that the everyday world fades away around you, replaced by a floating mist. Gradually the mist begins to clear, and you find yourself in a new landscape.

You stand within the papyrus swamps. It is night-time and the moon is full, so you can see clearly. The tall reeds rise all around you, their feathery heads wave far above your own and rustle in the night breeze. You can hear the sounds of marsh creatures all around you, moving amid the foliage and calling through the darkness. You know that venomous snakes and scorpions abound in this area, but these creatures will not harm you, as you are here to meet with Serket. You are surrounded by the pungent aroma of growing plants and the water of the swamps; within it is a tart, acrid scent, which is not unpleasant, but unusual.

You find a spot that you feel is appropriate, and here come to a halt. Raise your arms and call: *'Oh Serket, she of the sting and the balm, I call you to you! Come to me and reveal to me your mysteries!'*

For a moment, all goes quiet. The animals cease their noises and even the shivering papyrus falls silent. The acrid scent grows stronger around you. Strangely, it makes your mouth water, makes you want to swallow.

Then you hear rustling nearby and see that the tall reeds are shaking. Something approaches. The invisible form grows nearer, and the reeds shake more violently. Suddenly they part and a monstrous shape scuttles out of them. It is an immense armoured scorpion, its tail raised high as if to strike. It has the head of a beautiful woman, and well-shaped human arms held out in front of it. This is Serket. She exudes the powerful tart scent you smelled around you. The *neter* comes to a standstill a few feet away and says, *'Who is it seeking my remedy and my bane?'*

You bow to her and say, *'It is I (your name), great Serket. Look gently upon me. I seek the mysteries of your being. I seek your cleansing fire.'*

She laughs: *'Is that so? Do you know what you ask, and is it of your own free will?'*

You reply: *'I know what I ask, and it is of my own free will.'*

Serket says: *'Then step forward to receive my sting.'*

You do so, and although part of you is afraid another part welcomes what is to come, because it is a liberating process, a cleansing of the deepest kind.

Serket raises her tail higher and then it lashes forward, over her head, and stings you in the chest, above the heart. For a moment, you are stunned. But then a sharp pain shivers through you and your body arches against it. Then, as quickly at is came, the pain subsides and a strangely comforting numbness steals through you.

Your vision becomes blurry as if you're looking through rain-stippled glass. You can see Serket before you, but her form has taken on a greenish glow. As you look around you, so the whole landscape is tinged with this glow. You look inwards. The venom of Serket courses through you, riding in your blood, your breath. As it passes, so it burns away that which is harmful, or that which you might have stored, unable to let go of, but which has been slowly poisoning you from within. Serket's cold-burning fire expunges pockets of negativity and listlessness. It enlivens you as it moves onward. Feel it flowing through your entire being, flushing as it goes. It goes through every organ, up into your head, then down through your arms to your hands and down through your legs to your toes. From your extremities, the venom flows out of you, carrying with it all that is baneful. You see this as sickly green streams that trickle across the land, gradually turning into a greenish-grey smoke that dissipates completely.

You take some deep breaths and stretch your body. It feels wonderful, as if you've bathed in a magical pool with life-giving properties. You feel lighter, and nagging doubts, grievances and resentments have no hold over you. They have been flushed away by Serket's venom.

Serket steps forward, and now she has assumed a human form, a woman wearing a crown shaped like a scorpion. She takes your hands and gazes into your eyes. Spend some time communing with Serket, perhaps travelling with her. She may have a gift to impart to you.

When you are ready to depart, say to Serket:

'Oh, Lady Who Stings the Unrighteous,
Whose Bane is Also Balm,
I thank you for your cleansing fire
And for revealing to me your mysteries.'

Now, bid her farewell. She turns and walks back into the tall reeds. The scene before you fades into mist, bringing you back to the present time, and earthly reality. Return to normal consciousness and open your eyes. The cleansing fire of Serket still refreshes your body and will do so in the days to come. Record your experiences.

Ritual:
Drawing Out Poison

This ritual to Serket can be performed to help rid a situation of lingering bad feeling and resentment. It can also aid in undoing harm that has been done through people being 'poisonous' – the telling of lies or the spreading of misinformation. Serket's influence is uncompromising. Her instinct is to sting but she will not inflict physical harm. If anything, she simply forces participants in a situation to face the consequence of their actions.

If you wish to perform this ritual but are not in a situation where the specific abilities of Serket apply to you personally, then you can perform it for someone else – but only with their consent. You can also use it to detoxify situations in general. But bear in mind that people's interpretation of what toxicity is will vary. You should not, under any circumstances, act merely upon your own preferred opinions. You should act to heal situations rather than punish or avenge, for such actions go against Maat and will rebound to sting you.

Equipment Required

- The altar cloth should be green, symbolising venom, but as this is a benign colour all traces of harm are, removed. You may decorate the altar with green stones and crystals
- A sistrum
- Green candles
- An acrid, tart incense (or you can use a Scorpio incense)
- The hieroglyph of Serket's name
- An appropriate feast

The Ritual

Create your enclosure and enliven your altar statue with *heka*, if you have one. Light the altar candles and replenish your incense if necessary. Then sit down in the centre. Close your eyes and breathe deeply for a while to alter your state of consciousness.

(If you are working in a group, the person reading the visualisation should leave plenty of time at the appropriate moments for people to commune with Serket and complete the task of drawing venom. It is perhaps best if when participants have finished the venom-removal section, they should make a small signal to the reader to indicate they are ready to move on. The reader should only resume once everyone has indicated they are ready.)

Visualise your environment gradually changing. A mist fills your enclosure, so that objects around you disappear within it. Presently, the mist begins to clear, and you see a new landscape appearing around you.

You find yourself in the desert of Khemet. The sun is going down in the west. Serket had no great temples dedicated to her but even so she was widely worshipped by the Khemetu and priests worked in her name.

You walk along a rough road between high cliffs, carrying a satchel with offerings for Serket. Presently, you come to a small mudbrick dwelling upon a hillside above you, which seems strange, as it is out in the middle of nowhere. You see a young priest sitting on the ground before a fire, outside the building, mixing herbs, spices and some kind of fluid in a bowl decorated with hieroglyphs. You know he is a priest of Serket, and people come to him to heal the stings and bites of venomous creatures. Approach him and tell him you have come to seek the aid of Serket. He bids you to sit down and explain what it is you require of the *neter*.

After a few moments of speaking with the priest, he tells you to call upon Serket yourself, for he can see that you work in her name and that of the other *neteru*. You both get to your feet and raise your arms, facing one another. You say:

'Oh, Mighty Serket,
She Who Causes the Throat to Tighten
Yet Who Causes the Throat to Breathe,
I ask that you to come to me,
As She Who Pulls the Venomous Stings,
And work your magic for me.'

Chant: *'Serket Tchanri-metut sutcha'* for a minute or so.

(Pronounced Ser-ket Chan-ree met-ut soo-cha. Meaning (roughly) Serket, scorpion venom healer.)

Then, without opening your eyes, cast your inner gaze back to the image of Serket in your enclosure. Imagine it glows with soft light, as it brims with *heka*. Serket is alive in both inner and outer realities and will communicate with you.

A figure appears walking down a narrow path from the cliffs. This is Serket in her human form, wearing the crown in the shape of a scorpion. Eventually, she stands before you and says, *'What sting is that needs pulling, meruti?'*

Bow to her and describe what venom it is you need help with. Omit no detail. Show to Serket the exact circumstances and those involved. Try to do so without bias or judgement, merely present the facts.

She will then grant you her gift of removing poison. She hands to you a small vessel, like a jug with a spout. She gestures to the priest and he hands you a small pot containing some of the ointment he's been mixing.

Serket says to you: *'This balm is of my venom and my blood. Draw the sting and offer the balm.'*

The *neter* leads you up the cliff path. You come to a narrow opening in the rock and walk into a small, dark cave. There isn't much space to move and you wonder why you are here. Then, Serket takes your hand, and bids you close your eyes. You become aware the environment has subtly changed around you. Serket tells you to open your eyes and you find she has transported you to a large dark chamber where all the people involved in the situation you seek to heal are gathered. She remains with you but is silent while you perform the required actions.

It is a strange scene, like a shadowland. The people are indistinct, yet you know them. They're not aware of your presence. You see each of them speaking, gesticulating. Perhaps they are sad or angry or merely confused and frightened. As you walk among them unseen, you murmur Serket's chant beneath your breath *'metut sutcha'*. As you do so, a thin coil of steam pours from each individual, which finds the spout of the jar and flows down into it. Slowly, you draw the poison from everyone present, freeing them from pain or negative emotion. If they are people who seek to harm you, draw venom from the feelings that make them wish you harm. Why do they feel that way? Once the poison is drawn, you place balm on their foreheads, from the pot that Serket's priest gave to you. This glows with soft healing light. No matter what these people might think and feel, whatever they do, you heal them impartially in the light of Maat. Once you've placed the balm upon them, the figures dissipate like mist.

Spend some time now in free visualisation. Serket may take you somewhere or give you a gift.

When you are ready to conclude this part of the visualisation, tell Serket you wish to return with her to the house of her priest. She takes your hand and transports you back to where you began your journey. Here, take the offerings you have brought from the satchel and spread them before the *neter*. Open your eyes and come out of the visualisation, while imagining that part of you is still with Serket and her priest in Khemet. Say:

'Oh Serket, Wife of Heru,
Protector Against Venom,
I have brought offerings to you,
As symbols of thanks and respect.
Through me, may you experience their pleasures.
As I eat this food, may you relish its flavours,
As I drink, may your thirst be quenched with enjoyment.'

Now you will feast in her honour. Consume the offerings, concentrating on sharing the pleasure of doing so with Serket. Leave a small portion of everything you eat and drink. After this has been done, wrap the remains in paper and leave this parcel before the statue on your altar.

When you are ready, compose yourself and return to the visualisation. See your offerings around Serket, which she consumes with relish and shares with her priest. Bow to her and say:

'Oh Serket, Queen of Scorpions,
Companion of Isis,
Continue to share with me the ability to expel poison
Give me your ability to heal and to protect,
And to recognise when venom holds influence.
Grant me the vision to know myself as you know me.'

Then bid farewell to Serket and prepare to leave. She turns and walks away up the cliff path. The priest goes into his house and pulls a curtain across the door. The scene around you gradually dissolves into mist. Return to normal reality and dismantle your enclosure in the usual way. Then record the results of your work and dispose of the remains of your offerings appropriately.

From a Khemetic Wall Painting

The Sons of Horus and Serket

The Sons of Horus with Osiris venerated by a worshipper

Attributes of the Sons of Horus

The sons of Horus and Serket can be approached collectively. In Khemet, they had a shared purpose in being personifications of the canopic jars that housed the viscera of mummified bodies. They are also *neteru* of the cardinal points and have as guardians the four female *neteru* associated with the compass directions – Neith, Serket, Isis and Nephthys, only one of whom isn't directly related to them. (This set of female directional *neteru* differs to that addressed in the construction of the Sacred Enclosure.)

In ancient texts, these four sons are sometimes regarded as the offspring of Osiris and Isis, but this is undoubtedly to do with the multiple versions of the Ennead myths and that in some of them Horus the Elder was a brother to Osiris rather than a son. To avoid getting caught up in the tangles of the myths, we'll concentrate upon these *neteru* as being sons of Horus and Serket. Also the word for 'father' can mean 'ancestor' and the word 'son' can mean descendent, so I'll use the terms 'ancestor' and 'descendent' where it seems appropriate in translations of ancient texts, in respect of either gender.

Duamutef

Duamutef is associated with the east, the direction in which the sun rises. In the dawn, the air begins to grow warm after the cold of night. He was responsible for protecting the stomach of the dead. Grievous wounds to the torso and stomach were often the cause of death in combat, so in this sense Duamutef guarded those slain on the battlefield. He had the head of a jackal like his uncle Anubis and his protectress was the *neter* Neith.

One of Duamutef's epithets is 'He Who Worships His Mother', so we could imagine he was the favourite son of Serket. In a spell from *The Book of the Dead* he says, referring to Osiris: *'I have come to rescue my ancestor from his assailant'*, which we can take to mean the serpent Apep, who seeks to stop the sun's nightly passage through the Duat, which would prevent the resurrection of Osiris.

Imsety

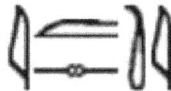

Imsety is associated with the south, and therefore the place in the sky where the sun is at its hottest during the day. He has the head of a man, wearing the false beard of a pharaoh, perhaps to represent Osiris, a *neter* connected in his aspect of fertility with the full light of day. Imsety protected the liver of the deceased and his guardian *neter* was Isis.

Part of Imsety's role was to help revive the body of the deceased. In the funerary texts, Horus instructs him to lift the dead person. In art, a prone position of the body indicated death, while a standing position indicated life. In a spell from *The Book of the Dead*, Imsety says: *'I am your descendent, Osiris. I have come to be your protection. I have strengthened your house enduringly.'* This could refer to him continuing the line of the Osirian dynasty or it could be a euphemism for resurrection. Making someone's 'house flourish' could be read as giving them life, the term 'house' referring to the physical body that houses the *ka*, meaning life-force or spirit.

Qebehsenuef

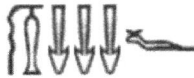

Qebehsenuef is associated with the west, where the sun sinks in the evening to begin its nightly journey through the Duat. This is the time when the air cools after the heat of the day. He has the head of a falcon, associated with his father Horus, and his guardian *neter* was his mother, Serket. He protected the intestines of the deceased.

His role was to refresh the deceased, to offer them water, and his name means 'He Who Offers Refreshment to his Brothers'. In the funerary text, Horus says to him: *'Come, refresh my father. Betake yourself to him in your name of Qebehsenuef. You have come that you may make coolness for him.'* This could refer to his cardinal direction and the time when the day cools down. Showering with water and libation, (which meant pouring it on the ground), were common forms of offering to the *neteru* in Khemet. Therefore, we can deduce that Qebehsenuef was responsible for both refreshing and cleansing the body of the deceased.

However, the most important role that Qebehsenuef had was ensuring the bodies of the dead were intact. This was no doubt invaluable when the deceased had died in battle and might have lost limbs or other body parts. In *The Book of the Dead*, Qebehsenuef says: *'I am your descendent, Osiris. I have come to be your protection. I have united your bones for you. I have assembled your limbs for you. I have brought you your heart and placed it for you at its place in your body.'*

Hapi

There are two *neteru* with this name in Egyptian myth, who have distinctly different attributes, functions and appearance. Both can be spelled Hapi or Hapy, or Hep. The androgynous *neter* associated exclusively with the River Nile will be referred to as Hapy in this system. The spelling Hapi will refer always to the son of Horus.

Hapi was associated with the north, when the sun is below the horizon, and the dark of the night. At this time, the air is cold. He has the head of a baboon, a creature associated with Thoth and therefore the moon. His guardian *neter* is Nephthys, herself a *neter* of the night. Hapi protected the lungs of the deceased.

Part of Hapi's name has been interpreted as referring to the steering of a vessel, resulting in him becoming associated with the navigation of ships. He was also mentioned in funerary texts as a 'runner', presumably being fleet of foot. Horus says to him: *'You are the great runner. Come, that you may join up my father and not be far in this your name of Hapi, for you are the greatest of my children.'* We can read from this that Hapi is the favourite son of Horus.

The lungs were associated with death by drowning, which again connects Hapi with water. Like, Qebehsenuef, he appears to have something to do with ensuring the body is intact, in particular guaranteeing that the head is connected to the body. In *The Book of the Dead*, Hapi says: *'I have come that I may be your protection, Oh Osiris. I have knit together your head and your members. I have smitten your enemies beneath you, and I have given you your head forever.'* This implies he wards the dead from their enemies, who perhaps might interfere with the process of resurrection.

The Magical Purpose of the Sons of Horus

In the modern world, we are not preoccupied with intricate preparations for the afterlife. Our internal organs don't end up in jars for eternity and need to be protected from harm. So in order for the Sons of Horus to have relevance for a modern practitioner, we need to delve more deeply into their meaning and functions, examine the symbols and reinterpret them for our times. Primarily, I believe they work best as *neteru* associated with health and the body. This ensures they do not move too far from their original meaning.

When thinking about pertinent functions for these *neteru*, the first thing that sprang to mind to me was that the Sons of Horus could be used as alternative directional *neteru* when building the Sacred Enclosure. They could be asked to attend during times of trouble when you feel more protection and force is needed than usual in your working, or else when you are focusing particularly on matters connected with health and wellbeing.

But they can have other functions in ritual. If we look at the sons individually, we can discern a suitable modern meaning for them. Duamutef of the east wasn't given secondary functions like the other three. In his speech in *The Book of the Dead* he merely says his job is to see off Osiris's assailant. So we can visualise him as a guardian against disease and sickness, and also the facilitator of precautionary action.

Imsety of the south is concerned with reviving the bodies of the dead. He is said to make your 'house flourish'. This can be interpreted as facilitating a vigorous and functional body. He promotes good health and wellbeing, and the efficient working of the internal organs.

Qebehsenuef of the north proffers refreshment – his offering of cool water brings a sense of invigoration and renewed energy. He is also responsible for the safety of the body and bones, keeping them intact. So, in tandem with his previous trait, we can regard him as not only being an invigorating influence but an encouragement for us to care for our bodies and keep them in good condition – muscles, skin and the tissues that connect muscle to bone. He reminds us to be attentive to what is good for the vessel that houses our ka, our life spirit.

Hapi of the north is associated with the night and fluid. He can be regarded as the neter responsible for the health of our bodily fluids – blood and lymph.

The sons of Hours may be visited in visualisation to help with healing, especially when you – or someone else – is suffering from an illness or injury. They are associated with physical illness rather than emotional or mental ailments. I do not regard them as *neteru* of healing in the way that Serket or Isis may be approached. They have a subtle influence rather than a direct effect.

Symbols of the Sons of Horus

The symbols of these neteru are the canopic jars bearing representations of their heads on their lids. You can acquire ornamental copies of these quite easily and cheaply online. Otherwise, a picture will suffice.

Epithets of the Sons of Horus

The titles below derive from both ancient times and modern magical practice.

They Who Abide in the Tresses of Heaven
Protectors of the Body
Sons of the Mighty Heru
Preservers of the Everlasting
They Who Bring Refreshment
They Who Stand Guard
Lords of the Chamber of Healing

Offerings to the Sons of Horus

Suitable offerings for the four sons reflect their purpose in being items used in their original function, but which are still pertinent to healing.

Duamutef – scented oil to represent an ointment or unguent
Imsety - natron
Qebehsenuef – spring water
Hapi – incense

The visualisation below can be converted into a full ritual, using an alternative construction of the Sacred Enclosure. You may, if you wish, include a feast in this expanded pathworking, in which case appropriate foods would be refreshing drinks, (since that is one of the sons' gifts), healthy fresh food, such as fruit, seeded bread, snacks made out of alternatives to potato, such as root vegetables.

Visualisation:
The Chamber of Healing

What follows is a pathworking for which you don't need to construct the sacred enclosure – although you can if you want to. Otherwise the procedure for creating lesser sacred space will suffice. Because this pathworking includes many small actions and speaking parts, if you are working alone, it is especially beneficial to record the instructions beforehand or else get someone else to read them to you.

You will visit the Sons of Horus to promote good health, to assist with healing in the case of disease, other physical complaints and injuries. They can help ameliorate long-standing physical conditions that cause pain. You don't have to be unwell to benefit from this pathworking. You can simply ask for the restorative energy of these *neteru* to purify and invigorate your body.

Prepare yourself for visualisation and charge the atmosphere with *heka*. Imagine that the everyday world fades away around you, replaced by a floating mist. Gradually the mist begins to clear, and you find yourself in a new landscape.

You find yourself in the outer precinct of a temple dedicated to Horus. It is dusk and you can hear the chanting of priests coming from somewhere deep within the temple. But you are not here to seek the inner sanctum. You are here to visit the Sons of Horus. Looking around, you are drawn to a dark entrance to the side of the courtyard. A set of four lamps are set across the threshold, burning with a dim light. At once, you're certain that beyond it lies a shrine to the Sons of Horus.

You step carefully over the lamps and enter a low-ceilinged corridor. The light is so dim you can barely perceive the murals upon the walls. Shortly, you come to a shrouded chamber that smells heavily of incense, with a hint of what smells like medicinal herbs and powders. The air is warm, almost of blood heat and very comfortable. There are carpets underfoot that feel like walking over a lush, springy lawn. The walls are painted with scenes of daily life in Khemet. In each of the quarters stands a pillar of around four to five feet high, coming to about chest height for you. On each of these stands a canopic jar, representing the sons of Horus in their appropriate direction. Raise your arms and say:

'Oh Sons of Horus, the Venerated Ones,
Guardians of the Body
Those Who Mend What is Hurt,
I call to you.
Come to me in this, your shrine,

in the temple of your father.
I ask for your powers of healing.'

After a few moments, a nebulous shape begins to form before each pillar, gradually solidifying into a humanoid form. The sons have appeared to you, each with the head appropriate to them: the jackal in the east, the human in the south, the falcon in the west and the baboon in the north.

Stand before Duamutef in the east and bow to him. He says to you: *'What ails you?'* Place before him the offering of scented oil. Explain what you want him to do for you in terms of preventative measures and protection against sickness, or whatever feels appropriate to you at the time.

Duamutef raises his hands and from him streams a healing energy. Close your eyes and allow this to flow into you. Feel it filling you with restorative light.

When you are ready, move on to stand before Imsety in the south. Bow to him. He says: *'How might I make you flourish?'* Place the offering of natron before him. Tell him what you want of him in terms of well-being and cleansing, or matters to do with internal organs, or whatever feels appropriate to you at the time.

Imsety raises his hands and, as with his brother, a healing energy pours from him into your body. Absorb this as before, feeling it doing its work.

When you are ready, move on to Qebehsenuef in the west and bow to him. He says to you: *'How might I strengthen the frame of your being?'* Place the offering of pure spring water before him. Tell him what you want of him in terms of your bones, muscles and skin, and the tissues that connect them, or whatever feels appropriate at the time.

Once again, the *neter* raises his hands and directs healing energy into your body. Absorb it as you did before. Feel it travelling along your bones and through your muscles and flowing over your skin.

When you are ready, move on to Hapi in the north and bow to him. He says: *'How might I purify the precious fluids of your body?'* Place the offering of incense before him. Ask him to invigorate the blood and lymph within you and the water of which your body is greatly comprised. Otherwise say whatever feels appropriate at the time.

Hapi raises his hands and his purifying energy flows into you. Feel it coursing through your veins and the lymph system. Feel your flesh tingling with the cleansing power of Hapi.

Go to stand in the centre of the chamber with the sons around you. Together they raise their hands and again direct energy into you. This doesn't feel as strong as what came before, but more like a soothing balm. They say to you that you may share their healing energy with others. Bow to them in turn and say:

'Oh, Sons of Horus,
Who Abide in the Tresses of Heaven,
Which are the flowing locks of your father,
I thank you for your gifts,
For the strength, vigour and health
You have imparted to my body.
May you continue to share with me
The attributes of healing you represent,
Oh, Venerated Ones, Who Bring Refreshment
Who Banish Sickness and Injury.'

If you wish to now, you may speak further with the Sons of Horus. This will be particularly appropriate if you follow the path of a healer in your magical work. They might have tasks for you or impart further gifts.

When you are ready to depart, thank the Sons of Horus and bid them farewell. They step backwards and dissolve into glowing mist, which flows into the jar that represents them.

The scene before you now fades into mist, bringing you back to the present time, and earthly reality. Return to normal consciousness and open your eyes. Record your experiences.

Ritual:
Guardians of Healing and Great Protection

I haven't included a separate full ritual of healing for the Sons of Horus, since the visualisation can be adequately adapted if needed and/or expanded to be a healing rite for yourself or others. To turn the pathworking into a full ritual include the alternative Sacred Enclosure creation at the start of the rite and make further adaptations, using all you've learned from the previous workings. By this time, you'll know the formula of the rituals well enough to write your own additions to the pathworking, tailoring it to the circumstances and needs of the individual being healed.

The canopic jars, or representations of them are placed in the quarter positions rather than upon the altar. If you will be working with another neter within the enclosure, once it has been constructed, you can place a statue of them upon the altar. If not decorate your altar with items that you feel are pertinent to the ritual.

Equipment:

- Four canopic jars with the heads of the Sons of Horus, or pictures to represent them
- Sistrum
- Natron for the altar and a smaller bowl for the offering
- Frankincense or healing incense for the altar and for the offering
- Spring water for the offering
- Scented oil for the offering
- The altar candles should be green
- 4 green candles placed at the compass directions
- A feast

Place the representations of the four sons of Horus in their appropriate quarters. Then stand in the centre of your sacred space and perform a breathing exercise for a couple of minutes to help change your state of consciousness.

When you feel ready, raise your arms and shake the sistrum to enliven the natural energy in the atmosphere. Then draw an ankh, and the Eye of Horus in the air before you, visualising them glowing with green-white light.

Go to your altar and draw an ankh over the natron, visualising that the energy of the symbol goes into the fluid. Then sprinkle a few drops over your altar and say: '*I purify this altar with sacred natron.*'

Dip a finger into the natron and draw an ankh on your

forehead, saying, '*I purify my body with natron.*'

Repeat, and dab your tongue with natron, saying, '*I purify my mouth with natron.*'

Take up the incense and walk around the enclosure in a circle, saying: '*With this perfume, I purify and sanctify this sacred enclosure.*'

Walk around the edge of the enclosure, drawing an imaginary line with your hand and say:

'*I draw the boundary of the sacred enclosure.*
Open the gates of the heavens!
Raise the gate of the sky!
Let the neteru come forth
And shower their blessings upon me!
Open, oh heaven!
Let the doors be flung wide,
That the neteru may come forth from their horizon,
On the boat of the morning and the boat of the evening.
Open the gates of the heavens and raise the gates of the sky!'

Visualise this circle of enlivened energy around you. Then proceed to acknowledging the *neteru* of the directions.

Go the east, shake the sistrum, raise your arms and say:

'*Hail to Duamutef*
The Son of Horus who stands in the East,
I ask that you come to me in this Sacred Enclosure.
Strengthen my work with your powers of healing.
Accept this offering of scented oil I give to you.
Bring the might of your protection to this place
So that no hostile energy may enter in.
Look upon me with gentleness and empower my work.'

Light the candle and place the scented oil before it.

In the south:

'Hail to Imsety
The Son of Horus who stands in the South,
I ask that you come to me in this Sacred Enclosure.
Strengthen my work with your powers of healing.
Accept this offering of sacred natron I give to you.
Bring the might of your protection to this place
So that no hostile energy may enter in.
Look upon me with gentleness and empower my work.'

Light the candle and place the natron before it.

In the west:

'Hail to Qebehsenuef,
The Son of Horus who stands in the West,
I ask that you come to me in this Sacred Enclosure.
Accept this offering of pure clear water I give to you.
Strengthen my work with your powers of healing.
Bring the might of your protection to this place
So that no hostile energy may enter in.
Look upon me with gentleness and empower my work.'

Light the candle and place the spring water before it.

In the north:

'Hail to Hapi,
The Son of Horus who stands in the North,
I ask that you come to me in this Sacred Enclosure.
Strengthen my work with your powers of healing.
Accept this offering of sweet incense I give to you.
Bring the might of your protection to this place
So that no hostile energy may enter in.
Look upon me with gentleness and empower my work.'

Light the candle and place the incense before it.

Take up the natron from the altar and, starting in the east, sprinkle it around the boundary of the enclosure, saying: *'I purify this sacred enclosure with natron. Let no ill enter in.'*

Light the altar candles and say:

'By the light of these illustrious flames, my ritual has begun!'
The enclosure is now ready for you to work in.

Perform the pathworking of the Sons of Hours, making adaptations where necessary. Using the other rituals as a template, write your own personalised working, including a feast. You can adapt the ritual to be pertinent to a particular person, including their name where appropriate. When performing a healing rite, it's helpful if the person can be present within the enclosure, so that they can receive the healing energy of the Sons of Horus direct, but if that's not practical you may visualise them receiving the energy at a distance.

Dismantling the Enclosure

When you have finished your magical work, dismantle the enclosure by bidding farewell to the Sons of Horus.

In the east, shake sistrum and say:

'Hail to Duamutef, who stands in the East.
I acknowledge your power
And thank you for your presence at this rite.
You are ever welcome in my enclosure,
Until we meet again, I bid you farewell.'

Repeat in the other quarters:

'Hail to Imsety, who stands in the South.
I acknowledge your power
And thank you for your presence at this rite.
You are ever welcome in my enclosure,
Until we meet again, I bid you farewell.'

"Hail to Qebehsenuef, who stands in the West.
I acknowledge your power
And thank you for your presence at this rite.
You are ever welcome in my enclosure,
Until we meet again, I bid you farewell.'

'Hail to Hapi, who stands in the North.
I acknowledge your power
And thank you for your presence at this rite.
You are ever welcome in my enclosure,
Until we meet again, I bid you farewell.'

Put out the altar and quarter candles, and say:

'The sacred enclosure is dismantled; my work is done. May the
light of the mighty neteru go in my heart, until I come once more
to walk the path to ancient Khemet. Ta Keper Sem.'

Anubis - Intermediary for the Dead

𓀭 𓅱 𓃣

Attributes of Anubis

Anubis's name in Khemetic is Anpu. He is depicted as a jackal, or a man with the head of a jackal. As the *neter* of the embalming house, he assists with the mummification of pharaohs. He helps weigh the hearts of the dead in the Hall of Two Truths and acts as a guide to lead the newly dead into the Duat. Originally, he was Lord of the Duat, a role later given to his father, Osiris.

In the outer world, Anubis and his consort Anput are also protectors of graveyards. This might explain their jackal connections, for this animal is a notorious forager in cemeteries, a scavenger who digs up and feasts on corpses if they aren't buried deeply enough. Anubis and Anput, as supernatural jackals intent on protecting the dead, would frighten these scavengers away. While there were royal tombs aplenty in ancient times, and soaring pyramids for pharaohs, ordinary folk were interred in vast necropolises. The better-off, such as nobles, officials and successful merchants and tradespeople, could afford to have elaborate tombs constructed, usually excavated from the hillsides and consisting of several chambers and corridors, packed with grave goods to assist the dead in the afterlife. The less well-off might have family tombs, with a single chamber covered by a mud brick structure called a mastaba. Sometimes such tombs had two chambers – the innermost as the resting place for the dead and the outer as a kind of chapel where relatives could leave offerings. The poorest people would be buried in shallow graves, perhaps covered with a structure of reeds to resemble a tomb.

The vast necropolises naturally attracted scavengers, especially around the less-secure graves of the poor. But scavengers didn't just come in the form of animals seeking food; tomb robbers were – and still are – a problem, since even the poorest person was buried with grave goods. For the very rich this included items of immense value. The Khemetu believed that corpses must remain intact in order for the dead to use them again in the afterlife, and the items placed with them were also for their eternal use. Destroying the mummies of the dead, as well as depriving them of their belongings, was an abhorrent crime. The Khemetu placed magical protections within the tombs, to try and prevent these desecrations. The jackal *neteru* of the necropolis were part of this protection. This function is aside from Anubis's role within the myths of the Ennead.

While the often-bloody contest for sovereignty raged between Set and Horus, Anubis kept his head down, as if simply getting on with his job and keeping a distance from the drama. He was the first son of Osiris, being born before his father's death, and you'd imagine that this would have given him high status among the *neteru*, an individual the tribunal should consult concerning his father's murder and his brother's future. You'd also think he'd have had a legitimate claim to the throne himself, not least because in one story Isis adopted him as her own son. Yet he's barely mentioned in the myths. The only full story about Anubis derives from the time of Greek rule and can be regarded as an attempt to attach firmly to the Heliopolitan dynasty a character who was previously an independent deity.

It was the Greek writer Plutarch who gave us the story of Anubis's childhood. In this tale, Isis realises Osiris loves

Nephthys when she notices he has given her sister a garland of clover – this must have had some special significance not mentioned in the story. But Isis is not angered by this, presumably because of her deep affection for both of her siblings. Clearly, she does not see their love as damaging to her own relationship with them, or her position within the Ennead. We can draw this conclusion because if Isis is upset about something, this is generally described unflinchingly in the myths. Nephthys becomes pregnant by Osiris. After the child is born, Nephthys hides him in the desert, away from Set, presumably to prevent Set harming her son. Isis has long wanted a child of her own, so decides to find the hidden baby. She's assisted by a band of dogs, who lead the way. Together Isis and her companions overcome many difficulties before finding the boy. She then raises him as her own son, naming him Anubis, which has been said to mean 'royal child' by Egyptologists. He is described as becoming Isis's 'shield and ally'. In this role, he'd surely have been at her side during the protracted court case that followed Horus's claim for the throne. In other accounts, Anubis helps Isis and Nephthys to recover the parts of Osiris's body, after they've been scattered by Set. But all such details are missing from the earliest versions of the myth simply because they are late additions. That doesn't detract from the fact they are now *bona fide* inclusions in the myth cycle as a whole. While Anubis is not strictly part of the Ennead, he is certainly an important member of the Heliopolitan divine family.

Anubis appears to be a *neter* who gets on quietly with his job, and representations of him in art often show him at work, tending to the dead. Therefore, we get the impression he is industrious and dependable, keeping apart from the politics around him. It feels appropriate to imagine he inherited a lot of his father's gentle nature, even if part of his role is to deter scavengers. He has some of

Nephthys's darkness about him and is associated with the night, in his aspect of companion to the dead. His wife Anput is a more belligerent counterpart of the jackal *neter*. They had a daughter named Kebechet, who was a gentle and soothing neter of refreshment.

I visualise the character of Anubis as being somewhat reserved and practical, someone who would prefer his later more subdued role to that of being Lord of the Dead. I imagine he would not have contested standing aside for Osiris and would have welcomed the change, as it allowed him to concentrate fully on the tasks he found most satisfying.

The Magical Purpose of Anubis

Some modern pagans have expanded the protective side of Anubis's nature to be a guardian of households, (specifically to deter intruders), in the shape of a visualised thoughtform that manifests as a black dog. I'm unsure about this interpretation. I'm all for reinterpreting the *neteru* to be pertinent to the times, but I can't help thinking that invoking a fierce canine minder into the home when you live with cats, for example, isn't a good idea. Also, I simply don't feel Anubis is muscle for hire. But this is merely my personal interpretation. It's down to individual preference as to whether you're comfortable with him possessing this guardian aspect and feel it's appropriate to ask him to protect your home. Personally, I think other *neteru*, such as Horus or Anubis's wife Anput, are more suitable for that task.

Anubis weighing hearts, with members of the Ennead seated above him. The dead awaiting judgment are represented by two figures in white to the left

Because Anubis had specific functions in Khemet that aren't relevant to us, we need to examine those original traits and decide how they might be adapted. We can see that Anubis was concerned for the dead and performed his job diligently to facilitate a smooth transition between a life on earth and the afterlife. He acted as guide for those taking their first steps into the Duat. So ultimately, we can say he *cared* for the dead. My friend and colleague, Louise Coquio, was the first to suggest that we could approach Anubis to commune with ancestors; he is the link between now and what – and who – has gone before. I felt this idea fitted well and from there more ideas came. Through his closeness to the dead, Anubis can see back into time. Nothing is forgotten because there are so many who lived through it, who remember.

As an 'Opener of the Road to the North', Anubis is thought to personify the Winter Solstice, so it would be appropriate to acknowledge him at this time of year. His colours are traditionally black and gold.

Symbols of Anubis

You can decorate your altar to Anubis with pictures of his symbols.

Nekhakha (the flail) - Anubis is sometimes depicted carrying a flail in the crook of his arm. This was a symbol also associated with Osiris, thought to represent an aspect of farming when the grain was threshed.

Imuit Fetish – sometimes called the Anubis fetish, this is a symbol associated with funerary rites. It consisted of an animal skin – leopard or bull – tied to a pole which was capped by the representation of a lotus bud and placed in a stand.

Epithets of Anubis

The titles below derive from both ancient times and modern magical practice.

Foremost of the Westerners
Lord of the Sacred Land
Governor of the Hall of the Neteru
He Who is Upon his Sacred Mountain
Ruler of the Nine Bows
The Dog who Swallows Millions
Master of Secrets
He Who is in the Place of Embalming
Foremost of the Divine Booth
Guardian of the Scales
Opener of the Ways
Opener of the Roads of the North
The Power of the Two Lands

Offerings to Anubis

Anubis enjoys bread and beer – the darker in colour the better. Some practitioners claim he prefers spicy foods and dark bitter chocolate, so you can bear that in mind when choosing snacks for your feast. He is said to like strong liquor, such as dark, spiced rum. If you can't drink alcohol dark, root-flavoured drinks such as dandelion and burdock or root beer can be substituted. As his colours are black and gold, you can reflect this in your preparation of the food – using food dyes or edible gold leaf where appropriate. Use alternatives where required for diet/ preference.

Visualisation:
A Visit to the Ancestors

What follows is a pathworking for which you don't need to construct the sacred enclosure – although you can if you want to. Otherwise the procedure for creating lesser sacred space will suffice.

This visit to Anubis takes you a cemetery of Khemet. Anubis and Anput had a duty to protect the dead and part of that involved seeing off intruders, but that's not the aspect of Anubis you'll visit in this pathworking. In this case, he will take you to meet your ancestors.

Prepare yourself for visualisation and charge the atmosphere with *heka*. Imagine that the everyday world fades away around you, replaced by a floating mist. Gradually the mist begins to clear, and you find yourself in a new landscape.

You stand before a vast, sprawling network of buildings at the verge of the desert. You carry a satchel of offerings for the dead. It is early evening. The sun sinks like a vast crimson eye into the west, staining the sky. Above, the first stars begin to shine. You realise what lies before you are mastaba tombs and, in between them, endless avenues of simple graves dug into the ground. It's like an enormous city of the dead. You notice white scavenger vultures flying above, no doubt hoping to find some carrion. There are a few hyenas skulking about too. Occasionally, you see the dim flare of a lamp among the shadows, perhaps others visiting family tombs or else those with ill intent, hoping to find loot among the dead.

You walk towards the necropolis, mindful of the wild

animals around you. As you enter among the eerily still avenues of graves and structures, you hear the shrill call of jackals, although none can be seen. Sometimes, they sound almost like cats and at other times like a choir of young wolves singing to the closing day. Whenever the hyenas and vultures hear the calls close to them, they hurry away.

You are drawn to the entrance of a tomb set into a hillside. Dim oil lamps flicker at the threshold. You walk inside and find a small chamber with a shelf cut into the wall where offerings have been laid out. The atmosphere is peaceful and the moment you step within you feel you're cut off from the outside world. Across from you is a dark doorway into a second chamber or perhaps a corridor that leads to it.

In the outer room, stand for a few moments in silence, taking in the atmosphere. You sense there are watchful presences here, who are wary but not outrightly hostile. Project to them that you intend no ill but are here with a valid purpose. Not to rob, or ruin, or disrespect but to meet with those who have gone before.

Raise your arms and say: *'Oh Anubis, Son of Osiris, Opener of the Ways, I ask that you come to me in this city of the dead, which you guard. Open the way for me to speak with my ancestors.'*

Presently, you see a dark shape emerging from the unlit doorway opposite. This figure stoops to step into the outer chamber because it is so tall. In the dim light you see it is Anubis, with the head of black jackal, but this seems more like an elaborate mask than a living animal head. It is stylised and painted with eye makeup. Anubis wears a pectoral collar and a kilt. His long dark feet are bare.

Anubis says to you: *'If you seek an audience with those who went before, you must follow me.'*

He gestures for you to follow him back into the dark doorway. Beyond its threshold there is no light at all, and you have to feel your way along the wall. This is indeed a corridor and is sloping downwards. From the look of the outside of the tomb, you expected it to be of modest size, but you have to walk for some time before you see a dim light ahead. This must be the tomb itself.

You expect quite a small space, but when you step into this chamber it's immense, which startles you. Its ceiling is high and supported by columns heavily sculpted with the images of *neteru* and their servants. The place is lit by the warm orangey glow of a multitude of lamps. There is no sarcophagus or other funerary paraphernalia. In the centre is a vast table, around which a large company is seated, conversing quietly. They look as if they are waiting for something.

'Approach,' Anubis tells you, *'for these are your ancestors. I have gathered them for you and now they wait to meet you and begin the feast.'*

With a little trepidation you draw closer. The people around the table appear to be from all eras, as they are dressed in many different historical costumes. There's no sign of any food upon the table, or of any servants waiting to bring some. You recognise someone seated nearby – perhaps a relative who died, or even an ancestor you recognise from an old photograph. The familiar face is enough to draw you to them. This person turns to look at you and smiles. They welcome you. You tell them you have brought gifts and open the satchel you have carried here. However, once you begin to draw out the modest amount of fruit, cakes, bread and ale you packed, it seems to be never ending. The people at the table pass it around – there is more than enough for everyone. Your ancestor laughs at your surprise. *'This domain is under the sovereignty of Osiris,'* they say, *'and he is the king of plenty, who would let none go hungry at a feast!'*

Now spend some time communing with your ancestors for as long as you wish. Share the feast with them. Move around the table. Anubis takes part in the conversation. To the people in this chamber he is a great friend and provider. The atmosphere is one of celebration and joy; there is nothing sorrowful here. The ancestors might ask you questions, as well as answering any you may want to ask yourself. They might have tasks for you to accomplish for them in the land of the living.

You may also use this time to speak with Anubis privately about any issues you feel he might help you with. He is a guardian and a *neter* who is able to see to the heart of any matter and discern what is truth and what is not.

When you are ready to depart, say:

'Oh, Anubis Master of Secrets,
Guardian of the Scales,
I thank you for allowing this meeting with my ancestors.
I thank also, all those who came to speak with me.
May the light of the neteru shine ever upon you.'

Bow to the company and return the way you came. Once you reach the open air, the scene before you fades into mist, bringing you back to the present time, and earthly reality. Return to normal consciousness and open your eyes. Record your experiences.

Ritual:
Festival of the Dead

If you wish you could utilise this ritual as an alternative to a Samhain rite, performed on 31st October, but it may be undertaken effectively at any time of year. In the previous visualisation, you met with your ancestors in their domain. In this rite, you will invite them to be with you and take part in your festival.

Rituals of this kind are best performed at what are known as liminal times, associated with thresholds in time and space, when transitions and crossings may occur. This is when the veil between our world and whatever lies beyond it is said to be thin. It doesn't apply solely to the land of the dead, but other realms and dimensions too. While Samhain in particular is seen as liminal, any seasonal festival possesses this attribute, because they all symbolise the turning of the wheel of the year. Liminal, in its literal interpretation, means a transition between one state to another.

The feast is of great importance to this ritual, as it is an offering to your ancestors. Anubis will also be present. When you consume and enjoy the food and drink, so will your otherworldly guests. Be as extravagant as you wish with the preparation. This is not an occasion to be mournful, but a time of happy reunion.

Equipment

- A sumptuous feast
- Sistrum
- The altar cloth should be black and gold/yellow
- Myrrh, frankincense, cedarwood incense
- The altar candles should be black and/or gold/yellow

- Gold stars may be scattered on the altar
- The hieroglyph of Anubis's name

The Ritual

Create your enclosure and enliven your altar statue with *heka*, if you have one. Light the altar candles and replenish your incense if necessary. Then sit down in the centre. Close your eyes and breathe deeply for a while to alter your state of consciousness.

Visualise your environment gradually changing. A mist fills your enclosure, so that objects around you disappear within it. Presently, the mist begins to clear, and you see a new landscape appearing around you.

You find yourself out in the desert with high mountains around you. It's late in the evening, and the stars blaze overhead. You're upon a road between rearing cliffs and can see an immense structure ahead of you. This is a hidden temple, dedicated to Anubis. Its purpose is for the Veneration of the Blessed Spirits – those who have gone before.

There are a great many people gathered in the outer courtyard of the temple. As you approach, a priest comes forward, treating you as if you are an honoured dignitary. It seems you have been expected. Say:

'Oh, Great Anubis,
Foremost of the Westerners,
Lord of the Sacred Land
I ask that you to join me in a rite of celebration,
For life, for death, for rebirth in the light of the neteru.
Open the way for my ancestors to partake of the feast of light
Walk with them along the paths that lead from this land
To the Fields of Aaru.'

Chant: *'Anpu Apuat'* for a minute or so and gently shake the sistrum.

(Pronounced Ann-*poo* Ap-*Oo*-At. Meaning 'Opener of the Ways'.)

Then, without opening your eyes, cast your inner gaze back to the image of Anubis in your enclosure. Imagine it glows with soft light, as it brims with *heka*. Anubis is alive in both inner and outer realities and will communicate with you.

The priests bring out what you think is a black and gold statue of the neter, but once they've set it down in the courtyard, Anubis rises to his feet and you realise this is the *neter* himself, not just a statue.

Anubis acknowledges your presence by inclining his head to you, but then walks away to greet all the guests. This night he wears a long, finely pleated robe of the softest linen. He wears a golden pectoral collar and bracelets of gold around his wrists and upper arms. The guests are pleased to see him, clearly eager for his attention. He has helped them all at one time. You also spend some time talking with those around you, a larger crowd than you met in the visualisation. These are not just your direct ancestors, but the many others who were close to them.

After a few minutes, Anubis walks to the centre of the court and summons you to him. As before, you have brought a satchel of gifts, but as you move to open it, Anubis stays your hand. *'Behold,'* he says, *'those who serve you have carried the feast to this place.'*

You glance round and see a retinue of richly dressed attendants, who are carrying food and drink on trays or carts or in their arms. These they begin to place upon an immense table to the side of the courtyard. If there is a face beneath the mask of the jackal, you cannot see it, but you sense Anubis is smiling at your surprise. You raise your arms to him and say:

'Oh Anubis, Son of Nephthys,
Governor of the Hall of the Neteru,
I have brought offerings to you,
As symbols of thanks and respect.
Through me, may you experience their pleasures.
As I eat this food, may you relish its flavours,
As I drink, may your thirst be quenched with enjoyment.
And may these offerings be shared among all
Who are gathered here.'

When you feel ready, open your eyes and come out of the visualisation, while imagining that part of you is still with Anubis. Now you will feast in his honour.

Consume the feast, concentrating on sharing the pleasure of doing so with Anubis. Imagine that your ancestors are with you. Toast them with a drink. Leave a small portion of everything you eat and drink. After this has been done, wrap the remains in paper and leave this parcel before the statue on your altar.

When you are ready, compose yourself and return to the visualisation. See your offerings upon the great table, with Anubis and your ancestors gathered around it, consuming the feast with great pleasure.

Now is the time for private communion – either with Anubis or with your ancestors. Spend as much time as you like doing this.

When you are ready to conclude the ritual, return to the centre of the courtyard and raise your arms. Everyone falls silent and turns to look at you. Anubis steps forward to stand before you. Say:

'Oh Anubis, Tep-Tuf,
He Who is Upon His Sacred Mountain,
I thank you for your presence,
For accompanying the ancestors here
And for sharing in the feast I offered.
Grant me the good judgement to know myself as you know me.'

Turn to your ancestors and bid them farewell. Bow to Anubis and prepare to leave. The scene around you gradually dissolves into mist. Return to normal reality and dismantle your enclosure in the usual way. Then record the results of your work and dispose of the remains of your offerings appropriately.

Ruins of a Khemetic Necropolis

Anput - She-Jackal Assassin

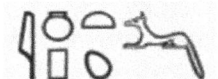

Not a great deal of information can be found concerning Anput, the wife of Anubis. Her name is the feminine form of Anpu, Anubis's name in Khemetic, meaning 'female royal child'. She could also be referred to as Anupet, Input and Yineput. She was a *neter* of funerals and, along with her husband, of mummification. Some writers believe that Anput was created only to give Anubis a female counterpart, rather than a wife or consort. Statues of Anubis as a jackal don't present him as overtly male, which was apparently unusual in Khemetic art. This has led to the speculation that he was once regarded as female, so therefore Anput could be his original form.

As a *neter* of the seventeenth nome (or district) of Upper Egypt known as Cynopolis, Anput was shown in group statues standing beside King Menkaure, with Hathor on his other side, as in the example to the left. Anput wears a headdress that

319

includes the form of a jackal lying upon a feather. The statues reveal that Menkaure regarded Hathor and Anput as his protectors.

Anput as knife-wielding jackal on a 21ˢᵗ dynasty papyrus

Anput could be represented in the form of a jackal, either as pregnant, or as a mother nursing her cubs. While she was sometimes shown as a woman with the head of a jackal, this wasn't very often. In the temple complex at Dendera, there's a carving of her as a jackal standing on its hind quarters, brandishing knives in its front paws. The text accompanying this depiction describes her vicious nature and that the fact that even when she's not wielding knives she's equipped with equally effective teeth. She uses both types of weapon to slaughter the enemies of Osiris. Text from the temple describe Anput thus:

'You are Anput, motionless on your belly, with teeth sharpened to ravage the Mischievous One.'

'...Anput, the bitch who barks against all who come with evil intentions, who cuts up the Wicked One in the back, so that he falls to the ground and so that he never exists again.'

And words accredited to Anput herself: 'I have taken apart Yash by driving a knife into his back.'

The first description suggests the image of a predator waiting in hiding, ready to leap out upon her unsuspecting target, while the other two quotes leave in no doubt her ferocious and brutal nature. In this role, she can be regarded as a protector, and may be invoked as such. I feel she is more suited to this task than Anubis himself. Her nature in this aspect can be likened to the viciousness displayed by a mother jackal when defending her cubs from harm.

Writer Bezenwepwy of the web site *Per Sabu – House of Jackals* – describes her interpretation of Anput as:

'...I've mostly come to know her as a shadowy assassin, who slips through shadows and avenges misdeeds. She also strikes me as being fairly territorial and certainly not adverse to running off trespassers or anyone looking to cause trouble...'

http://www.per-sabu.org/anupet.html

This certainly resonates with how I feel about Anput. But I also see her as having two sides to her nature: a ruthless assassin and a maternal figure. I don't regard her as being like a mother goddess in the accepted sense, but more of a protector and defender of the young. Louise Coquio offers the interpretation that Anput, in her connection with the dead, is concerned particularly with protecting deceased children, or those who died relatively young.

The Magical Purpose of Anput

As a neter of dual nature, Anput can either be a savage protector or a guardian with a more nurturing aspect. She personifies the urge to defend and to use force if necessary.

I also see Anput as a neter who helps us to help ourselves. She can instil courage when it is lacking. She can stand behind us, offering encouragement. Sometimes we all have to deal with situations in life that we'd rather not face but have no choice. We might have to confront daunting, intimidating individuals, undertake actions we feel we lack the ability to accomplish and so on. Anput can be called upon to give us strength and confidence. With her at your back, you don't have to feel intimidated by anyone or anything.

As Anubis is 'Opener of the Road to the North', Anput is 'Opener to the Road to the South', indicating that she personified the summer solstice. Therefore, you could venerate her at that time of year. Like Anubis, she is associated with Sopdet (Sirius) the Dog Star, so can be regarded as having a stellar aspect. The 'Dog Days' are also an appropriate time to celebrate her in ritual. This is the hot, sultry period when Sopdet rises at the same time as the sun, from 3rd July to 11th August. This time of year is particularly associated with the uncanny.

As a protector, especially of the young, Anput can be called upon as a guardian who will remain with someone until they no longer need her protection, until they can stand on their own feet. She guards the vulnerable and deters bullies. A dog is said to be vigilant by both day and night, so in this respect, in her form of jackal, Anput is the Lady of the Light and Dark.

Symbols of Anput

Jackal

Images of Anput's sacred animal, the jackal, are ideal for adorning your altar. Representations of the seated jackal are especially pertinent.

Ceremonial Blades

As Anput is shown at the temple of Edfu wielding twin blades, you can use ornamental knives to represent her defensive qualities on your altar. A blade used commonly in Khemet was in shape similar to the modern Khopesh knife, illustrated here.

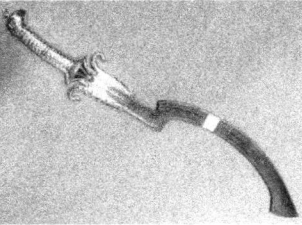

Epithets of Anput

The titles below derive from both ancient times and modern magical practice.

Opener of the Roads of the South
Opener of the Ways
Anput the Watchful
The Power of the Heavens
The She-Jackal Who Vanquishes Evil
Anput the Ravager
She Who Protects
The Guardian with Teeth and Knives
She Who Cuts the Wicked
She Who Watches the Necropolis
Dark Mother

Lady of the Light and Dark
She who is Crowned with Stars

Offerings to Anput

The offerings to Anput are the same as for Anubis. A theme of black and gold, dark-coloured food and drinks, with a touch of yellow or sparkle. Spicy snacks and dark chocolate, and dark, spiced rum. Use alternatives where required for diet/preference.

Visualisation:
Slaying the Monster of Ill-Intent

What follows is a pathworking for which you don't need to construct the sacred enclosure – although you can if you want to. Otherwise the procedure for creating lesser sacred space will suffice.

This visit to Anput will allow you to take on her aspect of protection when needed. You will face a representation of anything bad that you feel is threatening you or others close to you.

Prepare yourself for visualisation and charge the atmosphere with *heka*. Imagine that the everyday world fades away around you, replaced by a floating mist. Gradually the mist begins to clear, and you find yourself in a new landscape.

When the mist clears, you are in complete darkness, but from the echo of your breathing can tell you're inside a building. It feels deep underground but large. You sense an invisible presence nearby and can just about hear the soft pad of feet circling around you. Say:

'Oh, Anput The Watchful,
The She-Jackal Who Vanquishes Evil
I ask that you reveal yourself to me in this place of darkness.
Instil me with your strength and courage.
Stand by my side to protect me from harm,
In the name of Maat,
Oh, Lady of the Light and Dark.'

Gradually, a dim greenish-white light comes into the chamber. You can just about see the walls of a circular room, which is quite large. The ceiling is far overhead in darkness still. The walls are covered with bas reliefs and paintings, depicting those neteru and spirits who not only guard and protect the *neteru* but also humankind. You realise this is a kind of arena, and its purpose is for you to confront evil and vanquish it.

You also see – only a couple of feet away from you – two glowing greenish-white eyes that seem to have no body. But then a mist forms around them, gradually taking on shape. The figure of Anput is revealed as a jackal whose body is like a human's in some respects. She is covered in short black fur and has the hind legs of a jackal. Her head is also that of a canid. She wears a short, pleated kilt but is otherwise unadorned. She carries two long sharp knives.

She says to you, in an almost humorous tone, *'Greetings, meruti. Reveal to me your enemies. Let's see what can be done.'*

In your mind, now send pictures to Anput of those who oppose or threaten you, who are perhaps spiteful, cruel, bullying or in any other way harmful. If you have no need to ask for Anput's help in this way, you can work in the name of a friend or family member (with their consent), or else for the vulnerable in general. Adapt the visualisation as necessary. Make the pictures as clear as possible, showing each individual acting in the way that harms or hurts. Be objective about this, do not colour the picture with emotion, simply the facts of what you have witnessed and/or experienced.

When this is done, Anput nods her head, as if in thought. She says, *'Then we bring evil intention to us, in a shape we may slay. But you must know this beast is not the living people you showed me. It is merely the ill-shaped form of their ill will. This we will destroy and disempower. Are you in accord with this?'*

You give your assent to her.

Everything is quiet for a few moments, and then in the shadows you hear a strange rustle as of something heavy being dragged over the floor. Anput hands you one of her knives and puts a finger to her mouth to bid you be quiet. She stoops down and moves slowly to where the noise is coming from. You follow, in the same predatory position, holding the knife out before you.

You hear a long, low hiss and a swift slithering movement. A gigantic snakelike beast undulates from the darkness and rears up before you and Anput. Venom drips from its open jaws, its dull yellow tongue flicks out, and a terrible stench emanates from it. It represents Apep, the monster who attempts to devour the sun – the extinguisher of light bringing fear and darkness. It now represents the negative feelings directed at you or others. This creature might change in form as you look upon it, reflecting more intimately any difficulties you might face in your life at present.

The monster shows what evil thoughts look like when manifested into a shape. It is fashioned of mindless cruelty, greed, ignorance, envy and selfishness. You can see too that it is weak, because the badness was spawned from a cycle of malice spanning back through human history. Deep within this horrifying vision lies a kernel of fear, of terror.

'See how you humans must fight yourselves?' Anput says cynically, but with a wry smile. *'Now remove this abomination from your reality.'*

She leaps forward and you follow her. As you do so, you are filled with her strength and swiftness, her ability to see off trouble-makers. You chop at the monstrous beast, and as you do so parts of it fly off like dirty smoke. It has no real substance. As you do this, visualise strongly that those who wish harm and commit injury of any type lose the desire and will to do so. As the monster diminishes so does their power to wound and hurt, in whatever form. You are not smiting them in person but their actions, intentions and motives. Plans fail, gossip falls on deaf ears, anger dissipates, truth prevails. And for those whose intentions are darker and more dangerous, they have Anput to deal with, who fills them with horror and the urge to flee.

This is the time for you to put your own monsters to flight. The fear within can give others power over you. Take in Anput's fearlessness and determination to right wrongs. Spend some time doing this.

Eventually, the beast has been entirely dismantled. Anput changes her form to be that of a jackal-headed woman, dressed in a long robe of dark blue. Now she summons a light of protection around you and/or around those you championed. She says: *'Go forth from this place with my power within you. Take also my protection for I will watch over you.'*

She places both hands upon your shoulders and you feel a

soothing energy pass through you, calming you down after the fight, but even so you know that you are now strengthened and will remain so. Take a few minutes to commune with Anput further if you wish. She may have advice or information for you, and/or impart a gift.

When you are ready to depart, say:

'Oh, Anput, Dark Mother,
Lady of the Light and Dark,
I thank you for imparting your strength to me,
And for your help in vanquishing ill will.
Like you, I will work always to aid the vulnerable.'

Now bid Anput farewell. The scene before you begins to fade into mist, bringing you back to the present time, and earthly reality. Return to normal consciousness and open your eyes. Be aware your body is still invigorated with the power of Anput. Record your experiences.

Ritual:
Festival of Sopdet

Sirius rises late in the dark, liquid sky
On summer nights, star of stars,
Orion's Dog they call it, brightest
Of all, but an evil portent, bringing heat
And fevers to suffering humanity.

From *The Iliad*, Homer

The Dog Days, which follow the heliacal rising of the Dog Star, Sopdet, take place in high summer, between the dates of 3rd July and 20th August. This is the time when the season is at its hottest, and it is also a time when the land dreams beneath the sun, the air dances with summer-colts, and ghosts walk at mid-day. It is traditionally a time of feverish indolence, underscored by a wild excitement. It is a time when the land is exuberant, pulsing with power. For pagans, the pinnacle of the Dog Days is the festival of Lughnasadh (or Lammas) on 1st August. Gods and goddesses associated with this time are often mischievous and tricky, and Anput fits comfortably into this role. It's appropriate to venerate her at Lughnasadh, even if the landscape she once prevailed over was very different to that we inhabit ourselves. Anput, at this time, can be regarded in her protective aspect, a guardian of the land and of our selves. Wherever we live in the world, we can invite her into our lives and our landscapes.

The feast should include homemade breads, summer fruits, and other produce of the land, sourced from your local area, not imported or out of season.

Equipment Required

- The altar cloth should be black, which not only denotes Anput's colour, but also fertility of the lands. You can adorn this with green and gold/yellow items
- You may decorate the altar with green stones and crystals to symbolise growth
- Green and/or yellow candles
- Heavy, flowery, exotic incense
- The hieroglyph of Anput's name
- An appropriate feast

The Ritual

Create your enclosure and enliven your altar statue with *heka*, if you have one. Light the altar candles and replenish your incense if necessary. Then sit down in the centre. Close your eyes and breathe deeply for a while to alter your state of consciousness.

Visualise your environment gradually changing. A mist fills your enclosure, so that objects around you disappear within it. Presently, the mist begins to clear, and you see a new landscape appearing around you.

You find yourself in bright sunlight, in an idealised form of your native landscape on the day that Sopdet begins its seasonal journey. As usual, you carry a satchel of offerings. In the northern hemisphere, you may visualise lush, dense forests, untouched by humankind, spreading fields, vast heathlands baking beneath the sun, high mountains where birds of prey wheel and cry. The sun beats down, bringing a kind of ecstatic madness.

Find a spot that seems appropriate, raise your arms and say:

'Oh, Swift Anput,
Who defends the vulnerable,
And protects the land where you are called.
Come to me now at the brink of the Dog Days
When your star, Sopdet rises with the sun.
Walk in the summer fields of my land,
And reveal to me your mysteries.'

Chant: *'Anput, repit m'kit'* for a minute or so.

(Pronounced: rep-it, meh-kit. Meaning (roughly) Anput, protectress *neter*.)

Then, without opening your eyes, cast your inner gaze back to the image of Anput in your enclosure. Imagine it glows with soft light, as it brims with *heka*. Anput is alive in both inner and outer realities and will communicate with you.

You now walk through the landscape of the Dog Days. What do you see? What do you smell and hear? Explore this untouched landscape, which shimmers in the heat and burgeons with life – a perfect landscape before humankind encroached upon it. Spirits of the land are visible. Strange shadows flit at the edges of your vision and magic hums in the air. Presently, you become aware of a strange darting shape nearby, bounding through the fields or creeping through the trees. It's as if this being seeks to evade you, but then shows itself plainly, before slipping into the shadows once more. Eventually, you realise it is a black jackal – Anput in her full canine form. She seems to want you to follow her, pausing to wait for you.

You now transform into an animal yourself – one of your own preference. In this new form you catch up with Anput, who welcomes you. Now is the time to speak with Anput about the natural world and its preservation. Ask for her help in preventing its destruction, her guardianship. Spend some time in free visualisation. Anput may take you somewhere or give you a gift.

When you are ready to conclude this part of the visualisation, take the offerings you have brought from the satchel and spread them before the *neter*. Open your eyes and come out of the visualisation, while imagining that part of you is still with Anput in the idealised vision of summer. Say:

'Oh Anput, consort of Anubis,
Who guards and protects,
I have brought offerings to you,
As symbols of thanks and respect.
Through me, may you experience their pleasures.
As I eat this food, may you relish its flavours,
As I drink, may your thirst be quenched with enjoyment.'

Now you will feast in her honour. Consume the offerings, concentrating on sharing the pleasure of doing so with

Anput. Leave a small portion of everything you eat and drink. After this has been done, wrap the remains in paper and leave this parcel before the statue on your altar.

When you are ready, compose yourself and return to the visualisation. See your offerings around Anput, which she consumes with relish. Creatures of the land have come to her and she shares the feast with them. Bow to her and say:

'Oh Anput, Shield of Divine Power,
Ever watchful
Continue to share with me the ability to guard and protect
Give me the strength to stand up for those who need it
And to honour my home, the earth.
Grant me the self-awareness to know myself as you know me.'

Then bid farewell to Anput and prepare to leave. She runs off into the landscape and vanishes. The creatures who accompanied her disperse. The scene around you gradually dissolves into mist.

Return to normal reality and dismantle your enclosure in the usual way. Then record the results of your work and dispose of the remains of your offerings appropriately.

Egyptian Desert Cliffs

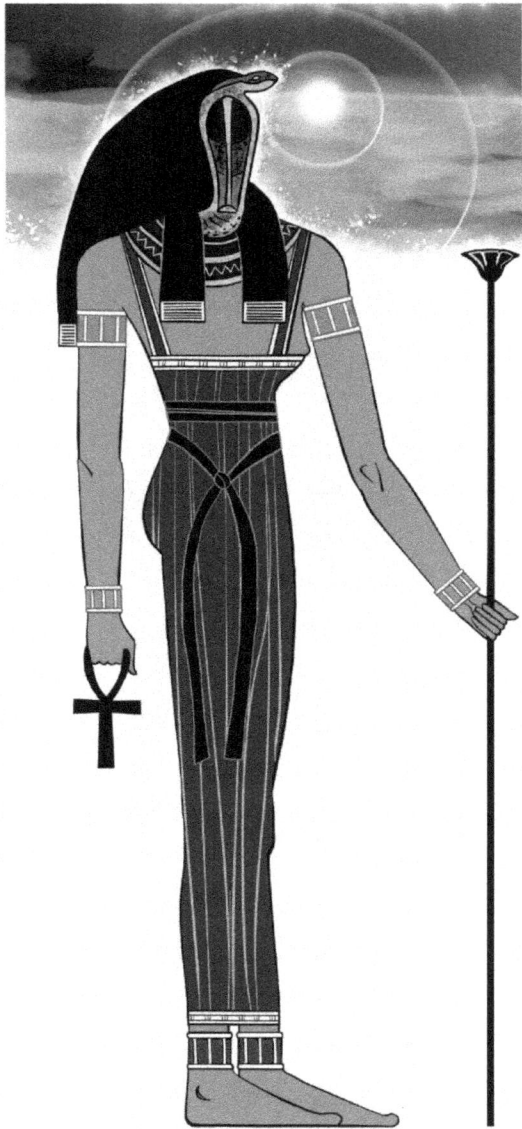

Kebechet - Neter of Freshness and the Celestial Realm

𝕂︎

Attributes of Kebechet

Kebechet's name in Khemetic was Qebhet, which can be pronounced as *Keb*-ek-het. She is also known as Khebhut, Kebehut, Kabehchet and Kebehwet. Her name means 'cooling water', and in one of her aspects she was associated with the fluids used in embalming. She assisted her father Anubis in mummifying the dead. Kebechet was generally depicted as a woman with the head of a serpent, but she could also be represented simply as a snake. She is known as the *neter* of freshness.

Sometimes, the 'cooling water' had a more literal meaning, since she was credited with refreshing and purifying deceased pharaohs with water. She also offered drinking water to the dead as they awaited judgement in the Hall of Truth. The offer of water was an important part of preparing for the afterlife. The family of the deceased could be comforted by the fact that Kebechet would be caring for their dead relative, not allowing them to go thirsty while awaiting rebirth. She was also said to be a neter who 'opened the windows of the sky', which meant she could free the spirit from the body.

Originally, Kebechet was a snake deity known as 'the celestial serpent', which is mentioned in *The Pyramid Texts*.

Only later did her role change and she became known as the daughter of Anubis and Anput, with her own part to play in the funerary process. As a *neter* of the heavens, Kebechet was connected with the Great Sky River (the Milky Way), itself appearing to those on earth as a serpent of stars stretching across the sky. She was also associated with the Nile, a river closely linked to the Great Sky River in spiritual lore.

In some versions of the Tarot deck, the Wheel of Fortune card (number 10 in the major arcana) shows a jackal deity and a serpent on the right and left of the wheel respectively and a female sphinx carrying a sword at the top of the wheel. The jackal represents Anubis and/or Anput, symbolising the evolution of consciousness from a lower to higher form. The celestial serpent, which we can imagine as Kebechet, represents cosmic energy flowing into reality and taking on form. The sphinx, presiding above, symbolises balance and justice.

Through her role as a purifier, Kebechet can be seen as a personification of harmony, characterising Maat. She is a benevolent *neter*, concerned with caring and nurturing. Her waters, whether offered as a drink or the Nile itself, are cool, clear and restorative. While her parents might focus upon the stages of preparation for life in the afterlife, Kebechet is the freedom beyond it. She's associated with the sky by day and night. In her aspect of the celestial serpent, she represents the evolution of the self, the knowledge the practitioner seeks through the Great Work.

How Kebechet became connected with Anubis and Anput is a mystery. At some point in Khemetic history, she was attached to their myth in the role of their daughter, yet there would seem to be little correspondence between them. Still, that is what she became and – to me – she fits comfortably into the stories of the Ennead. She has her own distinct role and brings to a close this exploration of the Heliopolitan divine family.

While her parents are creatures of black and gold, associated with the jackal, and in Anput's case with some quite aggressive traits, Kebechet seems a gentle soul. She is golden and dressed in white or blue. Her sacred animal, the cobra whose head she shares, might seem somewhat at odds with her attributes. While the serpent can impart wisdom and learning, it also has the reputation of being cunning or threatening, but Kebechet displays neither of those latter traits. She inherits her father's and grandfather's gentle nature but not Anubis's, or Anput's, defensive aspect. She swims in the Nile and the celestial river of the Milky Way, revivifying and soothing whoever needs her influence.

The Magical Purpose of Kebechet

Kebechet's prevailing quality is refreshment, in whatever capacity. She is like a fountain of energy, washing away dust, dirt, cobwebs or whatever other metaphors you can think of for feelings or situations that cause blockage and stagnation.

You can appeal to her when you feel listless, dull and without energy. She can also be asked to assist with depression and a general feeling of being low. Her influence brings refreshment, sparking renewed interest in life, flushing away melancholy.

She can also be asked to bring refreshment to any situation or project – reviving creative energy, stimulating fresh ideas. If you are revamping something – a business, a group effort of some kind – then Kebechet can bring her spark to it.

I feel also that Kebechet may be appealed to when you feel the need to calm down. Her soothing influence can dispel agitation and stress. Chanting her name may aid with this.

Symbols of Kebechet

The Serpent
Representations of snakes are appropriate for your altar, whether as pictures or ornaments and models.

The Milky Way – Stars in General
Representations of stars can be scattered upon the altar, and a picture of the Milky Way placed behind the image of Kebechet. A string of battery-operated fairy lights can be used to represent this too.

River Water
A bowl of water, perhaps taken from a spring or river rather than a tap or a bottle, may be placed before the image of Kebechet on the altar. This will represent the waters of The Nile.

Epithets of Kebechet

The titles below derive from both ancient times and modern magical practice.

She Who Offers Pure Clear Water
Opener of the Windows of the Sky
Celestial Serpent
She Who Banishes Thirst
Lady of the Great Sky River
Mistress of the Nile
The Serpent Who Spans the Sky
She of the Soothing Waters

Offerings to Kebechet

Food and drink offered to Kebechet should be of a light, delicate and refreshing nature. Small, light cakes or biscuits in the shape of stars are appropriate, along with fresh fruit. If you can get hold of star fruit, that is especially apt for a feast to Kebechet. The drink should be pale and sparkling, wine, water or fruit juice, or mixtures thereof.

Visualisation:
Swimming with the Serpent

What follows is a pathworking for which you don't need to construct the sacred enclosure – although you can if you want to. Otherwise the procedure for creating lesser sacred space will suffice. You will need a chalice of pure, iced water, preferably taken from a natural spring rather than purchased but bottled spring water will suffice, if necessary.

This visit to Kebechet will be purely to relax, to allow her soothing presence and the comfort of her waters to rid you of tension and anxiety. In her presence, you are at rest, free of all cares.

Prepare yourself for visualisation and charge the atmosphere with *heka*. Imagine that the everyday world fades away around you, replaced by a floating mist. Gradually the mist begins to clear, and you find yourself in a new landscape.

It is late evening, and the sun has almost sunk beneath the horizon. You are standing on the banks of the Nile, some distance from any village or habitation. You are alone. Then you hear an ethereal song, faintly on the air, that seems to come from everywhere and nowhere. You are drawn to walk into the river, which feels comfortably cool around you. You lie down in the water and float upon it like a feather. The sensation of riding upon the flow of the sacred river is immensely soothing. You feel all cares begin to drift from you. As you float, say:

'Oh Kebechet, Lady of the Heavens
Walker of the Roads Between the Stars,
Swimmer in the Great Sky River,
Come to me and grant me your refreshment.
Swim to me in these sacred waters,
Reveal to me your mysteries of the Heavens and the Earth.'

The ethereal song becomes clearer. You become aware of movement nearby and raise your head from the water. You see an immense serpent swimming towards you. It is very beautiful, with a pearlescent skin and eyes like opals. Its movement is sinuous and lazy. This is Kebechet.

She undulates around you in the water, creating soothing currents that massage your body, relieving any tension or stress you might still be feeling. You roll within the water, transforming into a serpent yourself, a long flowing muscle of power. Kebechet says to you, *'Swim with me, meruti.'*

Together, you and Kebechet swim upriver. This feels strange at first, because you're swimming against the current, but your strong muscles can do this with ease and you swiftly become used to it. As you travel, you glimpse upon the banks shadowy figures that represent aspects of your life that cause you worry or concern. They can be personifications of thoughts, emotions and situations – of your own or other people you care about. But for now these things are just shadows. They cannot touch you here for you are in the sacred waters, protected. Kebechet says to you, *'Wash away with my deluge that which causes pain.'*

She begins to thrash in the river, causing the waters to rise and flood over the banks. The water is crystalline as if stars are caught within it. Wherever it flows over the land, the shadows dissipate. You emulate Kebechet's movements, causing spray to spurt high into the air, falling like a fountain onto the banks of the river. It is cleansing, purifying. Nothing which causes uncertainty can exist within it.

Imagine your life with all the things that cause niggling discomfort or outright hurt washed away from it. Experience living in that reality. Believe it to be true, even for just these minutes within the pathworking. Draw strength from this experience. Take it into you, like a sparkling, refreshing mist, which you can carry back into reality with you to sustain you through darker days.

Now you swim once more with Kebechet, upstream to the south, for the Nile flows south to north. The land becomes more mountainous and uninhabited, the river narrower and faster. You see a building ahead of you above the banks of the river. It's a small temple that appears abandoned, out here alone where no one walks or lives. But this is a peaceful place, nonetheless. Here Kebechet bids you to leave the water. As you do so, you transform back into a human form. You go with the *neter* into the shrine, where there is a sacred spring rising from the rocky floor.

Kebechet now takes on the form of a woman with the head of a cobra. Her skin is golden, and she wears a white robe. She bends down and dips a clay cup into the pool of the spring. This she hands to you. She says: *'That which heals lies within the land. My waters flow all over the earth, and each river, each stream, each spring, each lake is a restorative balm. Drink now of my waters and be purified.'*

You drink the water. It is extremely cold, which almost burns you. For a moment it makes your head ache.

Open your eyes and come out of the visualisation, while imagining that part of you remains with Kebechet in the shrine. Take up the chalice and drink from it. Do this slowly and mindfully. Close your eyes as you do so and return to the visualisation. Imagine the water you drink is from Kebechet's sacred spring. As this cool pure liquid flows down your throat, you feel increasingly refreshed, well and alert. Any lethargy you might have felt is dispelled. You feel vital and surging with energy. Your body seems to sing with power. You could run or swim for ever. Joy and contentment flow through you. Spend some time experiencing this fully. Then say, *'I thank you, Kebechet, for the refreshment that you have given me.'*

Now you should take time to commune with Kebechet. She may take you to other places, reveal some important information or impart a gift to you.

When you are ready to depart, bid Kebechet farewell. The scene before you now fades into mist, bringing you back to the present time, and earthly reality. Return to normal consciousness and open your eyes. Be aware your senses are still enlivened by the power and protective love of Kebechet. Record your experiences.

Ritual:
The Great Sky River

This visit to Kebechet will take you into her realm of the Great Sky River. Its purpose is to experience her celestial energy and its capacity to evolve consciousness. You should place the Wheel of Fortune Tarot card upon your altar, but it doesn't matter if in the deck you posses the card represents something other than the image found in traditional decks like the Rider Waite and other decks based on that imagery. Imagine that the meaning of the card is that of the eternal turning of the heavens, with the jackal and serpent upon the wheel of fate.

Equipment Required

- The Wheel of Fortune Tarot Card placed upon the altar
- The altar cloth should be white and/or silver. You can adorn this with representations of stars in silver and pale colours, and a string of battery-operated fairy lights
- You may decorate the altar with blue stones, opals and crystals to symbolise the divine waters
- Blue, silver or white candles
- A light airy incense
- The hieroglyph of Kebechet's name
- Chilled, sparkling water in a chalice
- An appropriate feast

The Ritual

Create your enclosure and enliven your altar statue with *heka*, if you have one. Light the altar candles and replenish your incense if necessary. Then sit down in the centre. Close your eyes and breathe deeply for a while to alter your state of consciousness.

Visualise your environment gradually changing. A mist fills your enclosure, so that objects around you disappear within it. Presently, the mist begins to clear, and you see a new landscape appearing around you.

It is night-time and you stand within the desert of Khemet. Above you the stars cover the Heavens, and starlight casts stark shadows upon the ground. You're aware of a sense of immanence, which takes the form of a song you can only barely hear – the song of the celestial spheres. This song is at once lovely but eerie. Raise your arms and say:

'Oh, Kebechet, Celestial Serpent,
Opener of the Windows of the Sky,
Come to me now!
Take me to your realm in the sky,
To the shining waters of the Great Sky River.
Help me realise my potential,
And reveal to me your mysteries.'

Chant: *'Kebechet, skhaiu skhuit'* for a minute or so.

(Pronounced: Keb-eh-chet sky-oo, skoo-it. Meaning (roughly) Kebechet, celestial serpent *neter*.)

Then, without opening your eyes, cast your inner gaze back to the image of Kebechet in your enclosure. Imagine it glows with soft light, as it brims with *heka*. Kebechet is alive in both inner and outer realities and will communicate with you.

In the land of Khemet, you see above you, in the air, the form of a cobra-headed woman beginning to manifest. She seems to be comprised of motes of light, miniature stars and wisps of misty radiance. She says to you: *'Walk the road to the stars, meruti, to my temple in the heavens.'*

As you watch, she stretches out, growing larger and larger,

changing shape. She becomes an immense serpent of light reaching up into the darkening sky. Her body expands to become a road of stars that will lead to the Great Sky River.

You step upon this road and begin to walk up it. You move swiftly, as if floating. As you rise into the sky, you see a shape begin to take form among the stars. It is the Great Wheel of Fate, as symbolised in the Tarot. You see the jackal neter on the right of the wheel, representing Anubis and Anput. This figure represents evolving consciousness, your own mind opening up to unimaginable possibilities. On the left, the celestial serpent twines around the wheel. Kebechet allows us to manifest celestial energy into reality. She empowers our thoughts, our actions, and stimulates our creativity. Atop the wheel, an inscrutable female sphinx stares down. She carries a sword and represents Maat – balance and harmony.

This image hangs before you, a symbol of potential. You walk towards it and eventually pass right through it, as if through a great circular gate.

Beyond lies a palace of stars, so beautiful, yet almost beyond description. Its form is like nothing you've ever imagined. It seems to be in constant motion, as if comprised of countless motes of information. It is the Great Library where knowledge of all time and space is stored. You wonder whether the Ennead came from this place originally, a storehouse of desires and hopes, the impetus to expand and replicate. Kebechet's temple exists inside this structure.

You have taken on a form of light, like a spirit, and can move freely. You drift through the indescribable labyrinth of the palace, through chambers of light, through corridors of starshine, heading always towards an inner shrine. Kebechet's song calls to you. You hear it clearly now. She sings ideas into existence.

Eventually, you come to rest at the threshold to the shrine. It is quite dark within, yet there are glimpses of starshine. Kebechet has now transformed back into a cobra-headed woman, sitting upon a basalt throne at the end of the room. She beckons you forward, and when you reach her, she says, *'This is the temple of your initiation, meruti. Drink of my waters.'*

She holds out to you a chalice of glass or maybe it is ice, or even starshine itself. You take it in both hands.

'When you drink,' Kebechet says, *'you will see all. My mysteries will be revealed to you.'*

Keeping your eyes on her, you drink from the cup. It is water and starlight but teeming with invisible particles of knowledge. As its cold fire streams through you, you can feel your mind opening up. Ideas come to you like flowers opening within you. Now spend some time in this experience. Commune with Kebechet, travel with her. Discover what she wishes to give to you.

When you are ready to conclude this part of the visualisation, return to Kebechet's shrine. Take the offerings you have brought from the satchel and spread them before the *neter*. Open your eyes and come out of the visualisation, while imagining that part of you is still with Kebechet in her celestial temple. Say:

'Oh Kebechet, the Serpent Who Spans the Sky
She Who Quenches all Thirst,
I have brought offerings to you,
As symbols of thanks and respect.
Through me, may you experience their pleasures.
As I eat this food, may you relish its flavours,
As I drink, may your thirst be quenched with enjoyment.'

Now you will feast in her honour. Consume the offerings, concentrating on sharing the pleasure of doing so with Kebechet. Drink the chilled water you placed upon the altar. Pass this chalice around if you're working with others. Each should make a toast, stating an intention for the future concerning their magical work. Leave a small portion of everything you eat and drink. After this has been done, wrap the remains in paper and leave this parcel before the statue on your altar.

When you are ready, compose yourself and return to the visualisation. See your offerings around Kebechet, which she consumes with relish. Bow to her and say:

'Oh Kebechet, Lady of the Nile,
Mistress of the Great Sky River,
Continue to share with me the vision of the infinite.
Give me clear sight to follow my own path to the stars
To reach my full potential.
I stand in your presence, purified and strong.
Grant me the light to know myself as you know me.'

Then bid farewell to Kebechet and prepare to leave. When you turn from her throne, you transform into a being of pure energy, which flies swiftly from the shrine, and through the edifice of the celestial palace. When you reach the road of light, you skim down it, back to earth. Here, you step upon the firm ground and transform back into your usual form. The scene around you gradually dissolves into mist.

Return to normal reality and dismantle your enclosure in the usual way. Then record the results of your work and dispose of the remains of your offerings appropriately.

Further Journeys

This concludes the work of *Coming Forth By Day*. I hope you have enjoyed exploring this system of magic. All of the rituals and pathworkings may be adapted and changed to suit situations that might arise in life. You may also use the workings as a template to create your own rituals and visualisations.

All of the workings in this book follow a pattern you can easily replicate for any *neter* you choose, including those who are not included in this volume. Part of preparing a new ritual involves researching the divine beings with whom you'll commune. Which would be the best one for the problem you want help with? Think about the symbols you can include and what should be placed upon your altar. Read up on your chosen *neter* and find out if there are any ancient invocations associated with them that you can incorporate into your rite. Discover what other practitioners might have done by exploring online. All of these things will help you create vibrant and meaningful rituals of your own.

There will be at least one more volume in this system of Khemetic magic, in which I'll explore the *neteru* of other areas of Khemet and devise new rituals and pathworkings for them, as well as updating those I've used before.

May you walk the path of the neteru to ancient Khemet and witness wonders there. *Ta-keper sem.*

Appendix
Breathing Exercises

It's important to feel comfortable when meditating, otherwise bodily discomfort will interfere with the process. Wear loose-fitting clothes and take off your shoes. Your environment should be at a pleasant temperature – neither too hot nor too cold. The lighting too should be appropriate – not bright artificial light, for example. You can either sit with a straight spine in a comfortable seat or lie down. Your torso should be erect when sitting, or comfortably stretched when lying down, to enable your breath to flow freely. If you wish, you can play soft music in the background.

Breathing Down

Lie or sit down. Close your eyes as if you are preparing to go to sleep. Breathe normally but slowly for a while.

Now, listen to yourself breathe. Become aware of your chest rising and falling, feel the rhythmic movement it creates.

After a couple of minutes, begin to breathe more deeply, taking the breaths in through the nose and out through the mouth.

Continue to breathe as deeply as you can for another couple of minutes, listening to the increased noise that deeper breathing creates.

Try to concentrate on your breathing, keeping it as regular and deep as you can, ignoring any distracting thoughts that may come into your mind.

The next stage is to breathe in through the nose for the count of ten seconds, then out through the mouth for the count of eleven.

Then, inhale for nine seconds and exhale for ten.

Inhale for eight seconds, exhale for nine.
Inhale for seven seconds, exhale for eight.
Inhale for six seconds, exhale for seven.
Inhale for five seconds, exhale for six.
Inhale for four seconds, exhale for five.
Inhale for three seconds, exhale for four.
Inhale for two seconds, exhale for three.
Inhale for one second, exhale for two.
Inhale again and gently hold your breath for the count of three before breathing out.
Resume normal breathing.

If you find starting with a count of eleven too difficult – simply start at a lower count.

Practise this exercise until you feel adept at it. Its purpose is to relax the body, calm the mind and improve the flow of energy within you.

Breathing Vp

This exercise enlivens the energy in your body. Your breaths will get longer rather than shorter. Start by breathing deeply and regularly, again becoming aware of the sound and movement of breath in and out of the body.

Now breathe in sharply for the count of two and out for the count of one.

Increase the counts by inhaling on the next breath for the count of three and out for the count of two, then in for four and out for three, and so on.

As you increase the counts, your breath will change from short sharp bursts to deep inhalations and exhalations.

When you reach your maximum inhalation point, which should still be comfortable rather than a strain, breathe at that level for a few minutes.

If you should feel dizzy at any point, slow your breathing

down by reverting to the Breathing Down exercise. Be mindful of how your body reacts. Learn what's the longest inhale and exhale count you can manage. This is not an endurance test; you must find your comfortable level and stick to it.

After breathing exercises, your mind and body will be in a relaxed yet enlivened state and you can then move on to your magical work, whether that's a full-scale ritual or a visualisation. You'll learn from experience when Breathing Up or Breathing Down are appropriate, which depends greatly upon your state of mind before you begin. If you feel tense and agitated, breathe down. If you feel lethargic and tired, breathe up.

Body of Light

This is a basic cleansing visualisation, during which you'll take vibrant free-flowing energy into your body from outside, and 'clean out' any stagnant energy from within. Once you can visualise it clearly, you will have more control over the energy flow within your body.

Before beginning the visualisation, perform the Breathing Down exercise. When you reach the count of one for inhalation, gently hold your breath and then resume normal breathing.

Now, maintain a slow and steady rate of breathing, ensuring that it is still deep but gentle.

For a few moments, visualise that a cloud of radiant white, sparkling light is hanging over your head. Then, imagine that when you breathe in through the nose, you inhale the light. Try to perceive the air entering your nostrils as a stream of white glittery light.

As you carry on breathing, visualise the light travelling up your nose and down through your throat into your chest. Try to not only see this light, but to feel what it would be like to breathe it. It might be cool or warm or induce other sensations – this is up to your individual imagination.

Steadily, continue to visualise the light going in through your nose and down into your body. Feel it expanding your chest cavity and swirling around within you.

The inside of your body is best visualised as completely empty and dark. Do not focus on the physical contents of it – organs, blood, bones and such. Imagine yourself as an empty vessel, like a bottle being filled with the radiance of liquid light.

Visualise the light going down further into your stomach, then into your legs, feet, and upwards and outwards into your head and arms. Observe it moving into and filling all parts of your body.

When you feel completely saturated with this white light, imagine that when you breathe out, the white light leaves your body. As it does so, it transforms from a sparkling mist to a foggy grey smoke.

Begin to imagine that with each exhalation, the white light inside you is beginning to diminish. It is being used up, expelling stagnant energy as dirty smoke. Continue to do this, seeing the white light becoming dimmer and dimmer, until you feel that it has completely gone from your body. The exercise has cleansed you, leaving you feeling refreshed, relaxed and calm. There is no time limit to this exercise. It can take as little or as long as you need.

If you've not attempted visualisation before, you might find it difficult to keep the image consistent in your mind at first. But this gets better with practice. Do the exercises initially for no longer than ten minutes a day, to avoid feeling dizzy or disorientated. As with physical exercise, you'll eventually be able to perform them for longer, should you want to, without any discomfort.

Resources

Incense
Starchild, Glastonbury
https://starchild.co.uk/

It's best if you can source your incense (sticks or loose) and oils locally – so you can smell the product before purchasing to make sure it's what you want. But if that's not possible, I have used Starchild loose incense and oils for many years and can recommend them for quality and variety. All their products are ecologically sound. The astrological and planetary incenses can be used for the various neteru in the Khemetic system. You need only look at the Starchild web site for details on what each incense may be used for in magical sense, to find the right match. Kyphi, an incense based upon an ancient Khemetic recipe, can be used for all the workings in this book, if preferred. If you've not used loose incense before, bear in mind you'll need purpose-made charcoal blocks to burn it on and a suitable heat resistant incense burner to hold it.

Tarot Cards
Aeclectic Tarot
www.aeclectic.net/tarot/

When choosing a Tarot or Oracle Card deck for a specific purpose, Aeclectic Tarot is my web site of choice. The site lists over 1800 decks, providing example pictures, as well as user reviews and information on where you can buy the cards online, if they are still in print. You can search by 'theme' and explore the section dedicated to decks inspired by Ancient Egypt.

About the Author

Storm has practiced magic since her teens and has taught it for the past 30 or so years. She was the founder, along with Louise Coquio, of the Lady of the Flame Iseum, which ran for many years and was affiliated to The Fellowship of Isis. In 2000, Storm trained in Reiki to third degree and co-administered the Kether School of Reiki for over a decade. While primarily a writer of fiction, Storm has released several nonfiction titles, including *'Bast and Sekhmet: Eyes of Ra'* (with Louise Coquio), *'Sekhem Heka'* and the three *'Grimoire Dehara'* books, a series of pop magic titles based on her best-selling Wraeththu science fantasy novels.

Her fiction works cross genres from science fiction, to dark fantasy, to epic fantasy, to slipstream. She has written over thirty books, including full length novels, novellas, short story collections and non-fiction titles. Her short stories, which she continues to write prolifically, appear in diverse magazines and anthologies.

Storm is the founder of Immanion Press, created initially to publish her out-of-print back catalogue, but which evolved into the thriving venture it is today. Her interests include magic and spirituality, movies, music and MMOs. She lives in the Midlands of the UK with her husband and four cats.

Books by Storm Constantine

The Wraeththu Chronicles
The Enchantments of Flesh and Spirit
The Bewitchments of Love and Hate
The Fulfilments of Fate and Desire
The Wraeththu Chronicles (omnibus of trilogy)

The Wraeththu Histories
The Wraiths of Will and Pleasure
The Shades of Time and Memory
The Ghosts of Blood and Innocence

The Alba Sulh Sequence
The Hienama
Student of Kyme
The Moonshawl

Blood, the Phoenix and a Rose

The Artemis Cycle
The Monstrous Regiment
Aleph

The Grigori Books
Stalking Tender Prey
Scenting Hallowed Blood
Stealing Sacred Fire

The Magravandias Chronicles:
Sea Dragon Heir
Crown of Silence
The Way of Light

Hermetech
Burying the Shadow
Sign for the Sacred
Calenture

Thin Air

*Silverheart (with Michael Moorcock)

Short Story Collections:
The Thorn Boy and Other Dreams of Dark Desire
Mythangelus
Mythophidia
Mytholumina
Mythanimus
Mythumbra
A Raven Bound with Lilies (Wraeththu)

Wraeththu Mythos Collections
*(co-edited with Wendy Darling, including stories by the editors
and other writers)*
Paragenesis
Para Imminence
Para Kindred
Para Animalia
Para Spectral

Non-Fiction
Sekhem Heka
Grimoire Dehara: Kaimana
Grimoire Dehara: Ulani (with Taylor Ellwood)
Grimoire Dehara: Nahir Nuri (with Taylor Ellwood)
*The Inward Revolution (with Deborah Benstead)
*Bast and Sekhmet: Eyes of Ra (with Eloise Coquio)
Whatnots and Curios
Zodiac of the Gods (with Graham Phillips)
SHE: Primal Meetings with the Dark Goddess (with
Andrew Collins)

All books listed are available as Immanion Press editions
except for those marked with *

More Egyptian-Themed Magic
From Megalithica Books
www.immanion-press.com

Sekhem Heka by Storm Constantine

Drawing upon her experiences in Egyptian Magic and the energy healing systems of Reiki and Seichim, Storm Constantine developed this new system for practitioners of both magic and energy healing. Incorporating ritual and visualisation into a progressive journey through the seven energy centres of the body, Sekhem Heka can be practiced by those who are already attuned to an energy healing modality, as well as those who are simply interested in the magical aspects of the system. Sekhem Heka is designed to help the practitioner work upon self-evolution. Each of the seven tiers focuses upon a particular Ancient Egyptian god or goddess, including practical exercises and rites. ISBN pbk: 9781905713134, £12.99 $21.99

Zodiac of the Gods by Storm Constantine & Graham Phillips (writing as Eden Crane)

This book presents a new interpretation of the Dendera Zodiac, exploring character analysis for each birth sign, revealing your relationship with the god or goddess who presides over your month of birth. *Zodiac of the Gods* also offers a primer for Egyptian magic, focusing upon the deities of the year. The vivid pathworkings enable you to connect with these ancient gods and goddesses, and work with their energy to influence and improve your life, to help you realise your goals and desires. ISBN pbk: 9781912241033, £11.99 $16.50

The Travellers' Guide to the Duat by Kiya Nicoll

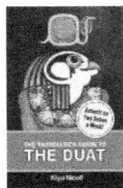

Planning a trip to the Egyptian spirit world? Like any responsible traveller, you want to know something about the history, geography, and politics of your destination. You want to know what documents you need to have in order for customs and immigration, what precautions to take, how to book a boat tour, where to stay, what to eat, and when you'll get the most interesting sightseeing opportunities. Laced through its humorous presentation you will find extensive information about ancient Egyptian religion and magical practice. Renditions of ancient spells in modern poetry mark each section, showing the ancient magical texts in a new light. The Beautiful West awaits! Book your tour today!
ISBN pbk: 9781905713738, $19.99, £10.99